INDIA

GOVERNMENT AND POLITICS IN A DEVELOPING NATION

Second Edition

Robert L. Hardgrave, Jr.

The University of Texas at Austin

Harcourt Brace Jovanovich, Inc.

New York / Chicago / San Francisco / Atlanta

COPYRIGHTS AND ACKNOWLEDGMENTS

For permission to use previously published material grateful acknowledgment is made to the following:
Hutchinson Publishing Group Ltd. For Tables 7–1 and 7–2 adapted from W. H. Morris-Jones, *Government and Politics in India*.
Princeton University Press. For Table 6–2 from Stanley A. Kochanek, *The Congress Party in India: The Dynamics of One-Party Democracy* (copyright © 1968 by Princeton University Press): Fig. on p. xxii, "The National Decision-Making Structure of the Congress." Reprinted by permission of Princeton University Press.
MAPS Harbrace

ISBN: 0-15-541351-1
Library of Congress Catalog Card Number: 74-20320
Printed in the United States of America

PREFACE

In may 1974, INDIA DETONATED AN UNDERGROUND ATOMIC DEVICE, BEcoming the sixth member of the world "nuclear club." At the same time, India confronts staggering economic problems, and close to half of its population remains inadequately nourished. *India: Government and Politics in a Developing Nation*, Second Edition, seeks to introduce the reader to the problems of political and economic development as shown through the experience of one nation. India, one of the first new states to emerge from colonial rule after the Second World War, has confronted a wide range of problems and dramatizes, perhaps more than any other developing nation, the crisis posed by the limited capacity of institutions to respond to expanding participation and rapidly increasing demands.

The book examines India's struggle for independence and national unity, its experience with democratic political institutions, its efforts to establish itself as a power in South Asia and the world, and its part in establishing independence for another South Asian country—Bangladesh.

Although the book reflects a particular theoretical perspective, it is not essentially theoretical, either in content or in purpose. It is designed to provide a sense of the cultural and historical milieu in which political development takes place and to give a balanced treatment of both structure and process, of both institutions and behavior, in Indian politics. India provides the framework, then, in which problems of political development common to a major portion of the world are explored, and in addition reflects the growing worldwide importance of non-Western nations.

In the five years since the first edition was published, India has experienced dramatic changes: the 1971 electoral mandate secured by Prime Minister Indira Gandhi; the Indo-Pakistani war and the liberation of Bangladesh; and a deepening economic crisis, described by India's president as "unprecedented." This new edition examines these changes in the broader context of India's political system and explores the impact they may have on the future of Indian democracy.

I wish to express my appreciation to those who assisted, through suggestions and criticism, in preparing the second edition: Mohammed Ayoob of the School of International Studies, Jawaharlal Nehru University, New Delhi; Bashiruddin Ahmed of the Centre for the Study of Developing Societies, New Delhi; A. P. Barnabas of the Indian Institute of Public Administration, New Delhi; Marguerite Ross Barnett of Princeton; Paul Brass of the University of Washington; James W. Bjorkman of Yale; Howard Erdman of Dartmouth; John O. Field of M.I.T.; Duncan Forrester of the University of Sussex; Henry C. Hart of the University of Wisconsin; Randir B. Jain of Delhi University; Rodney W. Jones of Pomona College; Ram Joshi of S.I.E.S. College, Bombay; K. P. Karunakaran of Delhi University; S. R. Maheshwari of the Indian Institute of Public Administration; Baldev Raj Nayar of McGill; Richard L. Park of the University of Michigan; William L. Richter of Kansas State University; Donald Rosenthal of SUNY at Buffalo; Ramashray Roy of the Indian Council of Social Science Research, New Delhi; Sunanda Sen Gupta of the World Bank, New Delhi; Grant Smith of the American Embassy, New Delhi; Paul Wallace of the University of Missouri; and Theodore P. Wright, Jr., of SUNY at Albany. Special thanks go to my colleagues at the University of Texas at Austin, Tom Jannuzi, Gail Minault, and James Roach. I am grateful to R. D. Sharma of the Election Commission of India for providing the provisional statistics on the 1972 elections, and to the Information Service of India in Washington, D.C., for helping me track down elusive facts and figures. For all my appreciation to those who assisted me and stimulated my work, however, I alone bear the responsibility for what appears here.

ROBERT L. HARDGRAVE, JR.

CONTENTS

LIST OF TABLES AND FIGURES

Tables

Figures

I

THE CHALLENGE OF DEVELOPMENT

INDIA, THE WORLD'S LARGEST DEMOCRACY, SUSTAINS A FRAGILE STABILITY and confronts an indeterminate political future—a future dominated by scarcity and by what Adlai Stevenson once called "the revolution of rising expectations." Politically conscious, increasingly participant, India's masses are an awakening force that has yet to find coherence and direction. The image of spiritual, Gandhian India pales before continuous agitation, intermittent rioting, and advocacy of violent revolution. The turbulence of modern India brings into focus processes of change experienced throughout the Third World.

The Process of Political Development

Seeking fulfillment of their aspirations after independence, the nationalist elites of the new states have committed themselves to rapid economic growth and social transformation. They aim to bring their countries into the modern world without loss of cultural integrity, to enable them to share what they see as the better life of an expanding technological-scientific world culture. The aspiration toward modernity is almost universal; few leaders are willing to relegate their nations to ethnographic museums—fewer still have the choice.

The desires for a higher standard of living, better health and education, the ease and efficiency of mechanical and electronic gadgetry, the delights of mass entertainment, and, above all, the ability to defend one's independence militarily have given compelling force to the push toward modernization.[1] But, as Rustow warns, "the effects of modernization are morally ambiguous." Together with unprecedented benefits, modernization "brings inevitable hazards and deprivations."[2] The process of modernization is disruptive; it is the source of discontent and social conflict. In those areas where modernization has proceeded most rapidly, conflict and discontent may be most evident. This arises, in part, because of differential access to the benefits of modernity and a new awareness of relative group differences. Also, modernization may well bring an absolute decline in the quality of life for those least able to take advantage of it. Beyond all this, however, even for the beneficiaries of modernization, the revolution of rising expectations may set goals that are unrealistic and simply unattainable. The hopes that modernization creates may then become the frustrations that feed political unrest and revolution.

Economic and social changes in the process of modernization may be more indicative of the disintegration of traditional society than of the creation of a viable modern society. The process may be highly disruptive, more productive of decay than of development. The essential quality of modernity lies in "an enduring capacity to generate and absorb persistent transformation."[3] The fundamental problem of the political system is to control and direct the process of change, to be its master, not its victim. Political development is "a process by which a political system acquires an increased capacity to sustain successfully and continuously new types of goals and demands and the creation of new types of organizations." This process may involve a common content, but it does not involve a definable "end product" or "final

---

[1] Baldev Raj Nayar writes, "The impulse for modernization thus emerges not *internally* from the demands of a socially mobilized population, nor from the humanitarian instincts of the political leadership, but *externally* from the security threat presented by the industrialized countries. . . . It is military security in its literal sense that propels nations to modernize and industrialize." For Nayar, the modernization imperative is: "Modernize or be subjugated. . . . This subjugation need not only take the form of physical occupation, but perhaps also political penetration and economic control." "Political Mainsprings of Economic Planning in the New Nations: The Modernization Imperative versus Social Mobilization," *Comparative Politics*, Vol. 6 (April 1974), pp. 346–47. See also his *Modernization Imperative and Indian Planning* (Delhi: Vikas, 1972).

[2] Dankwart A. Rustow, *A World of Nations: Problems of Political Modernization* (Washington, D.C.: The Brookings Institution, 1967), pp. 8–9.

[3] Manfred Halpern, "The Rate and Costs of Political Development," *The Annals* (March 1965), p. 22.

stage." It cannot be measured in terms of socioeconomic indicators, nor is the path of change unilinear. Political development is "a process of meeting new goals and demands in a flexible manner."[4]

No society is wholly traditional or wholly modern. The character and direction of change will be the product of a dialectical interaction between "tradition" and "modernity," as each infiltrates and transforms the other.[5] The relationship between tradition and modernity—the degree to which tradition is accommodated in the process of change, the ways it responds to the challenge of modernization—is a critical determinant of stability and development. The bargain struck with the forces of tradition may buy short-term stability at the price of revolution, but a failure to adapt to the context of tradition, to use traditional structures as the vehicles of change, may so undermine stability as to prevent the development of the institutional capacity to fulfill the promise of transformation.

The commitment to modernization in the new nations has given primacy to politics. "Seek ye first the political kingdom," Kwame Nkrumah of Ghana declared, "and all things shall be added unto you."[6] Development, however, involves not merely the will but the capacity to change, and the institutional capacity to absorb change may be disproportionately small in comparison to the aspiration after change. The forces of modernization are frequently initiated by a government to enhance its capacities, but once unleashed, these forces may proceed with autonomy and far outstretch the capacity of the government to control or regulate them, much less respond to them in any positive way.

Modernization represents both an opportunity and a challenge, for those forces that may enhance the capacity of the political system may at the same time heighten demands on the system. The same forces that serve to create for the people an identity with the nation-state may also sustain and strengthen primordial identities with religion, language, caste, and tribe. The same forces—education, communication, and economic growth—that may foster participant citizenship may act to increase the demands made on government beyond any capacity to meet them. The process of modernization may unleash a "revolution of rising frustrations"[7] as the gap widens between aspirations and achievement. The promises of political, social, and economic equality

---

[4] Alfred Diamant, "The Nature of Political Development," in Jason L. Finkle and Richard W. Gable, eds., *Political Development and Social Change* (New York: Wiley, 1966), p. 92.

[5] Lloyd I. and Susanne H. Rudolph, *The Modernity of Tradition: Political Development in India* (Chicago: University of Chicago Press, 1967), p. 3.

[6] *Ghana: The Autobiography of Kwame Nkrumah* (Camden, N.J.: Thomas Nelson & Sons, 1957), p. 163.

[7] Daniel Lerner, "Toward a Communication Theory of Modernization," in Lucian Pye, ed., *Communications and Political Development* (Princeton: Princeton University Press, 1963), pp. 327–50.

may serve to create an awareness of poverty among the poor, to sustain a sense of relative deprivation, and to deepen group conflict as inequalities of the society are exposed and sharpened. Regional, linguistic, religious, and cultural groups may become more self-conscious, and as such identifications are injected into political life, traditional communities may take on modern associational form or give rise to movements of xenophobia and separation. Conflict over scarce resources increases as new groups become participant, but if they lack the minimum consensus necessary for the orderly resolution of conflict, the political system may be unable to accommodate expanded participation by means of its institutions. Insofar as the system can respond to newly mobilized groups and to accelerating demands, participation strengthens the system and reinforces its legitimacy. When the system is unable—or unwilling—to absorb new demands, participation may simply overwhelm performance capacity.

"The primary problem of politics," writes Samuel P. Huntington, "is the lag in the development of political institutions behind social and economic change."[8]

> Political modernization involves the extension of political consciousness to new social groups and the mobilization of these groups into politics. Political development involves the creation of political institutions sufficiently adaptable, complex, autonomous, and coherent to absorb and order the participation of these new groups and to promote social and economic change in the society.[9]

The development of any political system depends upon the relationship between political institutionalization and political participation. As participation expands, the capacity of the political institutions to absorb change must also increase if stability is to be maintained.

A political elite committed to economic growth and modernization may stimulate the formulation of demands in the process of inducing social change. Development programs may seek to create "felt needs" within the traditional society in order to facilitate innovation, but modernization is itself destabilizing. In an environment of scarcity and limited resources the system will be most responsive to those commanding political capital—wealth, status, votes. When challenged the elite may seek to suppress widening popular involvement in order to insure stability and maintain their vested interests. Repressive rule supplants democratic response in the name of order. But stability bought through repressive order rather than secured through higher levels of institutionalization in response to expanding participation may be the harbinger of chaos.

[8] *Political Order in Changing Societies* (New Haven, Conn.: Yale University Press, 1968), p. 5.
[9] *Ibid.*, p. 266.

If any government is to confront effectively the challenge of modernization and meet the demands of expanding participation, it must have both the will and the capacity to initiate, absorb, and sustain continuous transformation. The critical factor in the developmental process is the ratio between capacity and demands. As demands increase, capacity must be enhanced to meet those demands. Development, defined in terms of the ratio between capacity and demands, may require a dynamic gap between the two variables. With participation somewhat beyond the capacity of the institutions to respond, the attempt to close the gap serves as a stimulus to higher levels of institutionalization. The interaction between capacity and demands, between institutionalization and participation, thus involves a staggered process of development, as each reacts to the other. The development process is dialectical, and the imbalance in demand serves as the incentive for enhanced capacity. The process involves a dynamic equilibrium, in which imbalance is the motivative force of change. Beyond a critical range, however, an imbalance may be increasingly difficult to correct. Overinstitutionalization is conducive to the establishment of repressive order; participation far beyond institutional capacity may foster unacceptable instability and political decay.

The success of a political system in coping with the challenge of development is dependent upon its capacity to affect horizontal and vertical integration. The task of horizontal integration, of nation-building, is the creation of a new sense of community and common destiny among those who previously may have shared only the oppression of a common colonial master. The people in the polyglot states of Africa and Asia must extend their identity beyond the primordial bonds of tribe, caste, language, and region to embrace a more inclusive national community. Horizontal integration does not require that traditional sources of identity be abandoned, but they must be transcended. Ideology, perhaps combining elements of tradition and modernity, is the instrument for the creation of a new political culture of shared values, common goals, and a minimum consensus on the institutions of conflict resolution.

Horizontal integration may take place only to the degree that vertical integration is extensive and penetrating. The capacity of the system to generate and absorb change, to respond to demands of expanding participation, requires effective channels of linkage between mass and elite. The institutions of government must command confidence and be regarded as legitimate. They must have the capacity to initiate change and to control its direction and intensity. Channels of access and communication must be available if the system is to respond successfully to change. The political system cannot be simply the dependent variable in a changing world; it must possess the will and capacity to intervene actively in its environment. Through the formal institutions of government, as well as through interest groups and parties, the political system must provide an infrastructure capable of accommodating the rapidly increasing numbers seeking entry. The success of the developmental effort, within the range of available resources, will depend upon the ability of these structures to acquire legitimacy and stability and to provide meaningful access and effective response.

What for the West took centuries, the new nations seek now to accomplish in decades. The fundamental crises of integration and institutionalization, met sequentially in the West, confront the new nations simultaneously and imperatively.[10]

The Context of Political Development in India

India, among the first of the colonies to emerge from the yoke of imperial rule, gained independence from Great Britain in 1947. Today it epitomizes both the problems of and the prospects for political development in the non-Western world. With more than six hundred million people, a population greater than that of Africa and Latin America combined, India is the world's largest democracy. Its leadership, committed to a fundamental transformation of the society, is confronted by an almost overwhelming cultural diversity, by often intransigent traditions rooted in the village and in religious values, and by poverty bred by scarcity of known resources, ignorance, and staggering population growth.

Jawaharlal Nehru spoke of the "essential unity" of India, of a civilization that was "a world in itself" and gave shape to all things: "Some kind of a dream of unity has occupied the mind of India since the dawn of civilization," he wrote.[11] But the unity of India was more a quest than a reality. The diversity of India has given richness and variation to its traditions, but diversity has been accompanied by patterns of social and cultural fragmentation, historically rooted in and sanctioned by religion. Almost every known societal division can be found in India: the Indian people are divided by religion, sect, language, caste, dress, and even by the food they eat. These divisions are compounded by the chasm between the rich and poor, between the English-speaking elite and the vernacular mass, between the city and the village.

Urbanization

More than one hundred million people in India live in cities. The rates of urbanization throughout India have not been dramatic, but the

---

[10] For an extended discussion of this development perspective, see James A. Bill and Robert L. Hardgrave, Jr., "Modernization and Political Development," *Comparative Politics: The Quest for Theory* (Columbus, Ohio: Charles E. Merrill, 1973), pp. 43–83.

[11] *The Discovery of India* (Garden City, N.Y.: Doubleday, 1959), p. 31.

largest cities have grown rapidly. Incredibly crowded, lacking in adequate housing, transportation, and sewerage, Indian cities have become almost ungovernable and for some unlivable. But because they offer new economic opportunities, rich and varied cultural experiences and intellectual stimulation, cities are for most urban dwellers preferable to rural areas. And in terms of relative deprivation, even the burdens of the poor in Calcutta, the problem city of the world, may represent an improvement over the marginal subsistence of the village. Nevertheless, with rapid social change, high levels of communication, and a frustrated middle class squeezed by rising prices and a deteriorating standard of living, India's cities suffer a deepening malaise. It is within the cities, where the government finds itself least able to respond to accelerating demands, that political unrest is most sharply evident.

Rural Society and Tradition

India, like most of the developing world, is overwhelmingly rural and agricultural. Eighty percent of India's population lives in some 550,000 villages, most with less than one thousand people. Village life was traditionally narrowly circumscribed, and even today the world of the average villager extends only a few miles beyond place of birth. Although the villages have now been penetrated by radio, film, and increasing contact with government officials and aspiring politicians, they remain the font of traditional values and orientations. If they are often eulogized as an ideal of harmony and spirituality, even by those who have chosen to leave, traditional villages are nevertheless bastions of parochialism and inequality.

THE CASTE SYSTEM

It is within the villages that the caste system, sanctioned by Hindu tradition, has its most powerful hold. There are more than two thousand castes, or *jati*, in India. Most are confined to relatively small geographical areas within a linguistic region. Marrying only among themselves, the members of each caste share, by tradition, a common lot and occupy by virtue of their birth a defined status and role within village society. Each caste is hierarchically ranked according to the ritual purity of its traditional occupation—whether or not the occupation is still followed. Castes can be distinguished from one another even in the same village by the manner of behavior and speech, the style of dress and ornaments, the food eaten, and the general life style. The behavior of each caste is restricted. Deviation may bring action from the caste itself through the *panchayat*, the council of caste elders, or it may incur the wrath of the higher castes and bring punitive measures against the aberrant individual or the caste group as a whole.

Although traditionally conflict between castes certainly occurred, caste as a *system* ideally presupposes the interdependent relationship of occupational groups, each functioning according to prescribed patterns of behavior, with the system providing both economic security and a defined status and role. The caste system is what Alan Beals calls "being together separately." "To survive," he says, "one requires the cooperation of only a few jati; to enjoy life and do things in the proper manner requires the cooperation of many."[12] Kathleen Gough, however, characterizes the system as one of "relationships of servitude."[13] A typical village might have from half a dozen to twenty castes within it. Traditionally, each by its ascriptive status occupied a particular position in relation to the land. In a system of reciprocity and redistribution, each caste provided the landlord with its services, agricultural or artisan, and received in return a portion of the harvest. The relationship of the lower castes to the high-caste landlord was hereditary, but their dependent status carried certain rights. All behavior within the system, however, served to emphasize superordination and subordination, congruent inequalities of power, wealth, and status. Control over land was the critical lever of social control, and today land remains the fundamental resource of political power.

The ascriptive identity of caste cannot be escaped, even by abandoning the traditional occupation. Although an individual cannot move from one caste to another, within the middle range of castes between the Brahmins and the untouchables there is considerable movement in the local hierarchy, as castes adjust their ritual position to accord with shifting economic status and political power. Such shifts, usually with a lag of several generations, are accompanied by changes in life style, such as the adoption of vegetarianism in "sanskritized" emulation of higher castes. This movement occurs within the framework of the *varna* system. Classically, castes have been divided into five divisions, the four varna and those beyond the pale of caste. The varna represented the classes of ancient Aryan society. Ranked hierarchically, the first three varnas included the Brahmins, who acted as the priests; the Kshatriyas, who were the rulers and warriors; and the Vaisyas, who were the mercantile classes. The Sudras, the lowest varna, were the common people, the agriculturists and craftsmen. Beyond the embrace of the varna were the outcastes, or untouchables, polluted by their life as scavengers and sweepers and therefore relegated to the lowest rungs of society.

HINDUISM AND THE CONCEPT OF DHARMA

Each person is born into a particular station in life, with its own privileges and obligations, and must fulfill an individual *dharma*, the sacred law or duty. It is better, according to the sacred Hindu text, the Bhagavad Gita, to do one's own duty badly than another's well. The suffer-

[12] *Gopalpur: A South Indian Village* (New York: Holt, Rinehart and Winston, 1963), p. 41.
[13] "Criteria of Caste Ranking in South India," *Man in India*, Vol. 39 (1959), pp. 15–17.

ings of people's existence can be explained by their conduct in past lives, and only by fulfilling the dharma peculiar to their position in life can they hope to gain a more favorable rebirth and ultimate salvation. There is a quality of resignation, of passiveness and fatalism, in this religious belief that has manifested itself in the political attitude of the many Indians who simply accept the government they have as the one they deserve. Expanding communications and political competition have, however, increasingly challenged the traditional order. The vote has brought a new sense of efficacy and power, and a willingness to question what was previously accepted simply as written by the gods.

Hinduism, while uniting India in the embrace of the great Sanskritic tradition, also divides the subcontinent. Each cultural-linguistic area has its own "little" tradition and local gods, and it is within the little tradition, rather than in the realm of Brahminical Hinduism, that most villagers live their religious life. The two levels of tradition penetrate each other, however, as the elastic pantheon of Hinduism absorbs the local tradition and is modified by it. Religion at the "higher" level need not be in conflict with the goals of modernization, Gunnar Myrdal argues, but the inertia of popular belief, giving religious sanction to the social and economic *status quo*, remains a major obstacle to social transformation. "Religion has, then, become the emotional container of this whole way of life and work and by its sanction has rendered it rigid and resistant to change."[14]

Poverty

Poverty is the omnipresent reality of Indian life. It is both the greatest impetus and the greatest impediment to economic and social progress. By almost every economic index India is among the poorest countries in the world. With more than half a billion people it has a gross national product of only fifty billion dollars—roughly that of Italy, which has one-tenth its population, and only a little more than half of what the United States *spends* in its annual defense budget.

THE CONDITION OF THE PEOPLE

The average annual income in India is less than one hundred dollars, and most of it goes to provide a meager diet. The average caloric intake is below the suggested minimum requirement of 2,250 per day.[15] But because of the stark inequalities, averages conceal the even greater poverty of the masses and a nutritional level far below that required to maintain health. Dandekar and Rath, in their study of

---

[14] *Asian Drama: An Inquiry into the Poverty of Nations*, Vol. 1 (New York: Pantheon, 1968), p. 112.

[15] As established by the United Nations' Food and Agriculture Organization. See Myrdal, *Asian Drama*, Vol. 1, p. 545.

poverty in India,[16] found that in 1961–62, for both urban and rural areas, two-thirds of the population fell below the average per capita consumer expenditure, a measure of the standard of living. Of the rural poor, 38 percent lived on less than 180 rupees per year, or about 10 cents a day per capita. The urban situation, with substantially higher prices, was even worse, with an estimated 50 percent of the urban population earning less than the 270 rupees required to maintain a standard of living equivalent to the rural poverty threshold. This income threshold represents the annual expenditure required to sustain an individual at the minimum caloric level. In other words, 40 percent of India's rural population and 50 percent of its urban population fell below this nutritional minimum.

In the decade of the 1960s the per capita consumer expenditure rose by only half a percent a year, but even this marginal gain was inequitably distributed among the different sections of the population. The gap between rural and urban areas narrowed, but largely at the expense of the urban poor and lower middle classes. In both rural and urban areas the rich disproportionately benefitted, and the poorest classes experienced an actual decline in per capita consumption, especially in the cities where wages remained depressed by the continuing emigration of the rural poor. For all the efforts of the Indian government, 40 percent of the population remain in abject poverty.

The diet of the poor is based on a single staple—rice, wheat, or, more likely, an inferior grain. It is both monotonous and nutritionally insufficient, and poor nutrition leads to what Myrdal has called hidden hunger—"a general state of weakness that impairs people's labor input and efficiency and decreases their resistence to disease."[17] There has been a dramatic decline in mortality in India as a result of advances in medical technology, but even with the control of epidemic and endemic diseases, sanitation and elementary hygiene have improved little. Life expectancy has risen from 20 to 25 years in the early part of the century to its present 46 to 50 years, but even this figure suggests a continuing high rate of infant mortality. India has only 23.7 physicians per 100,000 people (compared to 125 per 100,000 in the United States), and despite the effort to establish a system of rural health centers, most doctors practice in the major urban areas.

Poverty is a syndrome of cumulative and mutually reinforcing deprivations. In addition to low levels of nutrition and low standards of health, India is confronted by mass illiteracy. Education, in its strictly instrumental aspects of attitude change and dissemination of practical knowledge, is vital for progress and development. Primary education has expanded rapidly, from fourteen million children in school in 1951 to

[16] V. M. Dandekar and Nilakantha Rath, "Poverty in India," *Economic and Political Weekly*, Vol. 6 (January 2, 1971), pp. 25–48; (January 9, 1972), pp. 106–46.
[17] Myrdal, *Asian Drama*, Vol. 3, p. 1603.

more than eighty-five million today. But although the number of literates has doubled in India, the literacy rate is still only about 30 percent (40 percent for men; 19 percent for women.)[18] About 2 percent of the adult population is literate in English. Illiteracy sustains poverty, although it may reduce consciousness among the poor and render them less likely to be politically restless. Progress in education, a breakthrough in communication, and an incremental improvement in the standard of living for some, however, have raised the sights of the Indian people and stimulated their aspirations toward a better life. The possibilities of satisfying these demands depend upon both the will of the government to respond and its capacity to mobilize resources in a context of scarcity.

Ownership of land has been the traditional means to both wealth and power in India. Land reform has been more symbolic than substantive. Unimplemented by state governments politically dependent upon large landholders or evaded, often with the connivance of officials, reform in most states has little affected the radically unequal distribution of land ownership.[19] Over 95 percent of India's rural households own less than 20 acres of land; 43 percent own less than 5 acres; and 24 percent own no land at all. The disparities in land ownership are revealed in the fact that 30 percent of the rural families hold 70 percent of the cultivable land.[20]

THE CONDITION OF THE LAND

More than half of India's income is from the land, but there is little beyond the 325 million acres now under cultivation that can be redeemed for agriculture. The soil, though capable of being rejuvenated by rotation and fertilization, has been depleted by centuries of harvest, and the yield per acre is now among the lowest in the world. Rain is irregular, and the monsoon, which determines the difference between subsistence and famine, is uncertain. The uses of irrigation, improved seed grain, and modern agricultural techniques have increased India's agricultural output enormously without expanding present acreage, but most of India's peasants, with little access to credit and a tenuous hold on the land they till, cannot afford to assume the risks involved in innovation.

In raw materials, India possesses the resources for substantial industrial growth. In the Bengal-Bihar-Orissa triangle, coal, iron ore, and

---

[18] 1971 Census of India figures, inclusive of all ages from birth.
[19] For an account of the failure of land reform in one state, see F. Tomasson Jannuzi, *Agrarian Crisis in India: The Case of Bihar* (Austin: University of Texas Press, 1974).
[20] Francine R. Frankel, *India's Green Revolution: Economic Gains and Political Costs* (Princeton: Princeton University Press, 1971), p. 204; and Wolf Ladejinsky, "How Green Is the Indian Green Revolution?" *Economic and Political Weekly*, Vol. 8 (December 29, 1972), p. A-137.

transport facilities provide the base for a major steel industry. This region has the largest deposits of iron ore in the world; oil reserves have been opened in Assam and Gujarat; and India's rivers offer enormous hydroelectric potential that has only been touched. At the time of independence, India already had an extensive industrial base and one of the largest rail systems in the world. Under the Five-Year Plans, industry and transport have been greatly expanded. While India is the most industrialized nation in South and Southeast Asia and ranks tenth among the industrial nations of the world, it is backward in terms relative to size and population. Even with its potential in raw material, India is confronted with a scarcity of exploited resources that severely limits its capacity to invest in developmental efforts. Democratic commitment limits the system's ability to force saving and at the same time places rapidly increasing demands upon the capacity of the political system to distribute available resources.

POPULATION GROWTH

Competition for India's limited resources is intense, but there is no claimant greater than the growing population. Control of disease in the past fifty years has brought a rapid decline in the death rate, the Malthusian equalizer. From 251 million in 1921, India's population more than doubled by 1971, reaching 548 million. By the census of 1981, at the present rate of growth, India's projected population will be approximately 700 million. The annual rate of population growth has increased from 1.1 percent between 1921 and 1931 to 2.5 percent between 1961 and 1971. To reduce birth rates, the Government of India has undertaken the most extensive family planning program in the world. To overcome the fatalistic belief in "God's will," propaganda posters are omnipresent. Billboards, radio, and films proclaim: "A small family is a happy family." The campaigns have yielded impressive results. Eight million men have undergone voluntary sterilization—more in the past decade than in all other countries combined. Mobile vasectomy camps have been organized, and incentives of cash and even transistor radios have been offered to volunteers. More than four million women have had intrauterine devices (IUDs), or "loops," inserted, but the initial success of the IUD has succumbed to side effects. The condom (or *Nirodh*, "prevention") is being heavily promoted, and research is now underway to develop an antifertility vaccine that will bring temporary sterility.

The statistics pale, however, when matched with the yearly addition of fourteen million people to India's population. At the present rate, India's population will reach one billion before the year 2000—and perhaps much sooner. For all the government's efforts, many people, particularly among the poor, simply do not feel a compelling need for family planning. Aside from the fact that a male heir has ritual importance and additional future wage earners will augment family income, "those babies who are a planner's worry are also a parent's hope and joy."[21] Beyond this, the calculations of democratic politics have led many groups to consciously endorse population growth among their own so as to translate greater numbers into more power and influence.

The age structure of India's population is like a great pyramid, and half of the nation's population is below the age of 16. Thus, even with the most successful birth-control program, there would be little immediate impact on population growth. Moreover, as the young mature the demands of this expanding population for education, housing, government services, jobs, and, above all, food will place an increasingly heavy burden on India's limited capacity. Population growth has seriously undermined the economic progress made in the past two decades, and unless the population increase is drastically reduced, even an equilibrium of poverty will be impossible to maintain.

The Current Dilemma: "The Revolution of Rising Frustrations"

The challenge of population growth demands radical change in the form of a fundamental transformation of society. The inertia of tradition can be broken only by creating "felt needs," by stimulating discontent and aspiration toward a better life. The leadership of India, committed to goals of modernization, has sought to induce social change, and has succeeded to a considerable degree. It sought through the universal franchise to expand political participation in order to foster national integration, political legitimacy, and enhanced institutional capacity.[22] But its period of grace was short. The "revolution of rising expectations" has become a "revolution of rising frustrations" as the gap between aspiration and achievement has widened. As demands have increased, as new groups have entered the political system in the expanding participation, the capacity of the government to respond effectively has not kept pace. But beyond capacity, India has often lacked the *will* to initiate and respond to rapid change. Under pressure from sectors of society with a vested interest in preserving the inequalities of the *status quo,* Indian leadership has been emasculated by the paradoxical position in which it finds itself.

> On a general and noncommittal level they freely and almost passionately proclaim the need for radical social and economic

21 David G. Mandelbaum, "Social Components of Indian Fertility," *Economic and Political Weekly,* Vol. 8, annual number (February 1973), p. 171.

22 In a lucid discussion of democracy in India, John O. Field argues for the role of politicization in strengthening political institutions. His fundamental optimism, however, is not without caution: "A 'premature' democracy may create the conditions for its own survival, but it may also be buried by its limited successes." "Partisanship in India: A Survey Analysis," unpublished doctoral dissertation, Stanford University, 1973, pp. 38–115.

change, whereas in planning their policies they tread most warily in order not to disrupt the traditional social order. And when they do legislate radical institutional reforms—for instance in taxation or in regard to property rights in the villages—they permit the laws to contain loopholes of all sorts and even let them remain unenforced.[23]

Without the capacity and the will to respond to increasing demands and to fulfill their own hopes for the transformation of society, India's leaders may now be the victims of the change they once sought to induce. In a process of social mobilization, with the breakdown of traditional society, the expansion of communications and transportation facilities, and heightened political competition, more and more people have become participant and, at the same time, more highly sensitive to the poverty in which they live. How the Government of India responds to this situation is of more than academic interest; it is among the most critical questions in the world.

[23] Myrdal, *Asian Drama*, Vol. 1, p. 117.

RECOMMENDED READING

* Almond, Gabriel, and Powell, G. B., Jr., *Comparative Politics: A Developmental Approach*. Boston: Little, Brown, 1966.
> Advances an approach to political development in terms of political functions and system capabilities.

Apter, David E., *Choice and the Politics of Allocation*. New Haven: Yale University Press, 1971.
> A highly abstract, analytical theory of development.

*————, *The Politics of Modernization*. Chicago: University of Chicago Press, 1965.
> Analysis of modernization in terms of alternative types of political systems, drawing primarily on African field data.

* Bill, James A., and Hardgrave, Robert L., Jr., "Modernization and Political Development," Chapter 2 of *Comparative Politics: The Quest for Theory*. Columbus, Ohio: Charles Merrill, 1973.
> A critical analysis of concepts and theory in the study of political development.

* Binder, Leonard et al., *Crises and Sequences in Political Development*. Princeton: Princeton University Press, 1971.
> Examines the process of political development in terms of five key problems: identity, legitimacy, participation, distribution, and penetration.

Chaudhuri, Nirad C., *The Continent of Circe*. London: Chatto & Windus, 1967.
> A highly individual interpretation of Hindu personality by a controversial Indian intellectual.

* Available in a paperback edition.

* Cohn, Bernard S., *India: The Social Anthropology of a Civilization.* Englewood Cliffs, N.J.: Prentice-Hall, 1971.
>A succinct and thoughtful portrait of Indian civilization.

Finkle, Jason L., and Gable, Richard W., eds., *Political Development and Social Change.* New York: Wiley, 1966.
>An extensive collection of readings on the concept of development and various aspects of social change in developing areas.

* Huntington, Samuel P., *Political Order in Changing Societies.* New Haven, Conn.: Yale University Press, 1968.
>Explores the problem of political development in terms of the relationship between institutionalization and political participation, emphasizing the creation of stability and order.

* Lewis, John P., *Quiet Crisis in India.* Garden City, N.Y.: Doubleday, 1964.
>An examination of economic development in India and of American policy by the former director of the United States Agency for International Development in India.

Mandelbaum, David G., *Human Fertility in India: Social Components and Policy Perspectives.* Berkeley: University of California Press, 1974.
>A thoughtful examination of India's family-planning program and the obstacles it has encountered.

* ——, *Society in India,* 2 vols. Berkeley: University of California Press, 1970.
>A comprehensive survey of modern research on Indian society.

Moore, Barrington, Jr., *Social Origins of Dictatorship and Democracy.* Boston Beacon Press, 1966.
>The section on India examines the history of underdevelopment in South Asia.

* Myrdal, Gunnar, *Asian Drama: An Inquiry into the Poverty of Nations,* 3 vols. New York: Pantheon, 1968. Abridged one-volume edition, New York: Vintage, 1972.
>A vast study of poverty in South Asia by one of the world's most astute economists, encyclopedic in its breadth, depressing in its conclusions. See in particular the specific sections on India.

* Rustow, Dankwart A., *A World of Nations: Problems of Political Modernization.* Washington: The Brookings Institution, 1967.
>A very readable discussion of the political evolution of the newly independent and modernizing states.

Singer, Milton, and Cohn, Bernard S., eds., *Structure and Change in Indian Society.* Chicago: Aldine, 1968.
>A substantial collection of essays reviewing recent empirical studies that outline theoretical and methodological trends in South Asian anthropology.

* Welch, Claude E., Jr., ed., *Political Modernization.* 2nd ed. Belmont, Calif.: Wadsworth, 1971.
>A relatively slim but well-selected collection of readings on the problem of political development.

* Available in a paperback edition.

II

THE STRUGGLE FOR INDEPENDENCE

W HEN IT GAINED INDEPENDENCE FROM GREAT BRITAIN IN 1947, INDIA emerged as one of the first "new states." The society of the vast subcontinent is among the oldest in the world, although varied and complex in its rich heritage. Five thousand years of history have nourished the growth of a great civilization, vitalized through cross-cultural contact and characterized by diversities of culture and race, caste, religion, and language. In India there are examples of virtually every known type of societal division: six major religions—Hinduism, Islam, Sikhism, Christianity, Buddhism, and Zoroastrianism; two major language families, Aryan and Dravidian, with fourteen official languages and innumerable dialects and tribal tongues; three racial strains, Aryan, Dravidian, and proto-Australoid; and over two thousand castes, hierarchically ranked, endogamous, and occupational.

The great tradition of Hinduism unites the diverse cultural regions, but within its elastic framework are a myriad of sects and local traditions. Perhaps by more than anything else, traditional India has been characterized by localism, a fragmentation not simply of cultural-linguistic regions but of villages themselves. By no means completely isolated, the cultural world of the villages nevertheless remains narrowly circumscribed.

In the past the villages were little affected by the changes of governmental authority. For the villager, "it did not matter much who ruled in Delhi—Mughal, Maratha, or Englishman. His concern was with his crops, with the next monsoon, and with the annual visitation of the collecting officer."[1]

Even the most sophisticated administrative system, like that of the Moguls, penetrated the village for almost wholly extractive purposes. Neither the Moguls, the Muslim rulers who came to power in 1526 and reigned for over three hundred years, nor the great Hindu emperors before them extended their sway over the whole of India. India was a concept, not a political entity. Pockets remained beyond the reach of even Asoka, whose empire in the third century B.C. extended from the Hindu Kush to the Bay of Bengal. Islamic authority never established itself in the extreme South; and even as the Moguls attained the height of their power, they were faced by revolts among the Jats, Rajputs, and Sikhs in the North and challenged by the rising power of the Marathas in the West. These internal conflicts were both exploited and exacerbated by the appearance of the European powers in India in the fifteenth century.

The British Rise to Power

The British entered the struggle for a commercial foothold in India through the British East India Company, founded in London in 1600 during the reign of Akbar. Within a few years the company had secured limited trading privileges from the Moguls, and by the end of the century it had established commercial enclaves at Bombay, Madras, and Calcutta. As Mogul power declined in the eighteenth century, the British pushed for more extensive privileges and wider territories. The inability of the Moguls to control increasing disorder led the company, as early as 1687, to instruct its Madras representative "to establish such a politie of civil and military power, and create and secure such a large revenue to secure both . . . as may be the foundation of a large, well grounded, secure English dominion in India for all time to come."

In expanding their hold, the British played one ruler against another, annexing a widening range of territory. The princely states led a precarious and vulnerable existence. The price of preservation from Indian conquest was the acceptance of British suzerainty. Security of trade ultimately demanded that the powers opposed to the company be brought under control and that Pax Britannica be extended over the whole subcontinent. By the middle of the nineteenth century

1 Percival Spear, A *History of India,* Vol. 2 (Baltimore: Penguin, 1965), p. 43.

FIGURE 2–1

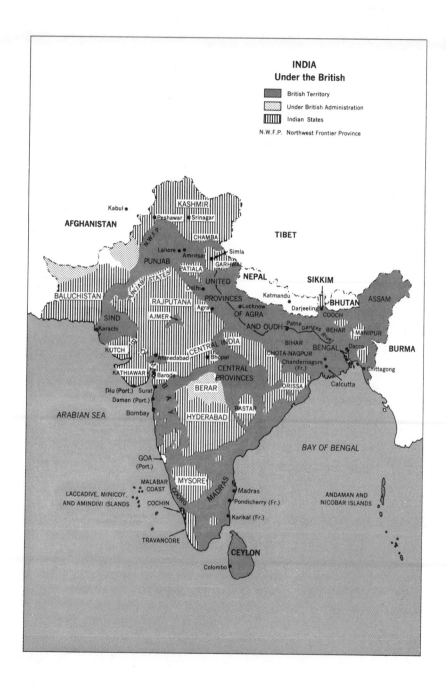

the company had assumed direct control over three-fifths of India, and the remaining areas were held by more than five hundred princely states subject to British control and intervention.

Westernization

As successors to the Mogul empire, the British sought to restore order and to reorganize the revenue system. Conditions were chaotic, and the opportunities for trade were restricted by inland transit duties, a wholly inadequate road system, and the constant dangers of *dacoity*, or gang robbery, which rendered safe travel almost impossible. In the course of pacification, however, the British began the construction of transport facilities—roads, canals, and railroads—opening the interior for the extraction of raw materials and the development of trade.

The British wanted to establish an equitable land and revenue system. In Bengal, revenues had previously been collected by hereditary *zamindars*, who as agents of the government also held police and magisterial powers. The British mistook the zamindars for landlords and under the Permanent Settlement confirmed them in their jurisdictions, thus creating a new class of wealthy landlords at the expense of the peasants. The mistake was soon evident, and subsequently in Madras the settlement was made directly with the peasant cultivators under the *ryotwari* system.

The British, content in the early years of company rule to let most things continue very much as before, had taken a position of neutrality with regard to the religious and social affairs of their subjects. In the early nineteenth century, however, demands for reform, voiced in England by the Utilitarians and the Evangelicals, were soon felt in India. The Utilitarians, committed to the rule of reason, sought to secure social harmony and justice through the free development of human virtue and common sense, unfettered by superstition and tradition. The Evangelicals, driven by a personal pietism and public humanitarianism, expressed horror at the abominations of the benighted heathen. Both Utilitarians and Evangelicals found little in India that they liked; both were ready to condemn and eager to change.

Under pressure from the English reformers, the Government took action against those Hindu customs offensive to Western sensibility. The reforms brought outcries of protest from the orthodox, particularly against the outlawing of *sati*, the self-immolation of a widow on the pyre of her husband. But the measures won the support of many reform-minded Hindus, notably Ram Mohan Roy, "the father of modern India." In general, however, the British sought to interfere as little as possible, and reform was largely negative. Not content with such limited response, the Utilitarians and Evangelicals introduced a new concern for education that was to have profound social implications. The Utilitarians advocated "useful knowledge"; the Evangelicals, "moral improvement." The English language was, in the words of Governor General Bentinck, "the key to all improvements." The whole of Hindu literature was seen as less valuable than any shelf of English books. Indeed, Lord Macaulay envisaged in his famous Minute of 1835, "a class of persons, Indian in blood and colour, but English in taste, in opinion, in morals, and in intellect."[2]

In 1835 English replaced Persian as the official language of government and thereby became the vehicle of advancement and progress. In establishing schools and, later, universities the British focused on the English education of the middle classes. The aristocrats for the most part held aloof; the masses, except for missionary concern, were largely ignored. The aspiring Hindu middle classes—particularly those castes with a literary tradition, like the Brahmins—were quick to respond to the advantages of English education. There were those of the *babu* stereotype who sought only a sinecure in the new bureaucracy, but others, like Ram Mohan Roy, were eager for the knowledge of the West —science, medicine, and the values of political liberalism.

The Persistence of Tradition: The Sepoy Mutiny

The rise of the new middle class, which Percival Spear has called "the most significant creation of the British in India,"[3] shifted the balance in the relationship of the various classes in Indian society. The old aristocratic landowning classes were rapidly losing their position of status and power. The changes introduced by the British, both by accident and by design, threatened the old order, and religion particularly was thought to be in danger. Brahmins, who served in large numbers as *sepoys*, or soldiers, were alarmed by rumors of Christian conversion in their ranks. They feared that they would have to serve overseas and thus break the religious prohibition against leaving India. Muslim resentments were stirred by the annexation of the state of Oudh for alleged misgovernment in 1856, and in an atmosphere of fear, mutiny broke out in 1857 when soldiers discovered that the cartridges of the new Enfield rifles were greased with animal fat of both the cow and the pig, polluting to Hindus and Muslims, respectively. "A consciousness of power," wrote one British official, "had grown up in the army which could only be exorcized by mutiny, and the cry of the cartridge brought the latent spirit of revolt into action."

In revivalist reaction Muslims rallied to the aged Mogul emperor of Delhi; Hindus, to the heir of the last Maratha *peshwa*, or head minis-

---

[2] John Clive and Thomas Pinney, eds., *Thomas Babington Macaulay: Selected Writings* (Chicago: University of Chicago Press, 1972), pp. 237–51. For a discussion of the Education Minute, see John Clive, *Macaulay: The Shaping of the Historian* (New York: Knopf, 1973), pp. 342–426.

[3] *India, Pakistan, and the West*, 4th ed. (New York: Oxford University Press, 1957), p. 110.

ter. Discontent was centered in Oudh, but among those in revolt there was no unity of purpose. The Maratha princes were not eager to see a resurgent peshwa and remained aloof from the mutiny. The Sikhs, though defeated only ten years before by the British, by no means wanted to resurrect Mogul power and thus gave active support to the British in crushing the revolt. The South remained virtually untouched by and uninvolved in the whole affair. Western education brought the Indian middle classes prospects for the enjoyment of status and privilege in a new order, and they pledged their loyalty and active support to the British. "So far from being the first war for independence or a national revolt in the modern sense, the Mutiny was a final convulsion of the old order goaded to desperation by the incessant pricks of modernity."[4]

The mutiny was, as Nehru later wrote, "essentially a feudal rising," and although it had directly affected only a limited area, "it had shaken up the whole of India."[5] The East India Company was abolished, and in 1858 the Crown assumed direct control over British India. The revolt, with all its savagery, marked a fundamental change in British attitude and in the relationship between the Indians and the English. The English became deeply distrustful of their native wards, particularly of the Muslims, who were believed to have been strongly committed to the mutiny. The manner of the British response to the mutiny reflected changes, conditions and attitudes that by 1857 were already well under way. The rise of popular imperial sentiments in England would soon have brought continued company rule into jeopardy had not the mutiny brought matters to a head.[6]

British Reaction and Awakening Indian Nationalism

The British were now determined to be in closer touch with established classes of traditional authority who could keep the masses under control. They rewarded princes for their loyalty during the revolt and guaranteed their territories. They secured landlords in their tenure on conditions of "loyalty and good service." Thus the relics of the past, the vested interests of conservatism, were tied to the British presence in India. At the same time the British exercised new caution in westernization. Their new policy reflected both a desire to placate the conservative upper classes and a certain disappointment and pessimism over Indians' inability to change. "Public works rather than public morals or western values was the guiding star of the post-Mutiny reformer."[7]

---

[4] *Ibid.*, p. 116.

[5] Jawaharlal Nehru, *The Discovery of India* (Garden City, N.Y.: Doubleday, 1959), pp. 239–40.

[6] Francis G. Hutchins, *The Illusion of Permanence* (Princeton, N.J.: Princeton University Press, 1967), p. 86.

[7] Spear, *A History of India*, Vol. 2, p. 114.

India was assumed to be changeless, perhaps irredeemable, and it was to be the "white man's burden" to bring enlightened rule to those incapable of governing themselves.

The British sought to reinforce traditional institutions, to minimize social change, and to soften the impact of the West. Their policy "went hand in hand with a new and avowedly imperial sentiment which glorified the British Raj and consigned the Indian people to a position of permanent racial inferiority."[8] While the British looked for support to the moribund traditional ruling classes, the rajas and zamindars, they virtually ignored the rising westernized middle class—the clerks and subordinate officials, the teachers and lawyers. "The fissure between the British and the new India began at this point."[9]

This new Indian class was characterized by a unity of sentiment, but at the same time, this unity was undercut by the growth of regional identity and of self-awareness and assertiveness among different communities, particularly in religion. The West had a double impact on India: it introduced Western liberal thought, but it also prompted the recovery of what was valuable in tradition. The Indian response to the West came in the forms of reform and revivalism. The movement for reform sought to reconcile tradition with modernity, to eliminate those elements of tradition repugnant to reason and liberal values and to reaffirm those that were compatible with them. Revivalism, in contrast, sought to regain the past through a traditionalistic reaction against the West, and while often involving radical reform, it was nurtured by the nostalgia for an idealized "golden age."

Reform and revival represented a quest for national self-respect and drew deeply upon both those who damned and those who praised Indian tradition and society. While often acutely self-critical, reformers and revivalists reacted sharply to the criticism of the Evangelicals, who saw only benighted heathen and a society of superstition and dark ignorance. They were unwilling to accept the latent, and often manifest, racism that relegated the Indian to a position of inferiority and described him, in Kipling's words, as "half devil and half child." In defense of Indian civilization, both reformers and revivalists drew upon the Orientalists, the European scholars who like Sir William Jones and Max Müller revealed the richness of Indian antiquity and the wisdom of the Sanskritic tradition.

Ram Mohan Roy paved the way for a century of social reform with the establishment of the *Brahmo Samaj*, or Divine Society, in 1830. The society, directed toward the literate middle classes, gained a small intellectual following, but under renewed leadership in the 1860s, it became increasingly vigorous in its advocacy of monotheism and social reform. Branches were established throughout India, but only in Bengal

---

[8] Thomas R. Metcalf, *The Aftermath of Revolt* (Princeton, N.J.: Princeton University Press, 1964), p. 324.
[9] Spear, *A History of India*, Vol. 2, p. 153.

and in Maharashtra, where it sparked the Prarthana Samaj, did it meet with significant success. The Prarthana Samaj become the center of social reform in western India under the leadership of M. G. Ranade. Believing revival impossible, Ranade sought to preserve tradition through reform. The Arya Samaj, founded in Bombay in 1875 by a Gujarati Brahmin, Swami Dayananda, took a more aggressive and revivalist stance. The Arya Samaj sought to lead India "back to Vedas," the earliest Hindu scriptures, in an effort to recover and restore the Aryan past. Like Roy and Ranade, Dayananda believed in one god and denounced the evils of post-Vedic Hinduism—idolatry, child marriage, and the restrictions of caste—but he also rejected Western knowledge, claiming that the scientific truths of modern thought were all to be found in the Vedas, if seen with enlightened eyes. The Arya Samaj reacted strongly to the influences of Islam and Christianity, and its proselytic fundamentalism contributed to the rise of enmity toward the Muslim community, particularly in the Punjab and in the United Provinces, where the society found its greatest success.

The conflict between Hindus and Muslims engendered by the activities of the Arya Samaj served only to underscore the alienation of the Muslim community in India. The collapse of Mogul rule brought confusion and doubt to the Muslims. The Muslim reaction to British rule was by no means uniform, but clinging to traditions of the past and to memories of their former glory, many Muslims remained unresponsive to the changes around them. Since they regarded English as "the highway to infidelity," they failed to take advantage of English education and were soon displaced in the civil services by the rising Hindu middle class. As the resentment of the Muslim community turned suspicion and hostility upon them, the Muslim reformer and educator Sayyid Ahmed Khan sought to convince the British of Muslim loyalty and to bring the community into cooperation with British authorities. At the same time, he warned of the dangers of Hindu domination under democratic rule. Hindu rule would fall more heavily upon Muslims than the neutral authority of the British raj.

Growing Political Consciousness

The rise of the new Indian middle class and the movements for reform, while regionally based and accentuating divisions within Indian society, nevertheless served as a catalyst for the development of a national self-consciousness. Upon Bengali and Marathi regionalism, the new class grafted an all-India nationalism. "Mother India had become a necessity and so she was created."[10] The obstacles to the growth of Indian nationalism were many and difficult to overcome—the divisions between British India and the various princely states, the divisions be-

[10] *Ibid.*, p. 166. See also Charles H. Heimsath, *Indian Nationalism and Hindu Social Reform* (Princeton, N.J.: Princeton University Press, 1964), pp. 135–36.

tween the linguistic regions, and the divisions of religion and caste within the society. The new middle class transcended these divisions, in part, through their unity of mind and speech. Their knowledge of English, commitment to liberal values, and pride in Indian civilization were the foundation for a common all-India view. Reforms served to offer the promise of a better future, and increasing opportunities were opening in the government services for educated Indians. At the same time, however, the British in India often acted without regard to Indian opinion. Indians were virtually excluded from the higher offices of the civil service, and the arrogant stance of imperialist responsibility cut deeply into Indian self-respect. That the behavior of the British in India contrasted so starkly with the values of English liberalism in which the Indian middle class had been steeped served to deepen their national consciousness.

In 1876 Surendranath Banerjea, dismissed—on insufficient grounds—from the Indian Civil Service, founded the Indian Association of Calcutta, which provided the groundwork for an all-India movement for the redress of wrongs and the protection of rights. "Indianization" of the Indian Civil Service was a central issue. The ICS had become the "steel frame" of British administration, and membership carried prestige and status. The Charter Act of 1833, introducing a system of competitive examinations for the service, provided that no Indian "shall by reason only of his religion, place of birth, descent, colour or any of them be disabled from holding any office or employment under the Company." This was reaffirmed in the Queen's Proclamation and in the Indian Civil Service Act of 1861.

There was, however, an obvious reluctance to admit Indians. The examinations were held only in London, and the examination itself virtually required study in England. As an increasing number of Indians successfully surmounted these barriers, admission was rendered more difficult when in 1878 the maximum age for application was reduced from twenty-two to nineteen.[11] The occasion served as an opportunity for Banerjea to organize a national protest. "The underlying conception, and the true aim and purpose of the Civil Service Agitation," he wrote, "was the awakening of a spirit of unity and solidarity among the people of India." The agitation demonstrated that "whatever might be our differences in respect of race and language, or social and religious institutions, the people of India could combine and unite for the attainment of their common political ends."

It was the Ilbert bill, however, which provided the catalyst for the development of an all-India organization. The bill, introduced in 1883,

[11] The Indianization of the ICS was negligible in the early years. In 1913, eighty years after the Charter Act, the proportion of Indians in the services was only 5 percent. By 1921, it was 13 percent, but by the time of independence, 48 percent was Indian. Naresh Chandra Roy, *The Civil Service in India* (Calcutta: Mukhopadhyay, 1958), p. 154.

was intended to remove distinctions between Indian and European judges, thus revoking the exemption of Englishmen in India from trial by native judges. The nonofficial English community in Calcutta exploded in an outburst of racial feeling. They formed a defense association and collected funds to support their agitation against the legislation.[12] The furor led the Government to withdraw the bill. The success of the agitation against the bill left the new Indian middle class with a sense of humiliation, but the effectiveness of organization as a political instrument had been impressed upon them.

THE CREATION OF THE CONGRESS

In response, Banerjea founded the Indian National Conference in 1883. In that same year a retired English civil servant, A. O. Hume, addressed an open letter to the graduates of Calcutta University, urging the organization of an association for the political regeneration of India —what, as he later said, might form "the germ of a Native Parliament." The first meeting of the Indian National Congress, attended by seventy-two delegates, was held in Bombay in 1885. Soon thereafter Banerjea merged his own association with the Congress.

The Congress affirmed its loyalty to the Queen, and with the dignity and moderation of a debating society, it sought by resolutions made at its annual meetings to rouse the British conscience to certain inequities of British rule and to the justice of Indian claims for greater representation in the civil services and in the legislative councils at the Center and in the provinces. The Indian liberals who dominated the Congress from 1885 to 1905 had an almost unlimited faith in British democracy. "England is our political guide," Banerjea declared. "It is not severance that we look forward to—but unification, permanent embodiment as an integral part of that great Empire that has given the rest of the world the models of free institutions." Even Dadabhai Naoroji, who formulated the "drain theory" of India's exploitation by British economic imperialism, remained "loyal to the backbone" and was the first Indian elected to the British House of Commons.

In these early years the Government regarded the Congress favorably as a "safety valve" for revolutionary discontent, but remained unresponsive to its polite resolutions and humble petitions. Indeed, Hume was led to remark that "the National Congress had endeavored to instruct the Government, but the Government had refused to be instructed." As Congress liberals sought to bring somewhat greater pressure on the Government, the raj expressed its official disapproval of the policy and methods of the association. The Viceroy denounced the Congress as reflecting only the interests of the educated middle class, who constituted but a rootless, "microscopic minority" that could hardly be taken as representative of Indian opinion. The British conceived them-

12 See Metcalf, *The Aftermath of Revolt*, p. 309.

selves to be the servants of truly representative Indian interests. The "real" India was not to be found among the effete babus of the city, but in the timeless villages, citadels of rugged peasant virtue.[13]

With growing disillusionment, the Congress assumed a stance of constitutional opposition to the Government, but such leaders as G. K. Gokhale retained faith in the "integrity and beneficence of that which was best in the British tradition."[14] Gokhale, friend and disciple of Ranade, was deeply committed to liberal reform and toward that end had founded the Servants of India Society in 1905. In that same year, as its dominant leader, Gokhale was elected president of the Indian National Congress.

THE RIFT BETWEEN MODERATES AND EXTREMISTS

Within Congress ranks, however, a militant Extremist wing grew impatient with the gradualism of the Moderates. The demand for administrative reform was replaced by the call for *swaraj*, or self-rule. Extremist suport was centered in the Punjab, Bengal, and Maharashtra, where the militants drew inspiration not from the ideals of English liberalism but from India's past. Reform appealed to the cultivated intellects of the English-educated middle classes, but only the passion of revivalism could capture the imagination of the masses and provide the foundation for wider participation. Aurobindo Ghose in Bengal infused the movement with a "neo-Vedantic" mysticism, and in western India, Bal Gangadhar Tilak evoked the memory of Shivaji, founder of the Maratha kingdom, and of his struggle against the Muslim invaders. Tilak recalled the days of Maratha and Hindu glory and, not without concern among Muslims, sought to stir a revival of Hindu religious consciousness to serve his political ends. Tilak castigated the Moderates for what he regarded as their cultural capitulation to the West. Struggle, not reform, was the keynote of his message: "Swaraj is my birthright and I will have it." In examining the role of Tilak, "the Father of Indian Unrest," Stanley Wolpert has written,

> His dream was not an India made in its foreign master's image, but one restored to the glory of its own true self. The quicker the British left, the happier he and his land would be. There could be no salvation for India in the self-deception of constitutional cooperation. Better to rely on the yoga of boycott.[15]

In 1905 Bengal was divided into two provinces; East Bengal comprised what is today Bangladesh. The partition gave impetus to the boycott of British goods and advanced the *swadeshi* movement for the use of indigenous products. The partition, designed solely with regard

[13] See Hutchins, *The Illusion of Permanence*, pp. 156–57.
[14] Stanley Wolpert, *Tilak and Gokhale* (Berkeley: University of California Press, 1962), p. 299.
[15] *Ibid.*, p. 304.

for administrative efficiency, completely ignored the renascent Bengali consciousness. A storm of protest, under the leadership of Surendranath Banerjea and such eminent Bengalis as Rabindranath Tagore, brought widespread popular opposition to the British raj. Boycott offered the possibility of mass participation. The emotion vented in agitation was accompanied by terrorism and, in the name of the demonic goddess Kali, assassination.

The Bengal partition brought a new urgency to the aspirations of Indian nationalists, and at their meeting in 1906 the Congress resolved to support the demand for swaraj. Gokhale and the Moderates envisioned responsible government within the British Empire—a position wholly unacceptable to the Extremists. The following year, the Congress meeting at Surat broke up in an uproar as the Extremists walked out, leaving the Moderates in control of the organization. Tilak, now in a political wilderness, was drawn increasingly toward the advocacy of violence in "political warfare" against the British. The Government enacted increasingly repressive measures to bring the wave of terrorism under control, and Tilak was arrested. Released after six years, he pledged his support and loyalty to the Congress. It was Tilak, however, given the title *Lokamanya*, or Honored by the People, who more than any of the early Congress leaders had sought to reach the masses, to transform the nationalist cause into a popular movement.

The Limited British Response

The Moderate position within the Congress was strengthened by the Morley-Minto Reforms of 1909 and the rescision of the Bengal partition. Since shortly after the assumption of direct rule by the Crown, there had been some degree of Indian representation in government, but as Morris-Jones argues, "whether or not the British Empire was won in a fit of absent-mindedness, such a mood seems to have had a good deal to do with the establishment of parliamentary institutions in India. . . ."[16] Under the Indian Councils Act of 1861, three Indians were appointed to the advisory Legislative Council at the Center as nonofficial members. Not until 1891, however, partly to placate the Congress, did the Government increase the number of members in the Central and provincial legislative councils and concede the principle of election, at least indirectly. The Morley-Minto Reforms, drafted in consultation with Gokhale and other Indian leaders, expanded the legislative councils, thereby increasing Indian representation, introduced direct election of nonofficials under limited property franchise, and in the provinces provided for nonofficial majorities. Recommendations of the councils, however, could be disallowed at the discretion of the Viceroy or of the provincial governor; thus the councils were to a degree representative,

16 W. H. Morris-Jones, *Parliament in India* (London: Longmans, Green, 1957), p. 73.

but not responsible. In fact, Morley declared that "if it could be said that this chapter of reforms led directly or indirectly to the establishment of a parliamentary system, I, for one, would have nothing to do with it."

The reforms provided limited institutional access to the new Indian middle class and sought to accommodate a range of moderate demands for representation. The Congress carried little weight, however, in the face of the highly institutionalized structures of the British raj. The repressive powers of the bureaucracy and the army could at any time be used against the few politically active Indians. The Congress had not yet gained the political capital of widespread popular support, of mass participation, that would allow it to challenge the British presence seriously. The Moderates were ready to work within the framework of imperial rule, making limited, though increasing, demands for greater access; the Extremists, lacking broad support and harassed by the Government, had been driven underground. The British lack of more genuine responsiveness to even the limited aspirations of Indian leaders and their readiness to use the power of repressive order to suppress opposition served, however, to awaken the political consciousness of the growing middle class.

The Morley-Minto Reforms, by their acceptance of Muslim demands for separate electorates, introduced the principle of communal representation. In presenting their case before the Government, the Muslim notables argued that without separate electorates the Muslim community would be submerged in the Hindu majority, which was becoming increasingly participant and vocal in its demands for representation. To advance their position, these notables organized the Muslim League in 1906 at Dacca. The League was the first real attempt by Indian Muslims to utilize an organization to secure a more favorable position. Its membership was middle class and concerned primarily with more jobs, better educational opportunities, and higher social and economic status. More a clique than a movement, it nevertheless reflected the awakening of Muslim political consciousness.[17]

The award of communal representation to the Muslims was attacked by Congress nationalists as an attempt to weaken national unity with the strategy of divide and rule. The British had found in the Muslim community a useful counterpoise to the growing force of the Congress. Within the League, however, the position of the loyalist Muslims was soon challenged by the Young Muhammadans, who sought political confrontation, rather than accommodation with the raj. By 1916 the Congress seemed prepared to accept separate electorates in exchange for the support of the Muslims, who because of the war between Great Britain and Turkey had been roused to anti-British feeling. The Luck-

[17] Wayne A. Wilcox, *Pakistan: The Consolidation of a Nation* (New York: Columbia University Press, 1963), p. 20. See also Khalid B. Sayeed, *Pakistan: The Formative Phase, 1857–1948*, 2nd ed. (New York: Oxford University Press, 1968).

now Pact, concluded in that year at a joint session of the Congress and the Muslim League, called for the achievement of self-government.

The Lucknow Congress, held a year after Gokhale's death, marked the reemergence of Tilak as Congress leader. In that same year Tilak founded the Home Rule League, and he was followed soon after by the English theosophist Annie Besant, who organized a Home Rule League in Madras. In alliance, Tilak and Besant reasserted the Extremist faction within the Congress, and in 1917, while interned by the British Government, Besant was elected president of the Indian National Congress. Moderate leaders soon withdrew to found the Indian Liberal Federation.

The Morley-Minto Reforms, while gradually moving India closer to responsible government, did not fulfill the rising expectations of Indian nationalists. India's involvement in the world war had brought a commitment of loyalty that soon turned to frustration and a diminished awe of imperial power, as the British called for sacrifice in exchange for vague promises of reform "after the war." Indian agitation for change was strengthened by Woodrow Wilson's declaration of the right of all nations to self-determination. As the demands for swaraj intensified with the home rule movement, Edwin Montagu, who had succeeded Morley as Secretary of State for India, announced in 1917 the Government policy "of increasing association of Indians in every branch of the administration and the gradual development of self-governing institutions with a view to the progressive realization of responsible government in India as an integral part of the British Empire."

The first step toward implementing this policy was the enactment of the Montagu-Chelmsford Reforms in 1919. Under the Act, authority was decentralized, with a division of functions between the Center and the provincial governments. At the Center, there was little substantive change. Bicameralism was introduced, with an elected nonofficial majority in the lower house, but the Governor General, responsible to London, retained the overriding powers of certification and veto. In the provinces, however, the reforms introduced *dyarchy*, or dual government, under which the governor retained authority over certain "reserved" subjects—largely in the areas of revenue and law and order—while "transferred" subjects, such as local self-government, education, health, public works, agriculture, and industry, came under the control of ministers responsible to popularly elected legislatures. Council memberships were enlarged, and the principle of communal representation was extended both at the Center and in the provinces.

The Congress Call for Swaraj

For many Congress leaders the reforms were just a sop. This seemed confirmed by the enactment of the Rowlatt Bills in 1919, extending the emergency powers assumed during the war to permit imprisonment without trial in political cases. In protest against the repressive "black bills," demonstrations and strikes were held throughout the country. Feelings were most intense in those more politically self-conscious regions where revivalism, and later Extremism, had gained a foothold among the masses. In the Punjab, where the situation was particularly tense, the arrest of two Congress leaders sparked a riot. Martial law was proclaimed and a ban on all public meetings was imposed. Defying the ban, an estimated 20,000 people gathered at the central park of Amritsar, Jallianwalla Bagh. Under the command of General Dyer, 150 troops suddenly appeared at the entrance and ordered the crowd to disperse. With the military blocking the only entrance, Dyer then gave the order to fire point-blank into the unarmed masses. When the ammunition was exhausted, 370 Indians were dead and some 1200 more wounded. Dyer intended the massacre "to teach the natives a lesson."

At the end of the year the Indian National Congress met at Amritsar in a mood of outrage and shock. The Montagu-Chelmsford Reforms were denounced as "inadequate, unsatisfactory and disappointing," but Tilak, who was to live less than a year, had mellowed, and he urged a policy of "responsive co-operation" with the Government. Indian restraint, however, was pushed beyond the limit of its endurance when in 1920 the House of Lords gave a vote of appreciation to General Dyer for his services. Mohandas Gandhi, the new Congress leader, proclaimed that "cooperation in any shape or form with this satanic government is sinful."

The Nationalist Movement

Gandhi's Philosophy of Satyagraha and His Role in the Congress

Gandhi was born into a Gujarati Vaishya family in Kathiawar, where his father was the *diwan*, or head minister, of a petty princely state. After completing university studies in Bombay, Gandhi read for the bar at the Inner Temple in London. After two years, still very much an Indian, he returned to India for legal practice. But the young barrister was soon invited to South Africa to plead the case of the Indian community against discriminatory legislation. He planned to stay one year; he remained for twenty.

In South Africa, with the Gita as his "infallible guide of conduct," he began his experiments with *satyagraha*, or nonviolent resistance, which he translated as "soul force."[18] It was satyagraha that was "to revolutionize Indian politics and to galvanize millions into action

[18] Mohandas Gandhi, *An Autobiography, or The Story of My Experiments with Truth* (Ahmedabad: Navajivan Publishing House, 1927), p. 195. See also Joan V. Bondurant, *Conquest of Violence* (Berkeley: University of California Press, 1965).

against the British Raj."[19] Already known for his South African victory, Gandhi was greeted upon his return to India in 1915 with the title *Mahatma*, or Great Soul. For the next three years, however, he remained a silent observer of the political scene, taking the advice of his political mentor Gokhale to keep "his ears open and his mouth shut" for a time.

During this period Gandhi became increasingly sensitive to the gap between the predominantly urban middle-class Congress and the Indian masses, and shifted his attentions to the villages and the peasants. In 1918, while introducing satyagraha in India, Gandhi courted arrest in support of the indigo plantation workers of Bihar. A year later, when the repressive Rowlatt Bills were introduced, Gandhi organized the Satyagraha Society, pledged to disobey the unjust law as a symbol of passive resistance. To mobilize mass support he called for a day of fasting and *hartal*, or general strike, in protest against the legislation.[20] The violence that marred the demonstrations led Gandhi to regard satyagraha as premature, as a "Himalayan miscalculation." For others, however, it marked the turning point in the struggle for sv araj.

Gandhi regarded his participation in the 919 Amritsar meeting as his "real entrance" into Congress politics. Thereafter, he became its guiding force. In seeking to mobilize mass resistance to the Government, Gandhi gained Muslim support through his appeal on the emotionally charged Khilafat issue, denouncing the dismemberment of the Ottoman Empire and the deposition of the Caliph, the religious head of all Muslims. The noncooperation movement was launched with the call for a boycott of the impending elections and the law courts, and for withdrawal from all government schools and colleges. Middle-class Indians, institutionally co-opted by the British raj, were now drawn into new patterns of political participation. Congress members were asked to resign from government office and to renounce all titles. More than thirty thousand Congressmen, including Motilal Nehru and his son Jawaharlal, courted arrest in defiance of "lawless laws" and gained honor through imprisonment. The civil disobedience was accompanied by the outbreak of sporadic strikes, by the rebellion of Muslims in Malabar on the southwestern coast, by no-tax campaigns, and on the visit of the Prince of Wales, by a nation-wide hartal. In February 1922, to the dismay of Congress leaders, Gandhi abruptly called an end to the movement, as he had done before, when mob violence in a small town in Uttar Pradesh left twenty-two policemen dead. Gandhi declared that he would not purchase independence at the price of bloodshed. Within days he was arrested and tried for sedition.

---

[19] Michael Brecher, *Nehru: A Political Biography* (New York: Oxford University Press, 1959), p. 59.

[20] Explaining this political tactic in the cultural context of India, Spear notes, "In theory, the soul is too shocked by some abuse to be able to attend to practical affairs for a time." *A History of India*, Vol. 2, p. 191.

During the two years that Gandhi was imprisoned, Hindu-Muslim unity was broken by the outbreak of communal rioting. Upon his release in 1924 Gandhi began a twenty-one-day fast for Hindu-Muslim solidarity, but to no avail. Thereafter, the Muslim League, representing the greater portion of the Muslim community, took an increasingly separate path from that of the Congress. The breach seemed irrevocable when the Congress refused in 1928 to accept separate communal electorates as part of the proposed constitutional change.

Within the Congress the solidarity forged during the noncooperation movement gave way to division on the issue of council entry. The legislative councils, boycotted by the Congress, were growing in importance and prestige under the provincial non-Congress ministries. While Gandhi was still in prison C. R. Das and Motilal Nehru led the Congress in the formation of the Swaraja party to contest the next council elections with the purpose of destroying the reforms from within by "uniform, consistent and continuous obstruction." The very entry of the Congress into the councils, however, increased their prestige and made them all the more difficult to subvert. Many Swarajists were led increasingly to favor a position of "responsive cooperation" with the Government for the achievement of swaraj. The Gandhians or "nochangers," opposed the Swarajist strategy and, losing their dominance in the Congress for the time, retired to engage in "constructive work." From his *ashram*, a retreat near Ahmedabad, Gandhi worked for the uplift of the untouchables, whom he called *harijans*, or "children of God," and with his own hands performed their "defiling" tasks. While the Swarajists debated in the councils, Gandhi led his swadeshi campaign for the use of *khadi*, a homespun cloth. Clothed simply in a loincloth and shawl, he would spin for a half-hour or more each day and urged all Congressmen to do likewise. The spinning wheel, emblazoned in the center of the Congress flag, became the symbol of the society Gandhi sought to achieve—a peasant society, self-governing and self-sufficient. Purity of the soul was requisite to the attainment of swaraj; only through self-discipline could India prepare herself and make herself worthy of freedom.

In accordance with the provision of the Montagu-Chelmsford Reforms for a parliamentary review after ten years, the Simon Commission was appointed for the recommendation of constitutional changes. The Congress regarded the commission's all-British membership as not in accord with the principle of self-determination and resolved to boycott its proceedings. In 1928 the Congress, the Muslim League, and the Liberal Federation came together in an All-Parties Convention to frame a constitution for an independent India. The report, drafted by Motilal Nehru, called for responsible government and dominion status. The young radicals Jawaharlal Nehru and Subhas Chandra Bose opposed the recommendation for dominion status. With the intervention of Gandhi the Congress agreed to accept the Nehru Report, but only if the proposed constitution were accepted in its entirety by Parliament before the end of 1929. Failing this, the Congress would launch nonviolent noncooperation in pursuit of independence.

The Governor General, Lord Irwin, announced that "the natural issue of India's Constitutional progress . . . is the attainment of Dominion status" and that toward that end a round-table conference would be held in London to discuss the recommendations of the Simon Commission. In accordance with its pledge, the Congress met in December 1929 at Lahore and there declared complete independence as its goal. It was resolved to boycott the legislative councils and the Round Table Conference and, under the direction of Gandhi, to begin a program of civil disobedience and nonpayment of taxes. At Lahore the elder Nehru, with little more than a year to live, passed the chair of the Congress presidency to his son. On December 29 Jawaharlal Nehru hoisted the national flag of India.

The Civil Disobedience Campaign

In launching the campaign of civil disobedience Gandhi announced his intention to violate the salt tax, a burden on even the poorest peasant and a source of bitter resentment against the raj. He would march from his ashram to the sea, a distance of 241 miles, and there, by taking salt from the sea, would disobey the law. The dramatic march lasted twenty-four days, and with this act of defiance, mass demonstrations, hartals, and civil disobedience began throughout India. The Government quickly responded with repressive measures. More than one hundred people were killed in police firings, and indiscriminate beatings of men and women were widespread. In less than one year some sixty thousand people were imprisoned.

During the Congress campaign, non-Congress representatives attended the Round Table Conference, but the Viceroy realized that any decisions would be hollow without Congress participation. In 1931 he released Gandhi and began a series of conversations that concluded in the Gandhi-Irwin pact. The Government agreed to withdraw its repressive measures and to release all political prisoners except those guilty of violence. Gandhi called off the civil disobedience campaign and agreed to attend the next round-table conference as a representative of the Congress. The London conference deadlocked on the question of communal electorates, and Gandhi returned "empty-handed" to India. With renewal of Government repression, the Congress reopened the civil disobedience campaign and called for the boycott of British goods. By March 1933 more than 120,000 people had been imprisoned.

At this inopportune moment, the Government announced its constitutional proposals, which included a provision for separate electorates for the untouchables. Believing the untouchables to be an integral part of the Hindu community, Gandhi, in jail, vowed to "fast unto death" against the provision. Gandhi began the fast despite the pleas of all. On the fifth day, as Gandhi's life was believed to hang in the balance, Dr. Ambedkar, leader of the untouchables, gave way and agreed to abandon separate communal electorates, but, to safeguard the interests of the untouchables he demanded that a number of seats be reserved for them within the allotment of seats to the Hindu community.

The fast, while stirring concern for the untouchables, diverted attention from the issue of independence and brought the collapse of the civil disobedience campaign. Radicals within the Congress declared that Gandhi had failed as a political leader and called for a new leadership. In the radical view the nationalist movement under Gandhi had become what was later described as "a peculiar blend of bold advances followed by sudden and capricious halts, challenges succeeded by unwarranted compromises. . . ."[21]

British Accommodation: The Government of India Act of 1935

The British sought to respond to widening political participation and increasingly vocal demands with the Government of India Act of 1935, which adapted the high levels of institutional capability to a changing environment. Abandoning its policy of repression, the Government sought to buy stability through accommodation; stability was the *raison d'état*. The Act abolished dyarchy and provided for provincial autonomy with responsible government, accountable to a greatly expanded electorate. The franchise continued to carry a property qualification, but by the Act, the electorate was expanded from six million to thirty million, one-sixth of the adult population. The federal arrangement—never actually brought into operation—provided for the integration of princely states with British India. The all-India federation, which provided the model for the federal structure of independent India, was to consist of governor's provinces, chief commissioner's provinces, and those acceding princely states. Legislative power was divided according to detailed lists, distinguishing Central, provincial, and concurrent jurisdiction. Representation in the federal legislature was heavily weighted in favor of the princes, giving a conservative cast to the Center. At the Center a dyarchical arrangement was introduced by which the Governor General, responsible only to the British Parliament, was invested with a number of discretionary powers and enjoyed "reserved power" over such departments as defense and external affairs. A. B. Keith, in his study of the constitutional history of India, argues that these provisions rendered "the alleged concession of responsibility all but meaningless."[22] Nehru termed the reform act a "slave" constitution—yet many features of the 1935 Act were later incorporated into the Constitution of the Republic of India.

---

[21] A. R. Desai, *Social Background of Indian Nationalism* (Bombay: Popular Book Depot, 1959), pp. 343–44.
[22] A *Constitutional History of India: 1600–1935*, a reprint of the 2nd, 1926 edition (New York: Barnes & Noble, 1969), p. 474.

In a very real sense the provincial autonomy granted under the Act was a substantive move toward meeting Congress demands for swaraj. Once again, as in 1922, the Congress resolved to work within the new reforms, and in 1937 it swept the provincial elections for Hindu seats and formed ministries in seven of the eleven provinces. The Muslim League fared poorly among the Muslim electorate and failed to secure majorities in any of the four predominantly Muslim provinces. Mohammed Ali Jinnah, the westernized leader of the League, offered to form coalition ministries with the Congress in each province, but the Congress refused to recognize the League as representative of India's ninety million Muslims. "There are," Nehru remarked, "only two forces in India today, British imperialism and Indian nationalism as represented by the Congress." History, however, bore out Jinnah's response: "No, there is a third party, the Mussulmans." The Congress was to pay dearly for its imperious attitude: "The opening shots had been fired in the calamitous Congress-League war which was to envelop north India in flames and ultimately result in partition."[23] In 1940 Jinnah declared that the Hindus and Muslims formed two separate nations. The Muslim League now adopted as its goal the creation of a separate and independent Islamic state, Pakistan.

During their term of office, the Congress ministries demonstrated considerable administrative ability and produced a distinguished record of achievements in social reform.[24] Inevitably, with their assumption of office, question arose as to the relationship between the ministries and the party. Participation in provincial government was only one aspect of the Congress struggle, and Nehru emphasized the primary responsibility of each ministry to the Congress high command from whom they would take directive. The high command itself was by no means united, but in 1939, with the resignation of Bose after his confrontation with Gandhi, the two main factions, the old guard (Rajendra Prasad and Sardar Vallabhbhai Patel) and the socialists (Nehru), united behind Gandhi's leadership.

Bose formed a new party, the Forward Bloc, and in 1941 appeared in Germany and later in Japan to secure support for the Government of Free India, which he proclaimed in Japanese-occupied Singapore. There Bose, now called *Netaji*, or Leader, organized the Indian National Army.

Renewed Demands for Independence

The tide of war imposed a new strain on the nationalist cause. In 1939 the Viceroy proclaimed India's involvement in the war without consulting Indian leaders. The Congress condemned fascist aggression

[23] Brecher, *Nehru,* p. 231.
[24] For a discussion of the Congress ministries, see Reginald Coupland, *The Constitutional Problem in India* (New York: Oxford University Press, 1944).

but declared that India could not associate itself with the war effort unless it was given immediate independence and equality as a free nation. When this demand was ignored the Congress directed the provincial ministries to resign in protest. In August 1940 Congress again offered complete cooperation in the war in exchange for at least a provisional national government. The Viceroy made vague allusions to independence "after the war," but went on to promise the Muslims and other minorities that Britain would not accept any constitutional modification to which they were opposed.

The Muslim League refused to cooperate with the Congress, and after the resignation of the Congress ministries, it proclaimed a "Day of Deliverance" from the "tyranny, oppression and injustice" of Congress rule. The departure of the Congress from provincial government at that critical time left the League in an advantageous position, one that by the end of the war would be virtually irresistible.

With the failure of the Congress offer, Gandhi again assumed leadership and opened a campaign of individual civil disobedience designed to symbolize Congress protest without disrupting the British war effort. Congress moderation was met by severe Government reaction. In 1942, however, as the Japanese advanced through Burma, Sir Stafford Cripps, on mission from London, promised the establishment of a constituent assembly and full dominion status after the war. Nehru and perhaps the majority of the Congress high command were responsive to the offer, but Gandhi, firmly opposed, held the balance. Nehru held out until the last, but finally submitted to Gandhi's persuasion. In August 1942 Gandhi demanded that Great Britain "quit India" or confront mass civil disobedience. The Government declared Congress illegal, and within hours Gandhi and the Congress leadership were taken into custody. They spent the rest of the war in prison. (C. Rajagopalachari, unable to support the resolution, resigned from the Congress.) The arrests set off a political explosion. Violence erupted throughout India, and by the end of the year, about one hundred thousand people had been arrested and more than one thousand killed in police firings.

The Quit India movement represented the apogee of the independence struggle in terms of mass involvement, but in a nation of nearly four hundred million people, the relative numbers of participants must have been small indeed. The various noncooperation movements beginning in the 1920s under Gandhi fundamentally changed the character of the Congress, transforming it from an urban middle-class coterie into a movement with an extensive social base reaching into the villages. If by 1942 Congress had enlisted four to five million members and widespread support, other millions, for various reasons of self-interest, remained loyal to British rule, and even greater numbers remained uninvolved or wholly unaware of the dramatic events transpiring around them. The nationalist movement, even in penetrating the villages, had limited impact. Those who were mobilized in the rural areas were far more likely to be the fairly prosperous peasants than the landless laborers. The mobilization of the still largely inert Indian masses to political consciousness and participation would remain the developmental task of India's leaders in the years after independence.

The Achievement of Swaraj

With the release of Gandhi in 1944, negotiations began again, as the Governor General proposed the formation of a national government. Discussions broke down when the Congress refused to recognize the League as the sole representative of the Muslim community. The war years had consolidated Jinnah's strength in the Muslim areas, however, and in the elections held at the beginning of 1946, the League swept the Muslim seats, as did the Congress the general seats. "The two-nations theory of Mr. Jinnah had found political expression."[25]

Prime Minister Atlee now announced the appointment of a Cabinet mission to India "to promote, in conjunction with the leaders of Indian opinion, the early realization of full self-government in India." Confronted with the widening gap between the Congress and the League, the mission sought to preserve a united India and to allay Muslim fears of Hindu domination through the proposal of a loose federation. Without satisfaction, both sides accepted the plan, but the Congress rejected the proposals for an interim government, again over the issue of allotment of seats; the Congress, representing all India, was unwilling to accord the Muslim League its claim to represent all Muslims and therefore to have the right to fill all seats reserved for Muslims in the Cabinet. The Congress announced that it would, nevertheless, participate in the Constituent Assembly to frame the constitution. Jinnah countered by declaring a day of "direct action," unleashing a wave of communal rioting.

In September 1946 Nehru took office as *de facto* Prime Minister of the interim government. Fearing isolation, Jinnah brought the League into the Government, but only to demonstrate that the Hindu and Muslim communities could not work in harmony and that the formation of Pakistan was the only solution. The obstructionist stance of the League brought negotiations to an impasse. At this point, on February 20, 1947, the British Government declared that it intended to quit India no later than June 1948 and that Lord Mountbatten had been appointed Viceroy to arrange for the transfer of power to Indian hands—however prepared they might be to accept it.

Communal rioting again broke out, and the Punjab approached civil war. Gandhi was prepared to see the whole of India burn rather than concede Pakistan. Congress power, however, lay with Nehru and the more traditional Sardar Vallabhbhai Patel, both of whom by this

[25] Spear, *A History of India*, Vol. 2, p. 231.

time had come to accept the inevitability of partition. With their agreement Mountbatten laid out the plan for the transfer of power. The predominantly Muslim provinces would be allowed to form a separate Islamic state and to draw up their own constitution. Bengal and the Punjab, where the two communities were almost equal in numbers, would be divided as defined by a boundary commission. In the Northwest Frontier Province, where a pro-Congress Muslim government had a precarious majority, a referendum would be held. The princely states, released from British paramountcy, would be given the freedom to accede to either India or Pakistan—or, presumably, to declare their independence. Moving with incredible speed, Mountbatten, who was to stay on as the first Governor General of the new India, moved up the calendar of British withdrawal. On August 15, 1947, India became an independent nation. "Long years ago," Nehru declared, "we made a tryst with destiny, and now the time comes when we shall redeem our pledge. . . ."

The Partition and Gandhi's Assassination

The achievement of swaraj was dimmed by the tragedy of partition and the assassination of Gandhi. The partition, in dividing Hindus and Muslims, had shattered Gandhi's dream of a free and united India, but the territorial division left millions of each community on both sides of the border. In the Punjab the boundary award, as anticipated, divided the cohesive and militant Sikh community almost equally between the two states. Here, in mounting hysteria, violence, and atrocity, Muslims fell upon Sikhs and Hindus in the West, and Sikhs and Hindus upon Muslims in the East. Before the end of the year half a million people had been killed. In the movement of refugees four and one-half million Hindus and Sikhs left West Pakistan for India; six million Muslims moved in the other direction. Rioting broke out in Bengal, but massacre was avoided, in part because of a Bengali consciousness that transcended religious division, but also because of the presence of Gandhi in Calcutta, "a one man boundary force." The costs of human suffering were, nevertheless, enormous: more than one million persons crossed the Bengal border from East Pakistan into India, leaving behind most of their possessions and bringing with them a bitterness that was to infect the communal life of Calcutta for years to come.

The Punjab was brought under control, but as hundreds of thousands of refugees poured into Delhi, the Muslims who either had chosen to remain or else could not leave, now faced a bloodbath of revenge. Gandhi sought to reconcile the two communities by his presence, to protect the Muslims and urge them to stay, and to calm the troubled city. On January 13, 1948, Gandhi began a fast, to death if necessary, to stir "the conscience of all"—Hindu, Muslim, and Sikh. The fast, which lasted five days and brought the Mahatma near death, ended only with the Indian Government's agreement to release Pakistan's share of the assets of British India and with agreement by representatives of all communities, led by Nehru, Prasad, and Azad, to "protect the life, property, and faith" of the Muslims.

Some within the Congress, such as Sardar Patel, did not approve of Gandhi's intervention on behalf of the Muslims. Others, the Hindu militants of the Mahasabha party and the Rashtriya Swayamsevak Sangh, openly denounced Gandhi for allegedly helping the Muslims against the Hindus. A bomb attempt was made on Gandhi's life, and then on January 20, twelve days after he had broken his fast, as he proceeded to his prayer meeting on the lawn of the palatial Birla House, Gandhi was shot by a young Hindu fanatic of the RSS. That evening, Nehru announced to the world, "The light has gone out of our lives and there is darkness everywhere. . . ."

Gandhi had served to mobilize widespread support for the Congress struggle for independence, and if he did not hasten its arrival, he nevertheless imbued the movement with moral concern and stirred the conscience of the world. By making the Congress a more representative organization, Gandhi fundamentally changed the character of the nationalist struggle for independence. He broadened the base of the party in his appeal to the masses, but at the same time served to "Indianize" the middle class. His vision of society, however, had turned him from the path of the modernists and their commitment to industrialization and Western parliamentary government, and with independence, he urged Congressmen to leave politics for "constructive work." Gandhi argued that the Congress "as a propaganda vehicle and parliamentary machine [had] outlived its use" and that "it must be kept out of unhealthy competition with political parties." Gandhi's death, mourned by all, brought a national reaction against the Mahasabha and Hindu extremism. It also served to free Nehru from the constraints of Gandhi's vision—but Gandhism had entered the political culture, more a charismatic memory than a revolutionary force, espoused by every shade of opinion and utilized for every purpose.

Formation of the Indian Union

In the wake of partition and Gandhi's death, India faced the problems of consolidation: the integration of the princely states and the framing of a constitution. Approximately two-fifths of the area under the raj had been made up of these 562 principalities, ranging in size from a few square miles to an area as large as Hyderabad, with seventeen million people. With persuasion and pressure, Sardar Vallabhbhai Patel succeeded by Independence Day, August 15, 1947, in securing the accession of all states with the exception of three—Junagadh, Hyderabad, and Jammu and Kashmir.

Junagadh was a tiny state in Kathiawar with a Hindu population and a Muslim ruler, surrounded by Indian territory. When the state acceded to Pakistan it was occupied by Indian troops, and after a plebiscite, Junagadh joined the Indian Union. Hyderabad, with a Muslim ruler, the Nizam, and a Hindu majority, presented a similar but more complicated situation. The largest of the princely states, Hyderabad, though landlocked in the heart of India, sought independence as a sovereign state and entered a one-year standstill agreement with India while negotiations proceeded. With increasing disorder in Hyderabad and the rising influence of paramilitary Muslim extremists, the Indian Government moved troops into the state in a "police action" to restore law and order. Hyderabad then acceded to the Indian Union.

The state of Jammu and Kashmir, contiguous to both India and Pakistan and acceding to neither, had a Hindu ruler and a predominantly Muslim population. The Muslims were centered in the central valley, The Vale of Kashmir, with the Hindu minority concentrated in the region of Jammu to the south. As invading Pathan tribesmen from Pakistan pushed toward the capital of Srinagar, the Maharaja called upon India for military assistance. India, on the recommendation of Mountbatten, refused to send troops unless Kashmir agreed to accede formally to India. With accession, India announced its intention, once peace was restored, to hold a referendum on the choice of India or Pakistan. Because of armed conflict between the two states over Kashmir in 1948 and the subsequent demarcation of a United Nations cease-fire line, the plebiscite was never held. Since then India, over the protest of Pakistan, has come to regard Kashmir as an integral part of its own territory, arguing that Kashmir legally acceded to India and that the large Muslim population of Kashmir serves as a force for secularity in India and as a protection for the forty million Muslims left in Indian territory after partition.

Once the princely states had acceded to India, the process of integration began. Smaller states were merged with neighboring provinces. Others were consolidated as centrally administered areas. States of another class, because of their affinity, were consolidated as new federal units; these included Rajasthan, Saurashtra, and Travancore-Cochin. Mysore, Hyderabad, and, in a separate class, the state of Jammu and Kashmir retained their integrity as separate states of the Indian Union. Each new unit developed from the former princely states was to have as its head a *rajpramukh*, elected by the Council of Rulers, which was made up of the former princes. Some princes, such as the Maharaja of Mysore, distinguished themselves in government service and others entered political life, but most of them, provided with special privileges and privy purse allowances, became relics of the past in a democratic state.

The man who guided the integration of states never captured the imagination of the Indian people or the attention of the world, as did both Gandhi and Nehru, but for the period of transition, 1947 to

1950, Sardar Vallabhbhai Patel shared power with Nehru in an uneasy alliance that Brecher has termed the "duumvirate."[26] Temperamentally and ideologically, the two men could hardly have been more unalike. Nehru, reflective and sometimes considered indecisive, was a man of international vision, a committed socialist, secular in approach, of aristocratic Brahmin background and European manner. Patel, of Gujarati peasant stock, plebeian and orthordox, "was a man of iron will, clear about his objectives and resolute in his actions."[27] He was the realist, the machine politician, the defender of capitalism, of Hindu primacy, and of traditionalism. In the duumvirate, created by Gandhi to hold the Congress together and sustained by his memory, Patel, the Deputy Prime Minister, held the critical domestic portfolios, which along with the party organization gave him effective control over domestc affairs. Nehru was responsible for foreign affairs. "In the broadest sense they were equals, with one striking difference. Patel controlled a greater aggregate of power in the short-run, through the party and the key ministries of government, but Nehru commanded the country at large."[28] With the death of Patel in 1950, Nehru assumed full leadership within the Congress, the Government, and the nation.

One of the most important achievements of this period of transition was the constitution. This document, symbol of India's new freedom, embodied the basic principles for which the Congress had long struggled and provided the institutional framework for the political life of modern India. Before the leaders of India lay the tasks of political development, of creating and sustaining an institutional structure designed not simply to maintain order, but to stimulate expanded participation, to provide access to increased demands, to secure social justice for all, and to effect a fundamental transformation of society.

[26] See Brecher, *Nehru*, pp. 389–425.
[27] Brecher, *Nehru*, p. 392.
[28] *Ibid.*, p. 400.

RECOMMENDED READING

* Brecher, Michael, *Nehru: A Political Biography*. New York: Oxford University Press, 1959.
　　　The best of many Nehru biographies, the book brilliantly utilizes the life of Nehru as the thread that weaves together the dramatic events of the nationalist movement and the first critical years of independence.

Brown, Judith M., *Gandhi's Rise to Power: Indian Politics* 1915–1922. Cambridge: Cambridge University Press, 1972.
　　　A study of political power and organization in Gandhi's assertion of leadership within the Indian National Congress.

* Available in a paperback edition.

* Erikson, Erik H., *Gandhi's Truth*. New York: Norton, 1969.
"The Event" of the 1918 Ahmedabad strike is the lens for this psychological and historical study of Gandhi.

* Gandhi, Mohandas, *An Autobiography, or The Story of My Experiments with Truth*. Ahmedabad: Navajivan Publishing House, 1927.
Although dealing only with his early life, the autobiography is a deeply revealing portrait of this highly complex and charismatic leader.

Gordon, Leonard A., *Bengal: The Nationalist Movement, 1876–1940*. New York: Columbia University Press, 1974.
An important and closely researched analysis of the nationalist movement within this turbulent region of India.

* Hardy, P., *The Muslims of British India*. Cambridge: Cambridge University Press, 1972.
Surveys Muslim-Indian history under the British, emphasizing the role of religion in the growth of political separatism.

Hodson, H. V., *The Great Divide*. London: Hutchinson, 1969.
One of the best studies yet written of the events surrounding partition.

Hutchins, Francis G., *Gandhi and the Quit India Movement*. Cambridge: Harvard University Press, 1973.
Argues for the view that Indian independence was attained through revolution, not through a benevolent grant from the British imperial regime.

————, *The Illusion of Permanence*. Princeton, N.J.: Princeton University Press, 1967.
An exploration of the changing self-image of the British presence in India and of the development of a fragile imperial confidence.

Menon, V. P., *The Transfer of Power*. Princeton, N.J.: Princeton University Press, 1957.
A detailed and dispassionate account by the man who served as constitutional adviser to the Governor General from 1942 to 1947.

Metcalf, Thomas R., *The Aftermath of Revolt: India, 1857–1870*. Princeton, N.J.: Princeton University Press, 1964.
An analysis of the impact of the mutiny on British imperial policy and on the people of India.

Moon, Penderel, *Divide and Quit*. Berkeley: University of California Press, 1962.
A moving, firsthand account of the tragedy of partition.

*Nanda, B. R., *The Nehrus: Motilal and Jawaharlal*. Chicago: University of Chicago Press, 1974.
A vivid portrait of Indian history, 1861 to 1931, through the ties and conflicts of father and son.

* Nehru, Jawaharlal, *The Discovery of India*. Garden City, N.Y.: Doubleday, 1959.
Written during the time of his imprisonment, this history of India reveals Nehru's understanding of its heritage and his perspective on the nationalist struggle.

_____

* Available in a paperback edition.

* Seal, Anil, *The Emergence of Indian Nationalism: Competition and Collaboration in the Later Nineteenth Century.* Cambridge: Cambridge University Press, 1968.
    Examines the social roots of the Indian nationalist movement.

* Spear, Percival, A *History of India*, Vol. 2. Baltimore: Penguin, 1965.
    An account of modern India, from the coming of the Moguls through the independence movement.

* Available in a paperback edition.

III

THE FRAMEWORK OF POLITICS

The constitution of india is among the longest in the world, with 395 articles and 8 schedules. It continued the constitutional development that took place under the British, retaining the basic precepts of the Government of India Act of 1935 and taking from it approximately 250 articles, verbatim or with minor changes. The "borrowed" constitution was attacked as "un-Indian" and unsuited to a people inexperienced in democratic self-rule. "Democracy in India is only a top-dressing on an Indian soil which is essentially undemocratic," Dr. B. R. Ambedkar argued; "constitutional morality is not a natural sentiment. It has to be cultivated."[1] The constitution was to be the agent of that cultivation. Democracy was to be achieved through its exercise.

The Constituent Assembly and the Drafting of the Constitution

The task of the Constituent Assembly was to draft a constitution that would provide a framework for democratic government and an institu-

[1] Constituent Assembly debates, quoted in M. V. Pylee, *Constitutional Government in India* (Bombay: Asia Publishing House, 1965), p. 8.

tional structure capable of both sustaining and accelerating change. It was to provide the instrument for stimulating increased participation and for securing the higher levels of institutionalization necessary to accommodate expanding demands.

Under the Cabinet mission's provisions for the transfer of power the Constituent Assembly was indirectly elected in 1946 by the provincial assemblies. Reflecting the Congress victories in the provincial elections the year before, the Congress commanded an overwhelming majority in the assembly, and Rajendra Prasad was elected president at its opening session. The boycott of the assembly by the Muslim League clouded the first sessions, however, and anticipated the settlement that was to divide India and provide a separate constituent assembly for Pakistan.

When India gained independence, the assembly, functioning under a modified Government of India Act of 1935, became the Provisional Parliament. Its fundamental task, however, remained that of framing the constitution. Dr. Ambedkar chaired the drafting committee and steered the document through nearly a year of debate over its various provisions. Four leaders, Nehru, Patel, Prasad, and the Congress Muslim leader Maulana Abul Kalam Azad, through their commanding grip on the Congress Assembly Party and the assembly's eight committees, constituted a virtual oligarchy within the assembly. Issues were openly debated, but the influence of the Congress leaders was nearly irresistible.[2] Although they themselves were by no means always of one mind, they sought to promote consensus, and in the end, the constitution was adopted by acclamation. On January 26, 1950, Republic Day, the new constitution went into effect.

The preamble of the constitution embodies the substance of Nehru's Resolution on Aims and Objectives and reflects the aspirations of the nationalist movement.

> WE, THE PEOPLE OF INDIA, having solemnly resolved to constitute India into a SOVEREIGN, DEMOCRATIC REPUBLIC and to secure to all its citizens:
> JUSTICE, social, economic and political;
> LIBERTY of thought, expression, belief, faith and worship;
> EQUALITY of status and opportunity; and to promote among them all
> FRATERNITY assuring the dignity of the individual and the unity of the Nation;
> IN OUR CONSTITUENT ASSEMBLY . . . do HEREBY ADOPT, ENACT AND GIVE TO OURSELVES THIS CONSTITUTION.

The new India was to be a parliamentary democracy, federal, republican, and secular. There were some members of the assembly who pushed for a Gandhian constitution, one that would provide for a decentralized state with the village panchayat as its nucleus. The vast ma-

[2] Granville Austin, *The Indian Constitution* (New York: Oxford University Press, 1966), p. 22.

jority, however, were committed from the beginning to a centralized parliamentary government. India had had a lengthy experience with representative institutions, and its leadership had been tutored in the liberal democratic tradition. The foremost task of the new government would be to restore order and unity to the nation. Only through the centralized authority of a modern state, they believed, could India achieve the stability requisite for economic progress. Only through democratic institutions could India begin to fulfill its aspirations after social revolution. The assembly, "with an abundant faith in the common man and the ultimate success of democratic rule,"[3] sought to break down the parochialism of local loyalties through the provision for direct election by adult suffrage.

Changes in the structure of India's government—the establishment of the dyarchy in 1919 and of a federal system in 1935—brought about a devolution of authority, but power remained centralized. To achieve the goals of social change and to overcome the "fissiparous tendencies" of communalism, the pattern of centralized authority was retained in the new constitution. The quest for unity was tempered, however, by demands to accommodate India's diversity. Provincial politicians, substantially represented in the Constituent Assembly, had had a taste of power and were therefore unlikely to yield to a purely unitary constitution. Moreover, there was a fundamental suspicion of the concentration of power that had enabled a handful of Englishmen to hold down a nation of four hundred million people. Most critical was the problem of integrating the princely states under a single constitution. With these considerations, the assembly concluded, "The soundest framework for our constitution is a federation with a strong Centre."[4]

The assembly determined also that India would be a republic, free and independent of the British Crown. After the transfer of power in 1947, India had become a dominion in the British Commonwealth of Nations. The head of state was the Governor General, appointed by the King on advice of the Indian Prime Minister. Lord Mountbatten, the last Viceroy, was asked to remain as the first Governor General, and he was succeeded by C. Rajagopalachari, who served until the promulgation of the constitution and the accession of Prasad to the Presidency. As India was to be a republic the Government sought to retain full membership in the Commonwealth without allegiance to the Crown. The formula was expressed in India's willingness to accept the King as the *symbol* of the free association of the member nations and as such the head of the Commonwealth. The first former British colony to request republic status within the Commonwealth, India served as the

---

[3] Alladi Krishnaswami Ayyar in the Constituent Assembly debates, quoted in Austin, *The Indian Constitution*, p. 46.

[4] Second Report of the Union Powers Committee, July 5, 1947, quoted in R. L. Watts, *New Federations: Experiments in the Commonwealth* (New York: Oxford University Press, 1966), p. 18.

example to others seeking a continued relationship with Britain that was compatible with nationalist integrity.

The Constitution of India provides for a secular state. Nehru, the architect of Indian secularism, rejected the demand for a restoration of Hindu raj as he had rejected, but without success, the notion that India was two nations, one Hindu, one Muslim. The creation of a Hindu nation, Bharat, as demanded by the Hindu communalists, would have vindicated the Muslim League and recognized the legitimacy of Pakistan as an Islamic nation. It would, as well, have placed India's religious minorities, particularly the forty million Muslims left after partition, in an unenviable, if not disastrous, position. Under the Constituent Assembly, communal tension had reached a peak and war with Pakistan was imminent. The Hindu right, including Sardar Patel, demanded, on the one hand, retaliatory action against Indian Muslims for expulsion of Hindus from Pakistan, and on the other, a favored position for Hindus in India. The assembly did not succumb to fanaticism, however, and adopted instead impressive guarantees of religious freedom and equal protection of all faiths. But the pressures of Hindu communalism have not subsided, and with the growth of the quasi-communal Jana Sangh party they have become an even more potent force in Indian political life.

The formal institutions of government established by the constitution provide a framework for political behavior. These institutions, often familiar in form, are frequently unfamiliar in operation. Traditional forms of behavior merge with the modern and adapt with resiliency to a changing environment. "Nothing in India is identifiable," E. M. Forster wrote in *A Passage to India*; "the mere asking of a question causes it to disappear or to merge in something else." If modern political institutions in India are often not what they appear, however, they are not mere façade to cloak a resurgent traditionalism. The structure of a political system is not simply passive and dependent. It not only responds to the environment; it also shapes the environment. In the process of development, the political system through its institutions will determine whether the nation has the capacity to meet the challenges of modernization and to change. The Constitution of India is a blueprint for institutionalization.

Fundamental Rights and Directive Principles Established in the Constitution

The Indian constitution, as Granville Austin states, is "first and foremost a social document."[5] The core of its commitment to a fundamental change in the social order lies in the sections on Fundamental

[5] *The Indian Constitution*, p. 50.

Rights and the Directive Principles of State Policy, "the conscience of the Constitution."[6]

The Fundamental Rights, embodied in Part III of the constitution, guarantee to each citizen basic substantive and procedural protections against the state. These rights, which apply to both the Center and the states, fall into seven categories: (1) the right of equality, (2) the right to freedom, (3) the right against exploitation, (4) the right to freedom of religion, (5) cultural and educational rights, (6) the right to property, and (7) the right to constitutional remedies. The right of equality guarantees equal protection before the law. It provides for equal opportunity in public employment, abolishes untouchability, and prohibits discrimination in the use of public places on the ground of religion, race, caste, sex, or place of birth. The rights of minorities are specifically protected in the provisions for freedom of religion and for the right of minorities to establish and administer their own educational institutions and to conserve a distinct language, script, and culture.

The Fundamental Rights reflect both India's assimilation of Western liberal tradition and its desire for the political freedoms it was denied under colonial rule. At the same time, however, these freedoms are not without their limitations. Under the Emergency Provisions of the constitution (Part XVIII) the President may suspend the right to freedom and the right to constitutional remedies in situations of national emergency. A national emergency was declared when the Chinese invaded in 1962 and was followed by the enactment of the Defense of India Act, which provided for the detention of any person

> whom the authority suspects on grounds appearing to that authority to be reasonable, of being of hostile origin, of having acted, acting, being about to act or being likely to act in a manner prejudicial to the defence of India and civil defence, the security of the State, the public safety or interest, the maintenance of public order, India's relations with foreign states, the maintenance of peaceful conditions in any part of India or the efficient conduct of military operations.

The emergency was revoked only in 1968, long after the immediate threat of invasion. On occasion, it was used by the Government to justify preventive detention (a legacy of British days) in cases like the language riots in Tamil Nadu (formerly Madras State) in 1965 that had little to do with the defense of India. The lifting of the emergency and suspension of the Defense of India Rules brought the release of 770 prisoners, the most prominent of whom was Sheik Mohammed Abdullah, leader of the Kashmiri Muslims, who had been held under house detention without trial. The threat of border disputes with China and

6 *Ibid.*

Pakistan and in particular the unsettled status of Kashmir, however, prompted Parliament to pass in 1968 the Unlawful Activities Prevention Act, which makes many of the emergency powers under the Defense of India Act statutory law. These include a provision to outlaw any organization or imprison any individual found guilty of disclaiming or questioning Indian sovereignty over any piece of India's territorial claims. The Defense of India Rules were again imposed during the 1971 India-Pakistan war. Though the emergency passed, the Rules remain in force and have been used for unintended and miscellaneous purposes, such as the arrest of striking railwaymen in 1974.

The constitution itself provides for preventive detention, sanctioning the confinement of individuals in order to prevent them from engaging in acts considered injurious to society. It was generally agreed in the Constituent Assembly that the times demanded extraordinary measures but that detention procedures should be strictly controlled.[7] In 1950 the Preventive Detention Act was passed to combat the dangers of communal agitators, urban *goondas,* and dacoits in the countryside. The most immediate justification for the measure was the Communist guerrilla activity in the Telengana region of Hyderabad State. Indeed, in the first year of the Act's operation, six thousand of the ten thousand arrests made were in Telengana. As the Government consolidated its position, the number of detentions declined, and it has stabilized at about two hundred each year.[8] Preventive detention has, on the whole, been used with moderation and restraint. Thus, even with these limitations, "the chapter on Fundamental Rights . . . remains a formidable bulwark of individual liberty, a code of public conduct and a strong and sustaining basis of Indian democracy."[9]

The Directive Principles of State Policy delineate the obligations of the state toward its citizens. Almost a platform of the Congress party, the Directive Principles direct the state "to promote the welfare of the people by securing and promoting as effectively as it may a social order in which justice, social, economic and political, shall inform all the institutions of the national life."[10]

The precepts of the Directive Principles are not justiciable—that is, they are not enforceable by a court, as are the Fundamental Rights. They are designed rather to serve as a guide for the Union Parliament and the state assemblies in framing new legislation. Although T. T. Krishnamachari, later Union Finance Minister, dismissed them as "a veritable dustbin of sentiment,"[11] the Directive Principles incorporated

[7] *Ibid.,* p. 111.
[8] See David H. Bayley, *Preventive Detention in India* (Calcutta: Mukhopadhyay, 1962), pp. 26–53.
[9] Pylee, *Constitutional Government,* p. 325.
[10] Constitution of India, Article 38.
[11] Constituent Assembly debates, quoted in Austin, *The Indian Constitution,* p. 75.

into the constitution the aspirations of a new nation and are, according to Article 37, "fundamental in the governance of the country." In evaluating the impact of the Fundamental Rights and Directive Principles, Austin doubts "if in any other constitution the expression of positive and negative rights has provided so much impetus towards changing and rebuilding society for the common good."[12]

The President and the Vice President

The executive power in India is vested by the constitution in the President, the formal head of state and symbol of the nation. He serves a five-year term and may be reelected. The President is subject to impeachment by Parliament for violation of the constitution.

Rajendra Prasad, who had presided over the Constituent Assembly, was elected by that body in 1950 as the first President of the Republic. Under the provisions of the new constitution, he was reelected in 1952 and again in 1957. Dr. Sarvapalli Radhakrishnan, a former Oxford philosopher who had served as Vice President under Prasad, was elected President in 1962. He was succeeded by his own Vice President, Dr. Zakir Hussain, in 1967. V. V. Giri, Congress labor leader, was elected Vice President. The 1967 presidential election was the first to be seriously contested by the opposition. Hussain, the Congress candidate and the choice of Prime Minister Indira Gandhi, was opposed by former Chief Justice Subha Rao. Hussain, a Muslim and a symbol of India's commitment to secularism, was returned by a substantial majority. In May, 1969, President Hussain died, and V. V. Giri took over as Acting President until elections could be held. The events that followed divided the Congress and underscored the potentially decisive position of the Indian President. (These events are examined in Chapter VI.)

The constitution specifies a complicated procedure for electing the President that is designed to insure uniformity among the states as well as parity between the states as a whole and the Union. The electoral college is composed of all elected members of the legislative assemblies in the states and of Parliament. Each elected member of a state assembly is given as many votes as there are multiples of one thousand in the quotient obtained by dividing the population of the state by the total number of elected members of the assembly. In 1969 the total value of all votes assigned to members of the legislative assemblies was 430,847, with a range in the value of each legislator's vote from 7 for Nagaland legislators to 175 for Uttar Pradesh legislators. The value of the parliamentary votes at the Center is derived by dividing the total allotment for the assemblies by the number of elected members in the Lok Sabha and the Rajya Sabha, the two houses of Parliament.

[12] *The Indian Constitution*, p. 115.

Thus, in 1969 the vote of each member of Parliament was worth 576.

Members indicate on their ballots their first and second preferences. If an absolute majority is not obtained by any candidate on the tabulation of first preferences, the second preferences indicated on the ballots of the candidate with the fewest number of votes are then transferred to the remaining candidates. The procedure is repeated until the sufficient majority is obtained. A candidate could conceivably win even with fewer first-preference votes than the major opponent.

In the balloting in 1969, minor candidates received scattered support in the states, but the contest was primarily between official Congress candidate Sanjiva Reddy, V. V. Giri, running as an independent with the silent support of the Prime Minister, and C. D. Deshmukh, candidate of the right-wing opposition parties. On the first count no candidate received the majority vote of 418,118, although Giri led with 401,515, followed by Reddy with 313,548, and Deshmukh with 112,769 votes. With the tabulation of the second-preference votes on the Deshmukh ballots, Giri went over the number of votes needed to win, securing a total of 420,077 to Reddy's 405,427.

The drama of the 1969 election was not repeated in 1974. Congress candidate Fakhruddin Ali Ahmed, a Muslim, won an easy victory over his single opponent, Revolutionary Socialist leader T. K. Chaudhuri.

The Vice President is elected for a five-year term by members of both houses of Parliament sitting in joint session. Votes are tallied according to the same system of simple majority and alternative preference. The 1969 vice-presidential election was held two weeks after the presidential election. The Congress candidate, G. S. Pathak, Governor of Mysore State, easily won over his three opponents, with 400 of 725 votes cast. In 1974, Congress vice presidential candidate B. D. Jatti, Governor of Orissa, overwhelmed his lone opponent. From the South, Karnataka, Jatti gave balance to Ahmed's North Indian origin. The Vice President is the ex officio chairman of the upper house of Parliament, the Rajya Sabha, or Council of States. During his term he may not also serve as a member of Parliament or of a state assembly. His functions are minimal, but in event of the death, resignation, or incapacity of the President, the Vice President assumes the responsibility of the office until a new President is elected. Under these circumstances a presidential election must be held within six months.

Powers of the President

The constitution confers an impressive list of powers on the President, but the Constituent Assembly determined that these powers should be exercised in accordance with the advice of the ministers. "Under the Draft Constitution the President occupies the same position as the King under the English Constitution," Dr. Ambedkar stated. "He is head of the State but not of the Executive. He represents the nation but does not rule the nation."[13] This view reflected a distrust of executive power nurtured by the colonial experience, but the constitutional conventions regulating the relationship between the King and Cabinet in Great Britain were not easily translated into written form. Although there were no specific provisions in the constitution, Prasad expressed the hope in the Constituent Assembly debates that "the convention under which in England the King acts always on the advice of his Ministers will be established in this country also. . . ."[14] It was Prasad, however, who sought as President to challenge this convention. Within two months after the preliminary draft constitution was published and subsequently throughout his tenure as President, Prasad argued that "there is no provision in the Constitution which in so many words lays down that the President shall be bound to act in accordance with the advice of his ministers."[15] He frequently spoke out on policy matters, such as the reform Hindu Code Bill governing marriage and inheritance, which he vigorously opposed, and would have assumed discretionary powers, but he was persuaded to accept a more limited role and exercise his power in accordance with convention. "For ill or creditable motives, Prasad attempted to read into the Constitution what was never intended to be there. Fortunately he failed. In fact, his efforts may have strengthened the Constitution by establishing the firm precedent that within the Executive the cabinet is all powerful."[16]

Even if the Cabinet is dominant the President is by no means a mere figurehead, however, for the political situation may provide a vast range of opportunities for presidential action. Both Prasad and Radhakrishnan exercised an independent role and sought on occasion to exert their influence on pending legislation. The undisputed position of the Congress before 1967 precluded the intervention of a strong presidential personality, but in a situation of instability, the President may have wide latitude and his actions may be decisive. The position of the President would be particularly critical if the states returned opposition parties to power and together in the electoral college elected a President over a Congress majority in the central Parliament, a situation foreshadowed by the 1967 elections. If Congress were to lose its majority in the Lok Sabha, the lower house of Parliament, the potential power of the President would become all the greater, particularly in the latitude he might exercise in his choice of the Prime Minister. The selection of the President in 1969, on the death of Hussain, was thus not merely a test of factional strength within the Congress, but a response to an uncertain political future, and it anticipates an increasingly important presidential role.

The President appoints the Prime Minister and on his advice then

---

[13] Quoted in Pylee, *Constitutional Government*, pp. 357–58.
[14] *Ibid.*, p. 358.
[15] See Austin, *The Indian Constitution*, pp. 135, 142.
[16] Austin, *The Indian Constitution*, p. 143.

appoints other members of the Council of Ministers. Under ordinary conditions, he has no discretion; his choice is the leader of the majority party in the Lok Sabha, for the Prime Minister is responsible to the lower house and remains in office only as long as he or she commands its confidence. If no party holds a clear majority, however, or if the majority party is torn by factional disputes, the President may play a critical role in determining who among the conflicting claimants might form a stable ministry. The Prime Minister holds office at the pleasure of the President. If the Council of Ministers has lost the support of Parliament by defeat on a major issue or by vote of no confidence, the Prime Minister must resign but may advise the President to dissolve the Lok Sabha and call new elections. While the President may accept such advice at his discretion, parliamentary convention would suggest that he do so only after surveying the possibilities for the formation of a new Government by the opposition. If formation of a new Government seems doubtful, he would then dissolve the lower house and call elections. The defeated ministry would then be invited to continue as a caretaker government until a new ministry could be formed. The President by oath of office must act "to preserve, protect and defend the Constitution." Presumably he is not bound by the advice of his ministers to take action he believes to be unconstitutional. The presidential position is by no means clear, but the President's actions will inevitably be determined by sensitivity and response to the political climate.

As intended by the Constituent Assembly, the convention that presidential power shall be exercised on the advice of the Council of Ministers has in the years of Congress dominance become well established. On the advice of the Prime Minister the President appoints the governors of the states, the justices of the Supreme Court and the state high courts, and members of various special commissions. He appoints the Attorney General, his legal advisor, and the Comptroller and Auditor General of India, who as guardian of the public purse sees that both Union and state expenditures are in accord with legislative appropriations. The President is the commander-in-chief of the armed forces and has the power of pardon. He calls Parliament into session and may dissolve the lower house. Every bill passed by Parliament must be presented to him for assent, and except in the case of a money bill, he may withhold assent or return the bill for reconsideration. Parliament can override his veto simply by passing the bill again in both houses.

Under Article 123 of the constitution the President may promulgate ordinances when Parliament is not in session if he is satisfied that circumstances exist that demand immediate action. A presidential ordinance has the same force and effect as an Act of Parliament, but the ordinance must be laid before Parliament within six weeks after it reconvenes. More extraordinary powers are given to the President in provision for three types of emergency: a threat to security by war or external aggression or by internal disturbance, a breakdown in the constitutional government of a state, and a threat to financial stability. Under proclamation of a war emergency, such as that invoked in 1962, the federal provisions of the constitution may be suspended and the area affected brought under direct Central control. Such proclamations must be laid before Parliament for approval within two months.

The President may declare a constitutional emergency in a state if, on receipt of a report from the governor, a situation has arisen in which the government of the state cannot be carried on in accordance with the constitution. The President may then (1) assume any or all of the state functions or may vest these functions in the governor, (2) declare that the powers of the state assembly shall be exercised by Parliament, and (3) make other provisions necessary to fulfill the objectives of the proclamation, including the suspension in part or whole of any constitutional body or authority in the state except the judiciary. The proclamation must be approved by Parliament; ordinarily it expires after six months, but it may be extended periodically by Parliament for a maximum overall period of three years. President's Rule in the years of Congress dominance was invoked sparingly. Its most dramatic use came in the 1959 supersession of the Communist government in Kerala, when the Center intervened in what it called a breakdown of law and order. In the months immediately following the 1967 elections, however, unstable coalitions in the North toppled one after the other, and within two years the Center had intervened in six states, initiating tremendous controversy over the specific events of each case and the wider problem of the Center-state relationship.

Fear has been expressed that the emergency provisions might provide the foundation for a police state or a presidential dictatorship, or at the least, might act as an instrument for the destruction of the federal system outlined in the constitution. Alan Gledhill was led in 1951 to conjure a Weimarian nightmare in which the President assumes dictatorial powers.[17] The check on executive authority is the Parliament, however, and thus far it has not abrogated its responsibility. "If the Federal Executive in India becomes autocratic," Granville Austin has written, "it will be because Parliament and the body politic have defaulted in their responsibility and have acquiesced in their own downfall, not because the intent of the Constitution has been 'constitutionally' circumvented."[18]

Parliament

The Parliament of India as defined by the constitution consists of the President and the two houses, the Lok Sabha, the lower house, and the Rajya Sabha, the upper house. The fact that the President is a part of

---

[17] *The Republic of India* (London: Stevens & Sons, 1951), p. 108.
[18] *The Indian Constitution*, p. 140.

Parliament stresses the interdependence, rather than separation, of the Executive and Legislative in the parliamentary system.

The Lok Sabha

The constitution as amended by the Fourteenth Amendment in 1962 limits the membership of the Lok Sabha, or House of the People, to 525. Of these, 25 seats are reserved for representatives of the Union territories to be chosen as specified by Parliament. In addition, the President may nominate not more than two representatives of the Anglo-Indian community if none have been elected to the house. The remaining seats are allocated among the states on the basis of population, and members are directly elected on the basis of adult suffrage. Each state is divided into territorial constituencies that are roughly equal in population.

The normal life of the Lok Sabha is five years, but in accord with parliamentary tradition, it may be dissolved earlier by the President. Under a proclamation of emergency the President may extend the life of the house for one year at a time, but not beyond six months after suspension of the emergency rules. The constitution specifies that the house must meet at least twice a year, with no more than six months between sessions. In practice, it has held an average of three sessions each year. The business of Parliament is transacted primarily in English or Hindi, but provision is made for the use of other Indian languages when necessary. While most members have been able to speak either English or Hindi, some have been determined to speak in their mother tongue. A few have had no other choice.

The Speaker, elected by the house from among its own members, presides over the Lok Sabha without political consideration. He is expected to stand above partisan conflict and is entitled to vote only in a tie. His powers are extensive, however, and his influence may be considerable. He is responsible for the maintenance of order and the conduct of business in the house. Twelve parliamentary committees carry the burden of most of the routine business in the Lok Sabha. Some, such as the Rules Committee and the Business Advisory Committee, are primarily concerned with organization and procedure. Others, however, act as watchdogs over the Executive. Specific committees scrutinize the budget and governmental economy, government appropriations and expenditures, the exercise of delegated power, and the implementation of ministerial assurances and promises. With regard to the financial committees, W. H. Morris-Jones writes that "this type of committee, inspired as it is by the idea not simply of economy nor even of efficiency alone but also of acting as a check against an oppressive or arbitrary executive, achieves a special significance as a substitute for a real Opposition."[19]

[19] *Parliament in India* (London: Longmans, Green, 1957), p. 308.

   The Lok Sabha may conduct business only with a quorum of fifty, but with low levels of attendance, even this small number is often not easily obtained. The first hour of the parliamentary day is devoted to questions that bring the Government to the dock of public scrutiny. At this time a minister responds to the questions that have been submitted in advance by members and faces supplementary questions from the floor that demand skill and quick judgment. As in Britain, the question hour supplies information to Parliament, but more significantly, it is an instrument of control over the Prime Minister and the Cabinet. The questions may highlight Government activity in a variety of areas, but they also serve to insure that the Cabinet will remain responsive to the opinion of the legislative majority and sensitive to the criticism of the opposition. In the hands of the opposition, questions may seriously embarrass the Government, revealing inefficiency, incompetence, or scandal. Revelations of this kind have forced the resignation of such important ministers as T. T. Krishnamachari in 1958 and K. D. Malaviya in 1963.[20] The question period illustrates the educative role of a parliament in a democratic society.

   The ultimate control of the Lok Sabha over the Executive lies in its power of censure, the motion of no confidence that can bring down the Government. The motion may be introduced only with the support of fifty members, and until 1967, because of Parliament's splintered opposition, it was brought on only one occasion, in 1963. It did not carry.

   The Lok Sabha was often criticized as Nehru's *durbar*, or princely court; but even though the Congress has had overwhelming dominance, the opposition has been respected, and Parliament has often been the arena of significant debate that the Cabinet has not ignored, While not genuinely a deliberative, policy-making body, Parliament has occasionally played an important role in modifying legislation submitted to it for ratification. Although Parliament has assumed a more important role since Nehru's death, it still remains under the shadow of the Prime Minister. However, the Lok Sabha debates are closely followed in the daily press, and through the pressure of this publicity, Parliament has been able to keep the Prime Minister sensitive and responsive to its opinion.

   For a group or party to be considered an "official" party, it must have at least fifty members in the house. From the time of independence, opposition at the Center has been weak and heterogeneous, and it was not until the Congress split and the breakaway Congress(O) emerged that any party other than Congress attained sufficient strength to meet the requirements for official recognition. Despite their lack of strength, members of the opposition have been consulted on the arrangement of business in the house, represented on various committees, and recognized by the Speaker in the course of debate. The fragmentation and

[20] Various "remarkable resignations" are discussed by R. J. Venkateswaran, *Cabinet Government in India* (London: George Allen & Unwin, 1967), pp. 73–93.

weakness of the opposition in the face of Congress dominance, its lack of experience and leadership, have tended, on the one hand, to make opposition criticism unrealistic and often irresponsible, and on the other, to predispose the Government to scorn of the opposition and unresponsiveness toward it.[21]

There is perhaps an inevitable tension between the Government and the members of Parliament, both in the opposition and the majority. It is after all the Cabinet that is the decision-making body of the political system, and a distrust of government lingers from the days of the nationalist movement. "This distrust is further aggravated by the lack of mutual respect between politicians and civil servants. This, too, is a relic of the past when the civil service was an arm of that foreign administration which put in prison a large number of those who are now the leading politicians."[22] When a member becomes a minister he is seen as having gone over to the other side and is viewed with a mixture of envy and antagonism.

The Rajya Sabha

The Rajya Sabha, or Council of States, consists of a maximum of 250 members, of whom 12 are nominated by the President for their "special knowledge or practical experience" in literature, science, art, and social service. The allocation of the remaining seats among the states corresponds to their population, except that small states are given a somewhat larger share than their numbers alone would command. The representatives of each state are elected by the members of the state legislative assembly for a term of six years. The Rajya Sabha is not subject to dissolution, and the terms are staggered, as in the United States Senate, so that one-third of the members stand for election every two years.

In the debates of the Constituent Assembly, some argued that second chambers were undemocratic bastions of vested interest and acted as "clogs in the wheels of progress." Others upheld the chamber as "an essential element of federal constitutions," declaring that it introduced "an element of sobriety and second thought" into the democratic process. In any case, as Morris-Jones wrote in his study of the Indian Parliament, "Whatever uncertainty there may have been on the purpose of an Upper House, there was at no stage any doubt that the House of the People would be the more powerful."[23] The Government rests on the confidence of the popular assembly. The Council of Ministers is responsible only to the Lok Sabha, and while the Rajya Sabha has the right to be fully informed of the Government's activities, it is not empowered to raise a motion of censure.

[21] See Morris-Jones, *Parliament in India*, pp. 153–54.
[22] Morris-Jones, *Parliament in India*, p. 152.
[23] *Ibid.*, p. 90.

The Legislative Process

Decision-making on public policy in India is concentrated at the highest levels of authority—with the Prime Minister, the Cabinet, and the top echelons of the bureaucracy. Policy is initiated primarily from within the Executive, but a fairly regularized policy process, providing an open hearing and wide consultation, has emerged in dealing with many major domestic issues. "The process begins," as Stanley Kochanek succinctly describes it,

> with the appointment of a commission of inquiry, composed of distinguished citizens, to investigate the problem. The commission takes public testimony from various groups and individuals and produces a report which includes a set of specific policy recommendations. The ministry concerned and the cabinet study the report, consider its recommendations, and note public reactions before drawing up a draft bill, which usually includes most of the recommendations of the commission. The draft bill is next submitted to Parliament. . . .[24]

It is the primary responsibility of the Government to draft legislation and introduce bills into Parliament, although private members' bills are considered in an allotted period once a week. Any bill other than money bills may be introduced in either house. Most bills originate in the Lok Sabha, however, and proceed through three readings, as in the British Parliament. The bill is introduced in the first reading, usually by title only and without debate. It may then be referred to a select committee of the house, appointed specifically for consideration of the bill, or in the case of bills of particular importance or complexity, to a joint committee of both houses. After the bill has been reported from the committee and accepted for consideration by the house, the second reading takes place; each clause is debated and voted on. Amendments may be moved at this stage. The third and final reading of the bill is the motion that the bill be passed. After passage, the bill is transmitted to the Rajya Sabha, where it follows the same procedure.

Differences between the bill as passed by the two houses may be resolved by sending the bill back and forth for reconsideration. If agreement is not reached, the President calls for a joint sitting of Parliament, and the disputed provision is decided on by a simple majority vote.[25] When the bill has passed both houses, it is sent to the President for his assent. He may return the bill to Parliament for reconsideration, but if it is passed again, the President may not withhold assent.

Bills for taxing and spending, money bills, may be introduced only in

[24] *Business and Politics in India* (Berkeley: University of California Press, 1974), p. 57.

[25] This occurred only once, in 1961.

the Lok Sabha. If amended or rejected by the Rajya Sabha, such a bill need merely be repassed by the lower house and sent to the President. Thre are certain powers relating to the position of the states, however, that are conferred upon the Rajya Sabha alone. It may, for example, declare by a two-thirds vote that Parliament should for a period up to one year make laws on the matters reserved by the constitution to the states. In most legislative matters, including constitutional amendments, the Rajya Sabha exercises the same power as the Lok Sabha. The two houses are similar not only in power but also in composition, and as Morris-Jones noted more than fifteen years ago, the Rajya Sabha "has, not surprisingly, failed to evolve a distinct role for itself."[26] It has provided neither the expertise for technical revision nor the atmosphere for more leisurely and considered debate. Indeed, the duplication and rivalry between the two houses has been criticized as "a most wasteful exercise of political energies [that] can only serve to lower Parliament as a whole in public esteem."[27]

Although the Supreme Court may hold an Act of Parliament unconstitutional, the Parliament may amend the constitution with relative ease. The Indian constitution combines both rigidity and flexibility in its amending process. The provisions may be amended in three ways: The greater portion of the constitution may be amended by a majority of the total membership of each house and by at least two-thirds of those present and voting. Some parts, however, may be amended by a simple majority of each house, the vote required to pass ordinary legislation. For example, the Parliament may by ordinary legislative procedure, create, reorganize, or abolish the constituent states and territories of the Union, if the President after consultation with the state assemblies so recommends. Other provisions, such as those dealing with the legislative powers of the Union and the states, may be amended only with a two-thirds majority in Parliament and ratification by not less than one-half of the states. Up to 1975, there have been thirty-five amendments to the constitution, a third of which were passed in rapid succession after the 1971 election securing a Congress majority.

Members of Parliament

Many of the individuals who have served as members of Parliament, in the opposition parties as well as in the Congress, were prominent leaders of the nationalist movement and had served in the legislative bodies both in the states and at the Center. Even in the first parliament, however, returned by the 1951–52 elections, more than half the members had never before served in a legislative body. An increasing number have been drawn into political life only in the years since indepen-

---

[26] *Parliament in India*, p. 257.
[27] *Ibid.*, p. 262.

dence, and these frequently have been without previous parliamentary experience.

Professionals, particularly lawyers, predominated in the first parliaments, but among the members, there have always been some of humble origin and little education. With each election, there has been a decline in the number of MPs who command English, and although three-quarters of the members of the current Lok Sabha have had some higher education, the average level of education has also declined. This decline in the level of education reflects increasing democratization as the representatives become more nearly like those they represent. The percentage of lawyers has steadily declined from 35 percent in the first Lok Sabha to 20 percent in the fifth. At the same time, landed agrarian interests have increased. The percentage of MPs giving agriculture as their main occupation has increased from less than one fourth in the first Lok Sabha to about one third in the fifth. They now constitute the largest occupational group in Parliament. The Congress party's rural base of support is distinctly represented in the Lok Sabha and is reflected in the fact that more than half of its members were born in villages. The opposition parties are more urban oriented, but their middle-class MPs draw little inspiration or sustenance from a working-class base. Satish Arora argues that with representation "systematically skewed in favour of some classes," the Indian political system "is dominated on all sides by the rural landed gentry and the urban middle classes who may have appropriated the symbol of socialism but lack the structured support which would be necessary to give it content and meaning."[28]

On the whole, Parliament still continues to draw members of exceptional quality, although in recent years, as the states have become increasingly important political arenas, many of the more politically able and ambitious men have been attracted to the state assemblies rather than to the Lok Sabha. As a result, many MPs find themselves in a dependent position. Unlike members of the legislative assemblies, they often lack a base of local power from which to bargain and are therefore likely to owe their seats to the chief ministers of their states. It was through the parliamentary delegations that the chief ministers exercised such a decisive role in the succession of Indira Gandhi to the Prime Ministership in 1966.

The Prime Minister and the Council of Ministers

Three Prime Ministers, Jawaharlal Nehru (1947–64), Lal Bahadur Shastri (1964–66), and Indira Gandhi (1966–   ), have served India. The constitution provides for the appointment of the Prime Minister

[28] "Social Background of the Fifth Lok Sabha," *Economic and Political Weekly*, Vol. 8, special number (August 1973), pp. 1433–40.

by the President, but because the ministers are responsible to the Lok Sabha, it is assumed that he will choose the leader of the majority party in that house or, if there is no clear majority, a member who can command the confidence of a sufficient coalition.

The Prime Minister selects ministers, who are then appointed by the President. They are not only responsible to Parliament, but are part of it. A minister must be a member of either the Lok Sabha or the Rajya Sabha. To draw on ministerial talent outside Parliament, however, the constitution permits the appointment of a nonmember if within a maximum of six months he becomes a member of Parliament, either by nomination or through a by-election for an open seat. Although a minister is entitled to vote only in the house of which he is a member, he may participate in the proceedings of both the Lok Sabha and the Rajya Sabha to answer questions or pilot a bill through passage.

The connecting link between the Ministry and the President as well as between the Ministry and Parliament, the Prime Minister is, in Nehru's words, "the linchpin of Government." The extensive powers vested in the President are in fact exercised by the Prime Minister, who, with the ministers, controls and coordinates the departments of government and determines policy through the submission of a program for parliamentary action. While commanding the majority in the Lok Sabha, the Prime Minister's Government is secure, but if defeated on any major issue, or if a no-confidence motion is passed, he must, by the conventions of cabinet government, resign. Custom in Great Britain has established that the Prime Minister shall be a member of the popularly elected lower house. It was presumed that the convention would be retained in India, and the selection of Indira Gandhi, a member of the Rajya Sabha, as Prime Minister was criticized as an unhealthy precedent. She subsequently was returned from a Lok Sabha constituency.

The Council of Ministers includes Cabinet ministers; ordinary ministers (called ministers of state); deputy ministers, who act as ministerial lieutenants; and parliamentary secretaries. In accommodating various party factions with office, as well as providing representation to different regions and groups, the Council has grown to the unwieldy number of sixty ministers. The ministers in theory are collectively responsible for all decisions of the Government, and no minister may publicly dissent from its policy. In fact, however, the Ministry does not meet as a body, and while every minister is expected to accept collective responsibility, the principle has not served to protect ministers from bearing individual responsibility for policy decisions. When heavy criticism has been leveled against a particular minister, he has frequently been dropped—as was Krishna Menon in the wake of the Chinese invasion—and the Ministry has thereby been vindicated. Rajni Kothari has written that "the collective responsibility of a council of ministers that never meets, has more the character of a coalition than a unified team, is divided into several layers of hierarchy, and allocates functions on a basis of drift and stop-gap arrangements, can neither be collective nor responsible."[29]

The Cabinet

The Cabinet is not mentioned in the constitution, but usage has equated its functions with those assigned to the Council of Ministers under the constitution. The Cabinet, the inner body of the council, is composed of the principal ministers who, while holding important portfolios, are responsible generally for Government administration and policy. The Cabinet has four major functions: to approve all proposals for the legislative enactment of Government policy, to recommend all major appointments, to settle interdepartmental disputes, and to co-ordinate the various activities of the Government and oversee the execution of its policies.[30]

The Cabinet must be small enough not to become unwieldy, but its size, which has ranged between twelve and eighteen, has more often been the result of political considerations than of decision-making efficiency. The composition of the Cabinet reflects a concern for a degree of regional balance and for the representation of important communities —Muslims, Sikhs, and untouchables. The Prime Minister's choice of Cabinet members is further constrained by the necessity to include those members of Parliament, across the political spectrum, who have distinguished themselves in party work and who command a position of factional strength. In the Cabinet, as in the larger Council of Ministers, the distribution of the major portfolios and ranking is determined largely by the political weight of each claimant. Each member of the Cabinet is formally ranked. "Ranking of members of the Cabinet," Michael Brecher notes, "appears to be based on a composite of the incumbent's political importance in the party and seniority, as intuitively perceived by the Prime Minister. . . . Yet formal status is not a measure of influence or involvement in the decision process."[31] As a "coalition," the Cabinet, which at times has included such polarities as Morarji Desai on the right and V. K. Krishna Menon on the left, has been disparate in character and frequently indecisive.

Only members are entitled to attend the weekly meetings of the Cabinet, but ministers of state, chief ministers, and technical experts may be invited to attend discussions of subjects with which they have special concern. Votes are rarely taken in the Cabinet; decisions usually are reached after discussion by a sense of the meeting. Only major issues

---

[29] "Administrative Institutions of Government," *Economic Weekly* (May 27, 1961), p. 823.
[30] Pylee, *Constitutional Government*, p. 377.
[31] *Nehru's Mantle: The Politics of Succession in India* (New York: Praeger, 1966), pp. 112–13.

are referred to the Cabinet, and frequently even these, such as the preparation of the budget, are decided by the appropriate minister in consultation with the Prime Minister. Most matters are resolved within the separate ministries and departments, and the work of the Cabinet itself is handled largely by committee.

The Cabinet committees, organized by the Prime Minister to coordinate the functions of the various ministries, have been largely dominated by the same few ministers. As Prime Minister, Nehru himself was chairman of nine of the ten committees, and the Home Minister was a member of all committees and was chairman of the tenth. The Finance Minister was a member of seven. "Appointments to these committees have been made more on personal considerations than on considerations of bringing only the ministers concerned together in relevant committees."[32] The Emergency Committee of the Cabinet, set up in 1962 and composed of six senior ministers including the Prime Minister, came in Nehru's last years to assume the role of an inner cabinet and took over many of the decision-making responsibilities of the whole Cabinet. As Prime Minister, Nehru exercised a preeminent role; his dominance of the Cabinet was overwhelming.

Under Shastri the Emergency Committee declined in relative importance. The Cabinet's primacy was restored in domestic affairs, as each minister was given a greater role of initiative and discretion. If under Nehru decisions had frequently been imposed from above, decisions under Shastri reflected more of a genuine consensus. The quest for consensus reflected as well the new balance of power between the Union and the states. What Brecher termed the "Grand Council of the Republic" was an informal body that came into being during the Shastri succession, made up of those who commanded decisive influence within the Congress—in the party and in the Government, at the Center and in the states. It was "the collective substitute for Nehru's charisma."[33]

The charisma of Nehru as a personality, however, has come to reside, in part, in the office of the Prime Minister, giving added strength and legitimacy to the most critical position in the Indian political system. With the authority of the office itself and her own charisma, augmented by considerable political skill, Indira Gandhi, daughter of Nehru, came to exercise enormous power, bringing the Cabinet into virtual eclipse as a source of policy influence. Through constant change and the reshuffling of portfolios Mrs. Gandhi deftly preempted the power of her lieutenants. Although by no means ever wholly free of constraints she commanded such unprecedented personal power in that brief period following the mandate of the 1971 parliamentary elections and the subsequent euphoria of the victory over Pakistan and the creation of Bangladesh that there were those who proclaimed her "Empress of India."

[32] Asok Chanda, *Indian Administration* (London: George Allen & Unwin, 1958), p. 91.
[33] Brecher, *Nehru's Mantle*, pp. 123–24.

In consolidating her power Mrs. Gandhi created the Political Affairs Committee, composed of a small group of senior cabinet ministers under her chairmanship. Responsible for the coordination of major cabinet concerns in domestic and international affairs and in defense, the committee became the "most important decision-making body in India after the Prime Minister herself."[34] A similarly constituted Economic Affairs Committee has been created more recently to give direction to Indian economic policy.

The Cabinet and its committees are assisted by the Central Secretariat, headed by the Cabinet Secretary, a senior member of the administrative service. In 1964, to ease the burdens of transition, Shastri set up the Prime Minister's Secretariat, analogous to the White House staff. While the formal functions of the secretariat involved the preparation "of important speeches, statements and letters," the office carried "the seed of influence," and recalling the days of the "steel frame" under the British raj, demonstrated "the re-emergence of the Civil Service as a powerful pressure group on policy."[35] The Secretariat has been augmented in technical expertise and strengthened under Indira Gandhi and has become the "nerve centre of political and administrative power" in India.[36]

In order to consolidate the nation in the first years of independence, 1947 to 1952, and in response to the fact that the Provisional Parliament had not been directly elected, Nehru brought into his first Ministry five non-Congressmen. Among them was Dr. Ambedkar, who had been a vigorous critic of Gandhi and the Congress, particularly in their policy toward untouchables. It was during this period also that Nehru shared power in the "duumvirate" with Sardar Patel. The post of Deputy Prime Minister had been created for Patel, and after his death in 1950 the post was not revived until Morarji Desai assumed that office under Prime Minister Indira Gandhi, serving until his resignation in 1969. Mrs. Gandhi's Cabinet contains, as Shastri's did, many of the ministers who served Nehru, and despite the death of many Congress stalwarts, ministerial resignations and the continued reshuffling of portfolios, there has been a remarkable continuity in Cabinet membership.

The ministries and departments, organized within the Central Secretariat, have expanded since independence in both number and scope. Each is responsible for the execution of Government policy in a particular area and is headed by a minister accountable for all that passes within his sphere of administration. A minister may be in charge of one or more ministries, some of which are then divided into departments. The ministry or department has as its permanent head a senior civil

[34] Kochanek, *Business and Politics in India*, p. 57.
[35] Brecher, *Nehru's Mantle*, pp. 115–20.
[36] C. P. Bhambhri, "A Study of Relationship Between Prime Minister and Bureaucracy in India," *The Indian Journal of Public Administration*, Vol. 17 (1971), p. 369.

servant, the secretary, who acts as the principal adviser to the minister in matters of policy and administration and who is responsible to the minister for efficient and economical administration.

The Public Services

During the struggle for swaraj the Indian Civil Service was condemned as an instrument of imperialism and exploitation, its Indian members as traitorous agents of a "satanic government." At the time of independence Sardar Patel rose to defend the service. "Remove them," he said, "and I see nothing but a picture of chaos all over the country." Nehru, who had once denounced the ICS for its "spirit of authoritarianism," declared, "the old distinctions and differences are gone. . . . In the difficult days ahead our Service and experts have a vital role to play and we invite them to do so as comrades in the service of India."[37] Those who had once governed were to become servants. The instrument for law and order was to become the agent of change and development.

The structure of the public services, the "steel frame" of the British raj, was left largely intact. The services are characterized by "open entry based on academic achievement; elaborate training arrangements; permanency of tenure; responsible, generalist posts at central, provincial, and district levels reserved for members of the elite cadre alone; a regular, graduated scale of pay with pension and other benefits; and a system of promotion and frequent transfers based predominantly on seniority and partly on merit."[38] The services are divided into three categories: state services, central services, and all-India services. Each state has its own administrative service, headed in most cases by the chief secretary to the government, and a variety of technical, secretariat, and local government services. The central government services, numbering more than twenty, include the Indian Foreign Service, the Central Secretariat Service, the Postal Service, and the Indian Revenue Service. Each has its own recruitment procedure, rules, and pay scales. There are also separate technical and specialist services. The constitution specifies two all-India services, the Indian Administrative Service and the Indian Police Service, but additional all-India services can be created by Parliament, provided there is approval by two-thirds of the Rajya Sabha.

With concern for national integration the States Reorganization Commission recommended in 1955 the creation of three new all-India services—engineering, health and medical, and forestry. The states have

---

[37] Jawaharlal Nehru, *Independence and After* (New York: John Day, 1950), p. 9.
[38] David C. Potter, "Bureaucratic Change in India," in Ralph Braibanti, ed., *Asian Bureaucratic Systems Emergent from the British Imperial Tradition* (Durham, N.C.: Duke University Press, 1966), p. 142. See also Hugh Tinker, "Structure of the British Imperial Heritage," in Braibanti, *Asian Bureaucratic Systems*, pp. 23–86.

generally opposed the creation of new all-India services, however. They have argued that the higher pay for all-India officers would impose a financial strain, but in fact, the states resist sharing control over the services with the central government. They also fear that local candidates may fail in an all-India competition and that the posts will be filled by candidates from outside the state.[39] Certain states have had a disproportionate number of direct recruits to the Indian Administrative Service. Tamil Nadu, for example, with its high standard of English, has supplied nearly a quarter of the recruits.

The Indian Administrative Service

At the time of independence the Indian Civil Service was 52 percent British in membership, but few chose to continue their service under the new government. With the departure of the British and the loss of Muslim officers at partition, the ICS cadre was reduced from nearly 1500 to 451. These officers retained their prestigious ICS designation and were integrated into the new Indian Administrative Service.[40] Most of the initial appointments to the IAS were made on an emergency basis without the usual examination, but the entrance examination was soon resumed. Out of a total of approximately ten million government employees in India, the IAS has a strength of less than three thousand officers, representing the elite cadre of the bureaucracy.

The IAS is composed of separate cadres for each state, and recruits are permanently allocated to a particular state by the Center. To promote national integration and to secure freedom from local influence, one-half of the IAS cadre in each state should come from other states. This provision is under increasing pressure, however, for with the reorganization of states on a linguistic basis, the vernacular became the language of administration within each state, displacing English and imposing serious hardships on those civil servants with less than perfect command of the local language. Moreover, the states have exerted increasing pressure for a policy of local recruitment. Seventy percent of the IAS officers serve the state governments and are under their administrative jurisdiction. There is no Central cadre for the IAS; senior posts are filled by officers on deputation from the states who rotate, at least theoretically, between their states and the Center. In practice the Center and the states are engaged in a "tug-of-war" to keep the best people. At both levels, IAS officers occupy the highest positions in the bureaucracy. In recent years, however, the states have drawn more heavily upon the state services to fill top administrative posts.

The Union Public Service Commission, an independent advisory body appointed by the President, is responsible for all matters relating

[39] Chanda, *Indian Administration*, pp. 102–04.
[40] Less than seventy of the old ICS officers, the elite of the elite, are now left. The last will retire in 1979.

to recruitment, appointment, transfers, and promotions, and its advice is generally decisive.[41] The commission also concerns itself with disciplinary matters affecting members of the services and functions to protect the services and the merit system from political interference. Its relations with the Government are coordinated by the Ministry of Home Affairs, but in its day-to-day work the commission deals directly with the various ministries and departments through its own secretariat.

The process of recruitment and training serves to reinforce the elitist character of the IAS. Approximately 25 percent of the yearly recruitment of less than one hundred are promoted from the state services, but the remainder is directly recruited through competitive examination. Competition is limited to college graduates between the ages of twenty-one and twenty-four. (The age limit is twenty-nine for members of Scheduled Castes and Tribes, those who because of their backward or depressed status are listed in government schedules for special protection or benefits.) Although once the highest position to which one might aspire, the IAS has lost much of its attractiveness for India's brightest youth, who may now find business offering both greater prestige and financial reward. The service continues to be dominated, nevertheless, by the urban, educated, and wealthy classes.

Studies of the social background of direct recruits reveal that most have come from high-income families—a significant factor in educational opportunity. Ninety percent are Hindu and nearly 45 percent are the sons of government officials.[42] The service, however, is no longer as homogeneous as the exclusive and internally cohesive ICS under the British raj. It is increasingly "a looser organization holding a more disparate collection of civil servants with different backgrounds and experience."[43] Approximately 20 percent of the direct recruits to the IAS are now women. A leveling process has also changed the character of its composition. There has been a dramatic increase in the representation of Scheduled Castes and Tribes, with about 25 percent of each year's recruits from these depressed classes.

The IAS examination reflects the generalist orientation of the service; English and general knowledge examinations and an essay that tests logic and expression are required. In addition, candidates may be tested on a wide range of nonadministrative subjects. Scores are considered in combination with a screening interview, but a candidate can no longer fail on "personality" alone. Recruits, on probation, receive a year of training at the service academy at Mussoori, where they take a foundation course that provides a basic background on the constitutional, economic, and social framework of modern India, broad principles of public

[41] See M. A. Muttalib, *Union Public Service Commission* (New Delhi: Indian Institute of Public Administration, 1967).

[42] R. K. Trivedi and D. N. Rao, "Regular Recruits to the I.A.S.—A Study," *Journal of the National Academy of Administration*, Vol. 5 (1960), pp. 50–80.

[43] Potter, "Bureaucratic Change in India," p. 156.

administration, and the ethics of the profession. On completion of the course, recruits must pass a written examination and qualifying tests in Hindi and the language of the state to which they will be allotted. A riding test lingers as a relic of the past.

After completing their training period the recruits are assigned to one of the state cadres for one or two years to receive training in the field. The state program is organized to provide on-the-job training at every administrative level in a wide range of practical problems.[44] In the British "tradition of the amateur" the IAS officer is a jack-of-all-trades, rotated between the district and the state secretariats, between the state and the Center. At each level the demand for specialized training is far greater than in the days of the British raj. The chief task of administration is no longer simply the maintenance of order, but the transformation of a traditional society. To overcome the rigidities of the parallel services, pools have been established to meet the demand for expertise. To handle economic matters the Central Administrative Pool was established to draw men from the IAS, the central services, and the top class of state services. Some qualified men have been directly re-cruited from business and academic life. A similar pool was formed for the management of state industries.[45]

Bureaucracy

"The well-ordered bureaucracy left by the British," Morris-Jones has written, "has not yet been replaced by an equally well-ordered one more fitted to the needs of the new planning and welfare state."[46] The elite IAS has nurtured an *esprit de corps* that has perhaps strengthened it against political interference, but it has cultivated what is often seen as a stance of arrogance. The separate services, with their wide disparity in pay scales, have become rigid and self-conscious "classes" and have stim-ulated jealousies and resentment. Paul Appleby, in his influential 1953 report on public administration in India, argued that "there is too much and too constant consciousness of rank, class, title and service member-ship, too little consciousness of membership in 'the' public service, and too little consciousness turning on particular job responsibilities."[47] It is no less true today. "The service has tended to become inward-looking, obsessed with questions of status, pay and promotion."[48]

The mistrust of the bureaucracy that characterized the period of the

---

[44] See S. P. Jagota, "Training of Public Servants in India," in Braibanti, *Asian Bureaucratic Systems*, pp. 83–84.

[45] W. H. Morris-Jones, *The Government and Politics of India* (London: Hutchin-son, 1966), pp. 127–28.

[46] *Ibid.*, p. 130.

[47] *Public Administration in India: Report of a Survey* (New Delhi: Government of India, Cabinet Secretariat, 1953), p. 11.

[48] A. H. Hanson and Janet Douglas, *India's Democracy* (New York: Norton, 1972), p. 149.

nationalist movement has been perpetuated in the public mind by the rigidities of the system, impersonal treatment, the preoccupation with form and procedures, and the unwillingness of lower officials to accept responsibility. The image of the officialdom has opened "a chasm between the administration and the general public."[49] The achievement of development goals, however, depends upon the growth of mutual attitudes of support and responsiveness between citizens and administrators. The results of various surveys, although inconclusive, suggest that increasing contact between a citizen and an official tends to mobilize the citizen's support *if* he believes the official responsive. If the official is unresponsive, as is often the case, increased contact can serve to widen the gap between aspiration and achievement, causing criticism, cynicism, and hostility.[50] Expanding participation has brought larger numbers of people into contact with the bureaucracy. If it is to cope successfully with the increasing demands made upon it, the bureaucracy must be more open, flexible, and less centralized in its decision-making responsibility. An increased specialization of function, with structural differentiation, a decline of the tradition of the amateur, and an opening of the ranks of the services to a broader social base have all served to enhance the capacity of the bureaucracy to meet the problems posed by expanded participation, but the bureaucracy remains essentially an instrument of order rather than of democratic responsiveness. It has not yet successfully adapted to the new political environment, and since it has lost much of its prestige and once legendary efficiency, some have argued that the "steel frame" has become a cheap alloy.

The structure of an administration is an important determinant of its capabilities. At the lower rungs of the bureaucracy, formalism has served to stifle bureaucratic initiative and imagination. Procedure involves what Appleby has called "the hierarchical movement of paper."[51] Unwilling to accept responsibility even for minor decisions, petty bureaucrats refer the files, neatly tied in red tape, to a higher level. In India, it is said, "the British introduced red tape, but *we* have perfected it." Responsibility is diluted in delay and inaction. "Red tape becomes a technique of self-preservation," writes Kothari, "and reverence for traditional forms is matched only by attachment to strict routine and an unwholesome

[49] Kothari, "Administrative Institutions of Government," p. 825.
[50] See Samuel J. Eldersveld et al., *The Citizen and the Administrator in a Developing Democracy* (Chicago: Scott, Foresman, 1968), pp. 133–34. John O. Field finds that

> those who are most inclined to make demands on government in the sense of believing it to be relevant to the solution of various problems and in the sense of actually participating in politics beyond mere discussion or voting, . . . are the people who are most likely to credit government with good intensions and satisfactory performance.

"Partisanship in India: A Survey Analysis," unpublished doctoral dissertation, Stanford University, 1973, p. 427.
[51] *Public Administration*, p. 18.

preoccupation with questions of accountability."[52] Appleby argues that it is not a question of too much hierarchy, but rather that there is an irregular hierarchy, disjointed and impeding effective communication.[53] Administrative structure is not truly pyramidal, for authority is overly concentrated at the top. The permanent secretary to a state or central government department or ministry is accountable to a minister who holds that portfolio. He may exercise considerable influence over the formation of policy through his advice; but more frequently, the minister intervenes in the administrative process to make particular decisions rather than general policy and, when criticized, shifts responsibility to the civil servants, a situation hardly calculated to sustain morale. In an atmosphere of distrust the civil servant may seek to separate policy and administration, sabotaging the former for the protection of the latter.[54]

A relationship characterized by mutual respect between the politician and the bureaucrat is critical. The civil servant must be neither arrogant nor slavish, but in a democratic system he is subject ultimately to nonbureaucratic control. In the years immediately following Nehru's death, particularly the instability following the 1967 elections, the administration assumed increasing importance and in the states, with the rise and fall of weak coalition governments, the bureaucracy managed to prevent major disruption. But the lack of decisive political leadership was reflected in bureaucratic indecision, in the refusal even to confront controversial issues. To pass the responsibility of governmental decision-making to administrators is likely to yield an order increasingly separated from the people, unaccountable to them, and unresponsive to their demands. The sphere of administrative decision-making has expanded in India, as elsewhere. In part because of the technical nature of so many decisions, what under Nehru might have been a political decision may now be bureaucratic, to a degree insulating the issue from the domain of public conflict.

One major element in the effective operation—and in the public image—of bureaucracy is corruption. While most people continue to see government service as prestigious, their confidence in it is low. Public servants are described as ineffectual, self-seeking, and dishonest. In a survey of residents of Delhi State, almost 60 percent felt that at least half the government officials were corrupt.[55] Corruption may be greatly exaggerated in India because economically frustrated individuals seek a scapegoat in official misbehavior, but A. D. Gorwala argues that "the psychological atmosphere produced by the persistent and unfavourable comment is itself the cause of further moral deterioration, for people will begin to adapt their methods, even for securing a legitimate right,

---

[52] "Administrative Institutions of Government," p. 824.
[53] Public Administration, p. 28.
[54] Morris-Jones, The Government and Politics of India, p. 133.
[55] Eldersveld, The Citizen and the Administrator, pp. 29–30.

to what they believe to be the tendency of men in power and office."[56] Moreover, the public may decry corruption, but traditional attitudes often condone it, and fatalism may lead many to accept it as inevitable. Nepotism is officially condemned, but in traditional terms it may be viewed as loyalty to one's family, friends, and community.

In India, as in any country in which the power of a public servant far exceeds his income, corruption is a major problem. The scope of corruption is greater at points where substantive decisions are made in such matters as tax assessment and collection, licensing, and contracts. "Speed money" to expedite papers and files, even when nothing unlawful is involved, is perhaps the most common form. And it probably takes its greatest toll from the poor, who can least afford it. The Government has engaged in vigorous anticorruption drives, yielding numerous complaints of petty graft. Less easily substantiated are the reports of corruption at the highest levels of government. Stories circulate in the bazaars of ministers who grow rich in office and favor their family and caste fellows. The most notable was Kairon, former Chief Minister of the Punjab, who was forced from office by the Nehru government on the charge of having "brought the State of Punjab to the verge of ruin by his systematic maladministration, the unabashed use of his official position and power to derive pecuniary gains for himself, the members of his family and relatives."[57]

Corruption in itself constitutes an informal political system. It opens channels of influence, but access is limited to only those with the right connections and the sufficient wealth to bend political decisions to their favor. Corruption serves to augment, through illegal means, the advantages those of wealth already command through more institutionalized means of access: the press, elections, and pressure-group activity. Its consequence is fundamentally conservative.[58]

The Supreme Court and the Judicial System

The Supreme Court of India stands at the apex of a single, integrated judicial system. Although India is a federation the centralized judiciary is regarded as "essential to maintain the unity of the country."[59] The Court has original and exclusive jurisdiction in disputes between the Union government and one or more states and in disputes between two or more states. It has appellate jurisdiction in any case, civil or crim-

56 *Report on Public Administration* (New Delhi: Government of India, Planning Commission, 1953), p. 13.
57 *Report of the Commission of Inquiry* (Das Report), Government of India publication, June 11, 1964, p. 27.
58 See James C. Scott, *Comparative Political Corruption* (Englewood Cliffs, N.J.: Prentice-Hall, 1972), pp. 2–35.
59 Dr. B. R. Ambedkar in the Constituent Assembly debates, quoted in Austin, *The Indian Constitution*, p. 185.

inal, that involves, by its own certification, a substantial question of law in the meaning and intent of the constitution. The Supreme Court is the interpreter and guardian of the constitution, the supreme law of the land. The Court is considerably less visible than its American counterpart and has yet to exercise a role in shaping Indian political life. Unlike Great Britain, however, where no court may hold an Act of Parliament invalid, all legislation passed in India by the Center or the states must be in conformity with the constitution, and the constitutionality of any enactment is determined under the power of judicial review by the Supreme Court.

The scope of judicial review in India is not as wide as in the United States. The detail of the constitution gives the Court less latitude in interpretation, and the emergency provisions have severely reduced the Court's review powers in the area of personal liberty. Through its power of judicial review, however, the Court exercises control over both legislative and executive acts. The Court first invoked its power of supremacy in 1950 when it held a section of the Preventive Detention Act invalid and unconstitutional. The Court has since held more than one hundred Center and state acts invalid, either in whole or in part, and most of its decisions have been unanimous.[60] Its decisions with regard to the protection of the Fundamental Rights, Articles 12 through 35, have been a source of particular controversy, leading Nehru to refer to the Court as the "third House of Parliament." When the Court invalidated the Zamindari Abolition Act on the basis of the equal protection clause of the constitution, Parliament enacted the first constitutional amendment, denying the Supreme Court power to declare government acquisition of property invalid on the ground that it abridges any of the Fundamental Rights. Two subsequent amendments, the fourteenth and the seventeenth, were required to free land-reform legislation from the Court's jurisdiction. Then in 1967, in the historic Golaknath case, the Supreme Court ruled that the Fundamental Rights cannot be abrogated or abridged by Parliament—even by constitutional amendment.[61]

The continuing controversy between the Court and Parliament has been over the right to property. The issue was again confronted dramatically in 1970, when the Supreme Court struck down the bank nationalization law and the Presidential Order abolishing the privy purse and privileges of the princes. The measures had been among the most popular of Indira Gandhi's new policy proposals, and they now provided the vehicle by which she could secure basic changes in the constitution. To

[60] Of the total decisions handed down by the Court—more than 3,000 since 1950—some 92 percent were unanimous. Two-thirds of these involved some level of government on one side, and in 40 percent of these cases, the government lost. See George H. Gadbois, Jr., "Indian Judicial Behaviour," *Economic and Political Weekly*, Vol. 5, annual number (January 1970), pp. 149–66.

[61] *All India Reporter*, 1967, *Supreme Court* 1643. See also G. C. V. Subba Rao, "Fundamental Rights in India Versus Power to Amend the Constitution," *Texas International Law Forum*, Vol. 4 (Summer 1968), pp. 291–339.

secure these changes the Prime Minister sought a mandate in the 1971 parliamentary elections. With an overwhelming majority in Parliament, Mrs. Gandhi led the passage of the twenty-fourth amendment, effectively securing for Parliament the power to amend any provision of the constitution, including the provisions of Part III relating to Fundamental Rights. The twenty-fifth amendment removed the Court's power of judicial review over property compensation, thus enabling the legislature, without impediment, to more fully implement the Directive Principles.[62]

The Supreme Court consists of the Chief Justice and thirteen associate justices (the constitution originally specified a total of eight judges, but this was increased in 1960 to fourteen). Each judge is appointed by the President after consultation with the judges of the Supreme Court and the high courts of the states, as deemed necessary. Consultation with the Chief Justice is obligatory. The judges hold office until retirement at age sixty-five, as specified in the constitution, and may be removed only by Parliament on grounds of "proved misbehaviour or incapacity." The appointments to the Supreme Court must be made on the basis of judicial distinction. Appointments are usually made from the benches of the high courts of the states. Although not constitutionally binding, the appointment of the Chief Justice had come to be automatic, with the elevation of the senior-most judge to that office on the retirement of the incumbent. Precedent was broken in 1973 when the President, acting on the advice of the Prime Minister, appointed A. N. Ray to succeed, superseding three senior judges, who then resigned in protest from the Court. The appointment provoked an outcry of "political motivation" from the legal profession. The Prime Minister defended the action—though hardly satisfying her critics—as in the interest of "social justice."

The judges of the high courts are appointed by the President, usually from lower benches, after consultation with the Chief Justices of the Supreme Court and the state high court and with the governor of the state. The number of high court judges varies from thirty-eight in the Allahabad High Court (the high court for the state of Uttar Pradesh) to three in the Himachal Pradesh High Court. The jurisdiction of the high courts is not detailed in the constitution, but it is provided that they retain their general appellate jurisdiction as established during British rule. In addition, the high courts have original jurisdiction on revenue matters, superintend all courts within the state, and have the power to issue writs or orders for the enforcement of the Fundamental Rights guaranteed under the constitution. Below the high courts are the district and subordinate courts, similar in structure throughout the country.

[62] For the background of the controversy, see S. P. Sathe, "Supreme Court, Parliament and Constitution," *Economic and Political Weekly*, Vol. 7 (August 21, 1971), pp. 1821–28, and (August 28, 1971), pp. 1873–80.

The Indian judiciary is a career service. Candidates for the State Judicial Service stand in competitive examination after at least three years' experience before the bar. Successful candidates are then given special training before their appointment to the service. Indian appellate courts are staffed not only from the career service but also, like the American judiciary, from practicing lawyers. The lower courts are staffed by career judges alone.

The "official" law of India may seem alien to most villagers, but they are increasingly ready to work within its framework. The modern judiciary, established by the British as a rule of law—universal, impersonal, and impartial—is today accepted as legitimate throughout India. While the modern legal system has largely displaced that of tradition, traditional society has not passively allowed itself to be regulated; it has used the modern system for its own ends. Traditional groups now find expression in litigation, but as Marc Galanter notes, "all contact with the legal system involves the translation of traditional interests and concerns into 'modern' terms in order to get legal effectiveness." In a sense, he argues, "the new system is Indian: it is a unique system, peculiarly articulated to many of the interests and problems of modern India; and it is a new kind of unifying network through which various aspects of the civilization may find new expression."[63]

Planning and Economic Development

The bureaucracy is the instrument by which policy is implemented, but the formation of policy is no assurance of its fulfillment. The gap between policy and implementation is nowhere clearer than in the broad area of the economy. The Congress, in its 1955 session at Avadi, committed itself in pursuance of the Directive Principles of the constitution to "the establishment of a socialistic pattern of society." For Nehru, this meant "a society in which there is social cohesion without classes, equality of opportunity, and the possibility for everyone to have a good life." Nehru remained "brilliantly vague," and the commitment to socialism was considerably diluted in response to the conservative base of Congress political support. The commitment to socialism reflected a symbolic emancipation from the "capitalistic-imperialist" past and involved fundamentally a pragmatic approach to democratic planning and a readiness to utilize political power to guide and control the economic and social development of the nation.

This commitment had been clearly evident in the establishment of the Planning Commission in 1950. The commission, an extraconstitu-

---

[63] "Hindu Law and the Development of the Modern Indian Legal System," unpublished paper presented at the annual meeting of the American Political Science Association, Chicago, September 9–12, 1964, p. 86.

tional advisory body under the chairmanship of the Prime Minister, was empowered to draw up plans for the effective and balanced use of the country's resources and to establish priorities within the development program. The composition of the commission, nominated by Nehru, gave it the quasi-political image of a "super-cabinet," but one removed from accountability to Parliament. The power and centrality of the Planning Commission reflected Nehru's involvement in it, but with Nehru's decline and death the commission found its political capital sharply reduced. While still important, the Planning Commission has today a more strictly advisory, technocratic role. The states have assumed increasing importance in the planning process, each seeking to maximize its own development allocation. The National Development Council, under the chairmanship of the Prime Minister, consists of the members of the Planning Commission, Union cabinet ministers, and the state chief ministers. It is here, with less regard to economic rationality than to political consideration, that the compromises between the Center and the states are formally agreed upon.

According to the First Five-Year Plan, "the central objective of planning in India is to raise the standard of living of the people and to open out to them opportunities for a richer and more varied life."[64] Poverty and inequality were to be fought by increased production and the redistribution of wealth. As Baldev Raj Nayar argues, however, "the planners were torn between the compulsions of production and the necessity of distribution. This dilemma has haunted the planners throughout the first two decades of planning, and the claims of production have consistently taken precedence over distribution."[65]

In 1951, at the beginning of the First Plan, India had a per capita annual income of only fifty-three dollars. Over 80 percent of the population was rural, yet only 48 percent of the national income was produced in the rural sector. There were major shortages of food and raw materials; industrial production was below capacity; urban unemployment was high, and what has been called concealed rural underemployment still higher;[66] inflation was beginning to accelerate; and the population increase cut deeply into any economic progress. The First Five-Year Plan drew together a variety of specific programs for coordinated investment, with a major emphasis on agriculture. Owing to good monsoons and sufficient reserves of foreign exchange the modest targets of the plan were fulfilled. During the plan years, 1951–56, national income rose 18 percent, with population growth only 6 percent, as then estimated.

---

[64] *The First Five-Year Plan: A Summary* (New Delhi: Government of India, Planning Commission, 1952), p. 1.

[65] *The Modernization Imperative and Indian Planning* (Delhi: Vikas, 1972), p. 32.

[66] The concept of underemployment is controversial and heavily value-laden, for it carries with it a cultural bias as to what full employment *ought* to be. Nevertheless, an adequate level of employment must be defined in terms of its capacity to provide a minimun standard of living. An objective measure of underemployment is that margin needed to secure such a minimum.

Buoyed by the apparent success of the plan, the commission drafted a Second Plan for the years 1956–61, which sought "to strengthen the foundations of economic independence" through rapid development of heavy industry, primarily within the public sector. It was directed by a "mobilization" strategy patterned after the Soviet model. Far bolder than the first, the Second Five-Year Plan doubled investment expenditure, but India's ability to mobilize and direct its own saving and investment potential was limited, and its hard currency reserves were rapidly declining. Within months it was clear that India had planned beyond its capacity. Deficits were met with inflationary deficit finance, with additional taxation, and with foreign aid, but even with midway adjustments the plan was only 70 percent successful. The problem of foreign exchange has always been critical for India. In order to buy the products necessary for its development effort it must use the "hard" currencies accepted as the media of international trade. With an unfavorable balance of payments—importing more than it exports—India has had to make up the difference through grants-in-aid and through a staggering burden of loans, the interest on which absorbs a major portion of its yearly hard currency receipts, sustaining a vicious circle of economic dependency.

The economic course upon which India embarked in the Second Plan involved a fundamental contradiction. The strategy to mobilize political and economic resources was not really compatible with the liberal democracy of the Indian political system.

> The Plan was inconsistent with the political framework in four important respects: one, it was an extremely ambitious need-based rather than resource-based plan, imposing "forced savings" on the community; two, the emphasis on heavy industry meant the postponement of immediate "pay-offs" or "gratifications"; three, the lack of emphasis on agriculture and consumer goods placed restraints on mass consumption; four, the burdens and tasks assumed by the government were beyond its skills and organizational resources.[67]

Despite the difficulties encountered in the Second Plan, its basic strategy and priorities remained essentially unchanged in the Third Plan (1961–66). The Chinese invasion, however, quickly shattered hopes of fulfilling the plan. Development funds were channeled into defense, foreign exchange reserves were exhausted in the procurement of new weaponry, imports ran 50 percent above exports, and inflation brought spiraling prices. The Indo-Pakistani war in 1965 brought further economic dislocation, and India's ability to recover its losses was seriously weakened by the extended interruption of the flow of American aid. This again underscored the vulnerability of the Indian economy

[67] Nayar, *The Modernization Imperative*, p. 54.

in its dependence on foreign support—a fact lost on neither the Government nor the opposition.

The cutoff in American aid, in response to the war, came in the midst of the worst drought of the century. The production of food grains fell nearly 19 percent in one year, and the shortage affected the entire economy. Food prices took a sharp rise, and the government, to curb runaway inflation, tightened credit and cut government spending. Reductions in investment, coupled with the loss of aid, brought an industrial slowdown and expanding urban unemployment. The gap between the plan expectations and realization, writes Rajni Kothari, "was filled by pious declarations, a continuous flow of new ideas which were never implemented, and a snobbish attitude on the part of planners and administrators who shifted the blame to the low motivation of farmers and rural people."[68]

In 1966, the rupee was devalued in response to pressure from the World Bank, but the devaluation failed to rally the economy from recession. Exports were not stimulated as expected, and the salaried urban middle class was caught in a tightening economic squeeze. The massive American wheat loan under Public Law 480 may have concealed the crisis in Indian agriculture, but the 1965–67 drought brought renewed emphasis on agricultural programs.

At the end of the Third Plan, the Planning Commission declared a two-year "plan holiday." One-year plans were considered, but in 1969, the Fourth Five-Year Plan, far less elaborate and ambitious than those that preceded it, began to take shape under the direction of a considerably less powerful Planning Commission. The strategy emphasized agricultural development, with balanced industrial support, and concentration in those sectors and among those individuals where development prospects were brightest—the rich peasants who were thus sustained in their traditional position of dominance. With limited investment resources India's planners confronted an apparent dilemma: they were committed to economic equality and social justice, but also to growth. Distribution would make only a minimal difference in the life of the poor, and it might well dissipate whatever opportunity there was to achieve a breakthrough to continuing economic growth. According to the Fourth Plan "the concern for achieving the desired increase in production in the short run often necessitates the concentration of effort in areas and on classes of people who already have the capacity to respond to growth opportunities."[69] Short-term growth and elite dominance, however, may have been purchased at the cost of economic polarization, increasing political dissent, and violence.

The new agricultural strategy affected at best only 20 percent of the total cultivated area of the country, but in these areas, the use of high-

[68] *Politics in India* (Boston: Little, Brown, 1970), p. 145.
[69] *Fourth Five-Year Plan, 1969–74, Draft* (New Delhi: Government of India, Planning Commission, 1969), p. 9.

yielding varieties of grain, fertilizers and insecticides, irrigation, and tractors produced enormous increases in agricultural output. In Ludhiana district of the Punjab wheat production quadrupled in six years to achieve the highest yield per acre in the world, and many assumed that a "green revolution" had occurred. The very success of the new technology, however, adversely affected many small cultivators and landless laborers. The industrial sector has been largely stagnant, and money that might have stimulated production has been diverted to rural areas for investment by large landholders in profitable agro-business ventures. The value of land in the areas of the green revolution has risen enormously, and the marginal peasants, unable to avail themselves of the new technology, are selling out—but there are no jobs in the urban, industrial sector to absorb them. Whether "pushed" or "pulled" from the land, the poor peasant and landless laborer are the victims of the green revolution, but their plight is shared by many within the cities who are squeezed by rising food prices and a staggering rate of inflation.

As the gap has grown between regions in terms of agricultural productivity, so too has the gap between the rich and the poor in those regions experiencing the greatest increases in productivity. Joan Mencher asks the purpose of growth: "Is it to feed people better, or is it to fill the shops with food that many people cannot afford to buy?"[70]

During the period of the first four plans India failed to fulfill its projected targets of growth. In the pursuit of often unattainable goals, resources have been wasted and hopes have turned to disappointment and cynicism. The record of India's achievements, nevertheless, has been impressive, even if punctuated by drought, war, and recession. There was an overall growth of 3.7 percent per year,[71] well below the plan target, but substantially above the 1 percent growth rate in the first half of the century. In spite of difficulties, agricultural production grew by 3 percent a year, and food-grain output doubled during the four plan periods. Industrial output more than tripled, with an annual growth rate of more than 6 percent. Coal production doubled; steel production increased sixfold; electric power, tenfold; and consumer goods made substantial, if less dramatic, progress. The availability of a rich variety of consumer goods, all made in India, contrasts sharply with the scarcities of even a decade ago.

In education, transportation, and communications, the period since 1951 has witnessed dramatic changes. Even the most isolated villages were penetrated, thus stimulating in the people aspirations for a better life and frustration at their inability to achieve it. The breakthrough in

---

[70] "Conflicts and Contradictions in the 'Green Revolution': The Case of Tamil Nadu," *Economic and Political Weekly*, Vol. 9, annual number (February 1974), p. 319.

[71] The Indian growth rate compares favorably with that of China. See Subramanian Swamy, "Economic Growth in China and India, 1952–1970: A Comparative Appraisal," *Economic Development and Culture Change*, Vol. 21, No. 4, Pt. II (July 1973), pp. 1–84.

communications brought to the Indian masses a new awareness of poverty and a sensitivity to the widening gap that separates them from the rich. The lot of most Indians improved in absolute terms in the years since independence, but the gains have not been equally distributed. Despite the slogans of socialism, government policy itself has often served to subsidize the fundamental inequities of the society. The very nature of liberal democracy, while sustaining personal freedom, has served to promote a pattern of consumption fundamentally inimical to economic development and social justice. Luxury goods whet the appetites of the wealthy few, who seek to emulate the West in wasteful private consumption.

During the period from 1961 to 1973, the increase in India's per capita income, at constant prices, was only 0.7 percent annually, a particularly disturbing figure considering the degree to which income growth has been unevenly distributed. Unemployment has gone up 400 percent, from 3.5 million in 1961 to 16 million in 1971. The number of unemployed grows yearly at an accelerating rate, for each year a larger number of young people enters a labor market that is not expanding fast enough to absorb them. Among the unemployed are increasing numbers of university-educated men and women, often highly trained engineers and technicians, who are unable to find work in the industrial sector, which continues to operate substantially below capacity. The urban unrest generated by deepening unemployment, especially among the young, is compounded by the deteriorating economic position of the lower middle classes, particularly salaried government employees, who have seen what little gains they have achieved swallowed by rapidly rising prices that have pushed them deeper into poverty.

In rural areas the largest estates have been reduced by a degree of land reform, but more to the benefit of rich peasants than the landless. Reforms have led to widespread eviction of tenants and to insecure seasonal employment for agricultural laborers. The poor, with no credit and little margin for risk, are often unable to take advantage of what new opportunities there are. The dominant agricultural classes, on the other hand, "have gained economically by access to credit, fertilizers, seeds, and implements, they have gained politically by control of a major source of influence and patronage, and they have gained socially by an improvement in their status as a result of their positions in the new institutions."[72]

By emphasizing growth as growth rather than growth as long-range development, India opted for production without social change, a policy that implicitly accepted the growing gap between the "haves" and the "have nots." The disparities of the green revolution underscore the tension between economic justice and a narrow production orientation.

Perhaps no one has been more sensitive to these contradictions than

[72] George Rosen, *Democracy and Economic Change in India* (Berkeley: University of California Press, 1967), p. 145.

Indira Gandhi. She sought and received a massive mandate in the 1971 parliamentary elections to remove poverty (*garibi hatao*). The draft for the Fifth Five-Year Plan (1974–79) reflected this commitment. The basic objectives of the plan were to remove poverty and achieve economic self-reliance.[73] With emphasis on overcoming income inequalities and regional disparities, the plan was to mount an "attack on the low-end of poverty" through heavy government expenditure on education and welfare. Critics attacked the Draft Plan as "unrealistic" and dangerously oblivious to the demands of increased agricultural productivity, industrial growth, and population control. For all her political skill, Indira Gandhi had no clear economic program. The burdens of refugee relief and of the war itself that had been imposed upon India during the Bangladesh crisis were compounded by the problems of severe drought in 1972–73. A situation was thus created that the President of India described as "an unprecedented national crisis"—a crisis soon exacerbated by the world energy crisis and the enormous increase in the cost of petrochemical fertilizers and fuel for the operation of tubewell irrigation pumps, upon which the new agriculture is dependent. Disillusioned in her own advisers and confronted by delegations of economists, industrialists, and bureaucrats, the Prime Minister yielded to the pressures for growth. The Fifth Plan began in 1974 with lower targets than set in the early draft. The emphasis was on the "core sector" of steel, oil, power, and fertilizers. The heart of Mrs. Gandhi's garibi hatao program was relegated to the lower priority of "nonessential items."[74]

The Responsive Capacity of India's Governmental Framework

The institutions of government, established by the constitution on the framework of the British raj, have taken root in the Indian soil. Although transplanted, they are today no longer regarded as foreign imports; they have gained legitimacy and widespread acceptance by political parties across the ideological spectrum. Their meaning and operation have been adapted to the Indian environment, and they are still taking form. The judiciary, developed under British tutelage, is at its highest levels considerably less important and less visible than in the United States. The lower courts, weighted with a backlog of litigation, are a widely recognized, and perhaps all-too-often employed, instrument of conflict resolution. The bureaucracy, in search of a new democratic role, has yet to find a clear identity and remains fundamentally an in-

[73] See *Draft Five-Year Plan, 1974–79* (New Delhi: Government of India, Planning Commission, Vol. I, 1973, Vol. II, 1974).
[74] See Marcus F. Franda, "India: 'An Unprecedented National Crisis,'" American University Fieldstaff Report, South Asia Series, Vol. 17, No. 5 (September 1973).

strument of repressive order. It has lost much of its former efficiency in the face of an increased load of demands, and perhaps also some of its quality, with a concomitant loss of respect. Occupants of the Presidency, while yet to face the test of coalition instability at the Center, have established conventions limiting the exercise of the post's potential constitutional power. The office commands national respect as symbol of the state. Parliament, particularly since the death of Nehru, has assumed greater importance. Although its debates rarely affect the character of legislation, they are closely covered in India's press, and the Prime Minister and the Cabinet are increasingly sensitive to Parliament's opinions. The impact of Parliament as an educative institution has been limited largely to the elite political culture. For villagers and many urbanites alike, it is a distant institution little affecting their everyday lives. For them the state legislative assemblies are of far greater importance. The Prime Minister, however, commands a powerful position. The charisma of Jawaharlal Nehru, Prime Minister in the nation's formative years, has become identified with the office itself. It is the symbolic repository of India's power and international prestige. While affected by the personal imprint of the great leader the office has transcended personality, and through the successions, from Nehru to Shastri to Indira Gandhi, the Prime Ministership has proved the most important position in the Indian government.

The political system has been resilient in the face of rapid change and increasing demands, but its increasing capacity is fragile, for India is only now beginning to feel the full impact of rapidly expanding political participation. The rising level of demands and their deepening intensity may strain the system beyond endurance. On gaining independence India inherited a highly institutionalized imperial regime. Relatively low levels of participation and demands provided India with a period of grace during which the institutions of repressive order were adapted to new democratic functions. But India has, if not fallen from grace, at least outrun its institutional advantage. The revolution of rising expectations now places continuous challenge upon these institutions to respond. It may well be, however, that the success of India's response will be determined not at the Center but in the states, through the development of state and local governmental bodies and of interest groups and political parties capable of ordering the newly participant society.

RECOMMENDED READING

Austin, Granville, *The Indian Constitution*. New York: Oxford University Press, 1966.
    An extremely well-written history of the Indian Constituent Assembly and an analysis of the constitution it created.

Bayley, David H., *The Police and Political Development in India*. Princeton: Princeton University Press, 1969.
> A study of the role police play in shaping and maintaining the Indian political system.

Bhambhri, C. P., *Bureaucracy and Politics in India*. Delhi: Vikas, 1971.
> Examines the Indian administrative system and its political environment.

Braibanti, Ralph, ed., *Asian Bureaucratic Systems Emergent from the British Imperial Tradition*. Durham: Duke University Press, 1966.
> A collection of essays dealing with various aspects of the history and structure of the government services in India.

Brecher, Michael, *Nehru's Mantle: The Politics of Succession in India*. New York: Praeger, 1966.
> A detailed account of the events surrounding the successions after the deaths of Nehru and Shastri.

Chanda, Asok, *Indian Administration*. London: George Allen & Unwin, 1958.
> A critical examination of the Indian administrative structure and the executive branch of government by the former comptroller and auditor general of India.

Frankel, Francine R., *India's Green Revolution: Economic Gains and Political Costs*. Princeton: Princeton University Press, 1971.
> A penetrating study of the political impact of the new agricultural strategy in five districts.

Hanson, A. H., *The Process of Planning: A Study of India's Five Year Plans, 1950–1964*. London: Oxford University Press, 1966.
> Although now dated, the major study of planning in India.

Jannuzi, F. Tomasson, *Agrarian Crisis in India: The Case of Bihar*. Austin: University of Texas Press, 1974.
> An account of the failure of land reform in one of India's most troubled states.

Kothari, Shanti, and Roy, Ramashray, *Relations Between Politicians and Administrators*. New Delhi: Indian Institute of Public Administration and the Centre of Applied Politics, 1969.
> A survey analysis of Meerut District, Uttar Pradesh.

Maheshwari, S. R., *Indian Administration*, 2nd ed., New Delhi: Orient Longman, 1974.
> A systematic and detailed description of Indian administrative structure, federal, state, and local.

* Malenbaum, Wilfred, *Modern India's Economy*. Columbus, Ohio: Charles Merrill, 1971.
> A broad view of the condition of the Indian economy, with an analysis of the record of development over the period of the first four plans.

Morris-Jones, W. H., *Parliament in India*. London: Longmans, Green, 1957.
> An extensive study of the Indian Parliament, now dated but still of great use in understanding the character and operation of this institution.

* Available in a paperback edition.

Nayar, Baldev Raj, *The Modernization Imperative and Indian Planning.* Delhi: Vikas, 1972.
 A compelling argument for a new perspective on India's economic planning.

Pylee, M. V., *Constitutional Government in India,* 3rd ed. Bombay: Asia Publishing House, 1975.
 A detailed analysis of the constitution and the formal structures of Indian government.

* Smith, Donald E., *India as a Secular State.* Princeton: Princeton University Press, 1963.
 A major study of secular government policy and its relationship to various aspects of Hindu religion and society, with a discussion of particular problems posed by Hindu communalism.

Taub, Richard T., *Bureaucrats Under Stress.* Berkeley: University of California Press, 1969.
 A careful and provocative study of administrators and administration in the state of Orissa.

Venkateswaran, R. J., *Cabinet Government in India.* London: George Allen & Unwin, 1967.
 An examination of cabinet operations under Nehru, Shastri, and Indira Gandhi in the first years of her leadership.

* Available in a paperback edition.

IV

FEDERALISM AND THE STATES

THE FEDERAL STRUCTURE IN INDIA IS CHARACTERIZED FORMALLY BY A bias in favor of the Center—a bias that has been the subject of controversy since the system's inception. Kenneth Wheare has described the system as "quasi-federal,"[1] and Asok Chanda, former Comptroller and Auditor General of India, has stated flatly that "India is not a federal state. In the final analysis," he says, "it is a unitary state in concept and operation. . . ."[2]

The Relationship Between the Center and the States

The unitary emphasis in the constitution, inherited from the Government of India Act of 1935, is to be found in the division of powers and in the various articles specifying the relationship between the Center and the states. The division of powers is laid down in the Seventh Schedule of the constitution in three lists exhausting "all the ordinary

[1] *Federal Government* (New York: Oxford University Press, 1951), p. 28.
[2] *Federalism in India* (London: George Allen & Unwin, 1965), p. 124.

activities of government." The Union List gives the Center exclusive authority to act in matters of national importance and includes among its ninety-seven items defense, foreign affairs, currency, banking duties, and income taxation. The State List, with sixty-six items, covers public order and police, welfare, health, education, local government, industry, agriculture, and land revenue. The Concurrent List contains forty-seven items over which the Center and the states share authority. The most important are civil and criminal law and social and economic planning. The residual power lies with the Union, and in any conflict between Union and state, Union law prevails.

The paramount position of the Center is underscored by the power of Parliament to create new states, to alter the boundaries of existing states, and even to abolish a state by ordinary legislative procedure, without recourse to constitutional amendment. Under a proclamation of emergency, Parliament is empowered "to make laws for the whole or any part of the territory of India with respect to any of the matters enumerated in the State List."[3] The President, if advised by his representative in the state, the governor, that "the government of the State cannot be carried on in accordance with the provisions of this Constitution," may by proclamation assume all executive functions to himself and declare the powers of the state assembly to be under the authority of Parliament.[4] In an emergency the Government of India in fact takes on a unitary form.

The constitution provides that the Union may give such directions to a state government as may be necessary "to ensure compliance with laws made by Parliament."[5] If a state fails to comply with such directions, the President may invoke emergency power to supersede the state government. In addition the Rajya Sabha may by a two-thirds vote resolve that it is "necessary or expedient" that Parliament make laws for a temporary period with respect to any mater on the State List.[6] The Rajya Sabha invoked this power on only one occasion. However, since state representation in the Rajya Sabha is unequal, larger states have the power to transfer a subject from state to Union jurisdiction if opposition parties should gain control of some of the smaller states.[7] A variety of other articles also reveals the constitutional imbalance between the Union and states: the amending process, the single judicial system, the all-India services, the single election commission, and the provision for reservation of certain state bills for presidential assent. The distribution of revenue resources is especially critical in determining the nature of the states' relationship to the Center. The Union's tax resources as specified in the constitution are considerably greater than those of the

[3] Constitution of India, Article 250.
[4] *Ibid.*, Article 356.
[5] *Ibid.*, Article 256.
[6] *Ibid.*, Article 249.
[7] Chanda, *Federalism in India*, p. 90.

states. Revenues collected by the Center are allocated in part to the states, on the basis of recommendations by the Finance Commission (an independent agency appointed by the President); thus the states are open to Union intervention. The states are further dependent upon the Center for grants-in-aid.

For all its unitary character, however, the Center is heavily dependent on the states for the implementation of its policies. The leaders in the states, sensitive to the base of their political support, have often remained adamantly independent, as, for example, in their refusal to levy taxes on agricultural income as the Center has recommended. Paul Appleby has argued that "no other large and important government . . . is so dependent as India on theoretically subordinate but actually rather distinct units responsible to a different political control, for so much of the administration of what are recognized as national programs of great importance to the nation."[8] Furthermore, for all its potential the Center has used its power to intervene in state affairs sparingly. This has led many scholars to stress "cooperative federalism," an interdependence of the Center and the states. India has been characterized by a dual process of centralization and decentralization—centralization in response to the exigencies of national planning, and decentralization as a result of the Center's dependence upon the states for administration, the increased solidarity of linguistic states, and the emergence of a new, regionally based state leadership.

The federal relationship is "a bargaining process between central and state leaders, one in which experiment, cooperation, persuasion and conciliation could describe both generally accepted norms and the usual procedural patterns of intergovernmental relations."[9] In a situation of limited resources each state seeks to maximize its advantage, stressing its needs and its potential. "Whereas the emphasis in the Constitution is on demarcation," says W. H. Morris-Jones, "that of practical relations is on co-operative bargaining."[10] In this bargaining process, the role of the Congress party has been critical. It has been widely held that the dominance of the Congress before 1967, when it controlled both the Center and the states, brought the state governments under effective Central control through the exercise of party discipline. However, on the basis of an examination of West Bengal–Center relations, Marcus F. Franda argues that the state Congress party organization may serve to impede Central control; party cohesion within the state and the ability of the party to mobilize the populace for political action are major sources of state autonomy.[11] In West Bengal before 1967, the threat of

[8] *Public Administration in India: Report of a Survey* (New Delhi: Government of India, Cabinet Secretariat, 1953), p. 21.

[9] Marcus F. Franda, *West Bengal and the Federalizing Process in India* (Princeton, N.J.: Princeton University Press, 1968), p. 179.

[10] *The Government and Politics of India* (London: Hutchinson, 1966), p. 143.

[11] *West Bengal and the Federalizing Process*, pp. 201–24.

the leftist opposition, supported by a volatile middle class, increased the state government's dependence upon the Union for support in maintaining order. But at the same time, the Bengal Congress used the "extenuating circumstances" of the situation to maintain its independence from central party discipline. Because of the threat posed by the left, the national leadership was more willing to allow a wide range of discretion in policy and behavior by the state party organization.[12]

The instability that followed the 1967 elections brought increased Central intervention, but if instability at the state level facilitates Union dominance, the capacity of the Center to intervene effectively may well be declining. The stability of the Center itself is no longer fully secure, and the states, both Congress and non-Congress, have exercised increased autonomy since States Reorganization in 1956. Their political weight, as seen in the role of the states in the successions, for example, is substantial. The emergence of a new state leadership, more politically sensitive to traditional bases of support, has served to strengthen state party organization. With a regionally based machine the Congress derived its electoral success more from local than from national sources. It may be, however, that the local base of party effectiveness makes the party more highly vulnerable to displacement by regional opposition parties, as happened with the victory of the Dravida Munnetra Kazhagam (DMK) in Tamil Nadu in 1967. The federal system serves, nevertheless, to quarantine state crises, for the local character of political conflict may have little effect on the stability of a neighboring state.[13] The states are the arena of the most dramatic increases in political participation, the focus of rising demands, and the critical testing ground of political development in India.

States Reorganization

With the accession of the princely states in 1947 the process of integration began. The components of the new Union were divided into four categories, depending upon both their makeup and relationship with the Center. Some, former governor's provinces and princely states alike, retained their boundaries. Others, however, were formed from the union of various contiguous states. A number of the smaller territories remained under Central administration.

The twenty-seven states of the Indian Union were heterogeneous linguistically and, except for their common link with the past, culturally. From the 1920s, and as late as 1945, the Congress party had called for the formation of linguistic provinces. The provincial branches of the party itself had been reorganized in 1921 on a linguistic basis, with units

[12] *Ibid.*, p. 190.
[13] Myron Weiner, *Party Building in a New Nation: The Indian National Congress* (Chicago: University of Chicago Press, 1967), p. 117.

established for what are today the states of Andhra, Kerala, and Maharashtra. With independence the Dar Commission was appointed to advise the Constituent Assembly in its deliberations on demands for linguistic states. The commission's report, submitted at the end of 1948, warned that linguistically homogeneous provinces would have a "subnational bias," threatening national unity, and that, in any case, each state would have minorities. The report was received with general disappointment. The issue had become critical, and the Congress appointed Jawaharlal Nehru, Vallabhbhai Patel, and the party president, Pattabhi Sitaramayya, "to examine the question in the light of the decisions taken by the Congress in the past and the requirements of the existing situation."[14] The "JVP" Committee, fundamentally concerned with the problem of national unity, reaffirmed the position of the Dar Commission. "It would unmistakably retard the process of consolidation [and] let loose, while we are still in a formative stage, forces of disruption and disintegration. . . ."[15] It conceded, however, that a strong case might be made for the formation of Andhra from the Telugu-speaking region of Madras, and that, if public sentiment was "insistent and overwhelming," this and other cases might be given further consideration. "This was the opening wedge for the bitter struggle over States Reorganization which was to dominate Indian politics from 1953 to 1956."[16]

The demand for a separate state of Andhra had deep roots among the Telugu people. It had won the agreement of the Madras government and obtained the support of the Tamilnad Congress Committee, but only after a fast-unto-death by one of the leaders of the Andhra movement did the Center finally respond. In 1953 the state of Andhra was created. Nehru argued against the "foolish and tribal attitudes" of provincialism. The states, he said, were only for administrative purposes —but the demand had been recognized, and other linguistic groups would now have nothing less.

The States Reorganization Commission, appointed by Nehru to examine the question, sought a "balanced approach" between regional sentiment and national interest. The commission, in its 1955 report, rejected the theory of "one language one state," but recognized "linguistic homogeneity as an important factor conducive to administrative convenience and efficiency. . . ."[17] The commission recommended that the political divisions of the Union be redrawn generally in accordance with linguistic demands. The States Reorganization Act, as it was finally

[14] Quoted in Joan V. Bondurant, *Regionalism Versus Provincialism: A Study in Problems of Indian National Unity* (Indian Press Digests—Monograph Series, No. 4; Berkeley: University of California Press, 1958), p. 29.
[15] *Ibid.*
[16] Michael Brecher, *Nehru: A Political Biography* (New York: Oxford University Press, 1959), p. 481.
[17] *Report of the States Reorganization Commission* (New Delhi: Government of India, 1955), p. 46.

FIGURE 4-1

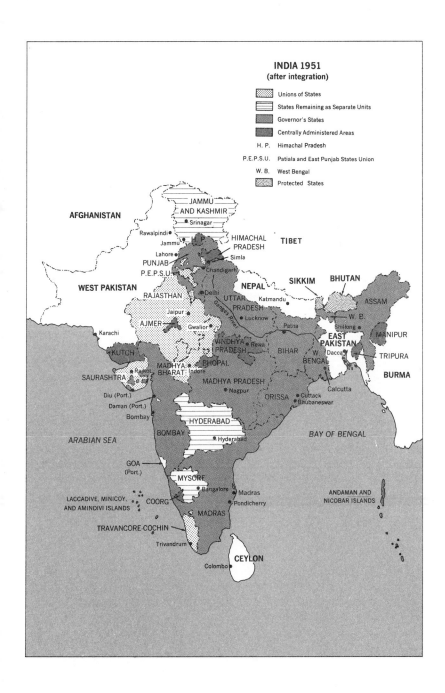

passed by Parliament in November 1956, provided for fourteen states and six territories. The boundaries of each state were to be drawn so that they would conform with the region of a dominant language. Following the recommendations of the commission, however, Bombay and the Punjab, two of the most sensitive areas, were not reorganized on a linguistic basis. The demands for separate tribal states, including Jharkhand and Nagaland, were also bypassed.

The commission opposed the division of Bombay into Marathi and Gujarati states largely because of the critical question of Bombay City. Marathi-speakers constituted its largest language group, but the city was dominated by Gujarati wealth. In the Marathi-speaking districts of Bombay State, widespread rioting broke out, and eighty people were killed in police firings. Under pressure the Center offered, then withdrew, a proposal that the state be divided but that the city of Bombay be administered as a separate state. During this period of indecision and vacillation on the part of Nehru and the Congress high command, the rioting spread to Gujarat. Bombay politics polarized linguistically; two broadly based language front organizations, the Samyukta Maharashtra Samiti and the Mahagujarat Janata Parishad were formed. In the 1957 elections the Congress majority in Bombay was seriously threatened. Agitation continued, and in 1960 the Congress gave way to the demand for reorganization. Gujarat and Maharashtra were constituted as separate linguistic states, with the city of Bombay included as part of Maharashtra.

In the Punjab, the Akali Dal, the paramilitary political party of Sikh nationalism, had long demanded a Sikh state, if not the independent Sikhistan it sought at the time of partition. The demand for a separate state of the Punjab (Punjabi Suba) was voiced not in communal but in linguistic terms. There was no real language problem in the Punjab, however; it was rather a problem of script and, fundamentally, of religion. Punjabi is the mother tongue of Sikhs and Hindus alike, but communal passions had led large sections of the Hindu community to renounce the Punjabi language by naming their mother tongue as Hindi for census tabulation. The languages as spoken are very similar, but Punjabi is distinguished by the use of Gurmukhi, the script of the Sikh holy books. Hindus in the Punjab write in Urdu or in Devanagari script. "The only chance of survival of the Sikhs as a separate community," it was argued, "is to create a State in which they form a compact group, where the teaching of Gurmukhi and the Sikh religion is compulsory. . . ."[18]

The States Reorganization Commission contended that the formation of a separate Punjabi-speaking state would solve neither the language nor the communal problem, but "far from removing internal tension, which exists between communal and not linguistic and regional groups,

[18] Khushwant Singh, *A History of the Sikhs*, Vol. 2 (Princeton, N.J.: Princeton University Press, 1966), pp. 304–05.

it might further exacerbate the existing feelings."[19] In the 1956 reorganization the states of PEPSU (Patiala and East Punjab States Union) and the Punjab were merged into a single state; the Sikhs, forming only about one-third of the population, were concentrated in the western districts. Punjabi and Hindi were both official languages. But the Akali Dal, encouraged by the bifurcation of Bombay in 1960, began agitating for Punjabi Suba. Akali volunteers courted arrest and filled the jails, while Sikh leaders Sant Fateh Singh and Master Tara Singh engaged in abortive fasts. Agitation continued, but without response from the Government. Then abruptly in 1966, supposedly as a concession to the valor and suffering of the Sikhs in the Indo-Pakistan war of 1965 but partly in response to the growing demand in the Hindi areas for a separate state of Haryana, the Government announced that the Punjab would be divided into two units, Punjabi Suba and Haryana, corresponding to the regions of language dominance. The Sikhs at last constituted a majority in the Punjab—55 percent of the population. The hill districts of the old Punjab became part of Himachal Pradesh, stimulating a demand there for full statehood that was fulfilled in 1971. Chandigarh, the modern capital designed by the French architect Le Corbusier, was made a Union territory and joint capital for the Punjab and Haryana.

The demand for the creation of Jharkhand out of the Chota-Nagpur region of southern Bihar and the contiguous tribal districts of Orissa was a product of the increasing self-consciousness of the six million members of the scheduled tribes in the area. The Jharkhand party, organized by a wealthy, Oxford-educated Munda tribesman, Jaipal Singh, secured various concessions from the Bihar government, but it did not succeed in its demand for a separate state.[20]

The demand for the creation of Nagaland posed a more serious problem. The Naga tribes in the hills along the Assam-Burma border had never been completely brought under control by the British, and they were eager to assert their independence from the new Indian government. The situation was further complicated by the conversion of many of the Nagas to Christianity by American Baptist missionaries. Their missionary tie gave the Nagas outside leverage. When the Government sought to bring formerly unadministered areas of the Naga hills under its control the Nagas appealed to the United Nations, protesting what they called an Indian invasion, and the Naga National Council was organized to function as a parallel government with Assam. With money and arms secured by the Naga leader A. Z. Phizo, who later set up an exile government in London, the rebellion became increasingly serious. In 1956 the Indian government sent in troops to pacify the area. The Naga People's Convention, representing the more traditional

---

[19] *Report of the States Reorganization Commission*, p. 146.
[20] See Myron Weiner, *The Politics of Scarcity* (Chicago: University of Chicago Press, 1962), pp. 41–43.

TABLE 4–1

STATES AND TERRITORIES OF THE INDIAN UNION

States	Principal Languages
Andhra Pradesh	Telugu
Assam	Assamese and Bengali
Bihar	Hindi
Gujarat	Gujarati
Haryana	Hindi
Himachal Pradesh	Hindi and Pahari
Jammu and Kashmir	Kashmiri and Urdu
Karnataka (formerly Mysore)	Kannada
Kerala	Malayalam
Madhya Pradesh	Hindi
Maharashtra	Marathi
Manipur	Manipuri
Meghalaya	Khasi and Garo
Nagaland	Naga and English*
Orissa	Oriya
Punjab	Punjabi
Rajasthan	Rajasthani and Hindi
Tamil Nadu (formerly Madras)	Tamil
Tripura	Tripuri and Bengali
Uttar Pradesh	Hindi
West Bengal	Bengali

Union Territories

Andaman and Nicobar Islands	Goa, Daman, and Diu
Arunachal Pradesh	Lakshadweep Islands
Chandigarh	Mizoram
Dadra and Nagar Haveli	Pondicherry
Delhi	

* English is the language used for administrative purposes as a result of both practical necessity and missionary influence.

leadership of the Naga tribes, opposed Phizo and proposed a settlement "within the Indian Union." The Nagas were finally released from Assamese administration, and in 1963 the state of Nagaland came into being.

Violence among the tribes continued, however, and Mizo rebels launched guerrilla action in a bid for secession. In 1972, the northeastern region was reorganized in an attempt to secure the support of moderate tribal leaders. The Union Territories of Manipur and Tripura and the Meghalaya section of Assam gained full statehood, the North East Frontier Agency (NEFA) was formed into the Union Territory of Arunachal Pradesh, and the Mizo district of Assam became the Union Territory of Mizoram.

Regionalism and the Politics of Language

India's political map has been modified in the years since States Reorganization, so that the Indian Union is now composed of twenty-one states and nine Union territories (see the map inside the front cover). The formation of new states cannot be ruled out, but the argument for smaller, more administratively viable states is countered by concern that the smaller state may be more easily dominated by vested interests. Prime Minister Indira Gandhi has strongly resisted the demands for the bifurcation of Andhra Pradesh. Initially a movement for the separate statehood of Telengana (the area that was part of old Hyderabad State), the struggle was joined by coastal Andhra when it appeared that the balance of power between the two regions had shifted in Telengana's favor. The demands of each region for separate statehood, led largely by urban, middle-class interests, have been accompanied by demonstrations, strikes, hartals, and widespread rioting, with a loss of life estimated to have passed one hundred.[21] Similar separate statehood movements, varying greatly in support and intensity, exist throughout India. Frequently involving depressed regions, these include tribal areas of Bihar, Orissa, and Madhya Pradesh; the hill districts of Bengal; the eastern districts of Uttar Pradesh; and the Saurashtra region of Gujarat. Of a different character is the demand by some in Haryana for adjacent districts of Rajasthan and Uttar Pradesh so as to create Vishal (greater) Haryana. Such an enlarged state, they argue, would become the "granary of India."

Disputes over the boundaries between the linguistic states have also

21 For a discussion of the two movements, see Hugh Gray, "The Demand for a Separate Telengana State in India," *Asian Survey*, Vol. 11 (May 1971), pp. 463–74, and "The Failure of a Demand for a Separate Andhra State," *Asian Survey*, Vol. 14 (April 1974), pp. 338–49; and G. Parthasarthy, K. V. Ramana, and G. Dasaradha Rama Rao, "Separatist Movement in Andhra Pradesh: Shadow and Substance," *Economic and Political Weekly*, Vol. 8 (March 17, 1973), pp. 560–63.

stirred violence, as in the case of the continuing conflict between Maharashtra and Karnataka over the district of Belgaum. Awarded to Karnataka in the 1956 States Reorganization, the city of Belgaum is linguistically heterogeneous, and its largest community, which speaks Marathi, wants to merge with Maharashtra. In late 1973, the struggle between the Marathi nativist Shiv Sena party and an equally chauvinistic Karnataka group turned Belgaum into a madhouse of linguistic rioting.

The creation of linguistic states has reinforced regionalism and has stirred demands for increased state autonomy—expressed most stridently by the Communist Party of India (Marxist) in West Bengal and by the DMK in Tamil Nadu, evoking its earlier call for secession and the creation of an independent Dravidian state.[22] Almost every state has spawned a militant nativist movement directed against outsiders. The fundamental issue has been employment for local people, and many state governments, either officially or unofficially, have supported the protection of jobs for the "sons of the soil." Of the movements, the most virulent has been the Shiv Sena, founded in 1966 in Bombay. Exploiting Maharashtrian grievances and economic frustration the Shiv Sena, under the banner "Maharashtra for the Maharashtrians," has directed its attack, both verbal and physical, primarily at South Indian immigrants.[23]

Language has been the subject of continued conflict among the states of the Indian Union. India has 1,652 "mother tongues," and of these, fourteen constitute the major languages around which the states were reorganized in 1956. During the years of British rule, the language of administration and that of the educated elite was English. For Mahatma Gandhi and the Congress, English had usurped the rightful place of the indigenous languages. Hindi, as the most widely spoken of the Indian languages, was to replace English with the achievement of independence. The constitution embodied this aspiration in Article 343, which stipulated that "the official language of the Union shall be Hindi in the Devanagari script." The constitution also provided that English should remain the language of administration for no longer than fifteen years.

The South, where English standards in school remained high and where there was little knowledge of Hindi, was uneasy. The changeover from English to Hindi would place those for whom Hindi was not a mother tongue at a severe disadvantage, especially in competition for coveted positions within the public services. In response to growing opposition—especially in Tamil Nadu—to the "imposition" of Hindi,

---

[22] For a discussion of the Dravidian movement and the rise of the DMK, see Chapter VI, pp. 170–72.

[23] See Ram Joshi, "The Shiv Sena: A Movement in Search of Legitimacy," *Asian Survey*, Vol. 10 (November 1970), pp. 967–78; and Mary F. Katzenstein, "Origins of Nativism: The Emergence of Shiv Sena in Bombay," *Asian Survey*, Vol. 13 (April 1973), pp. 386–94.

Nehru assured the South that English would remain "as an alternative language as long as the people require it. . . ." In 1961 the National Integration Council recommended the adoption of the "three-language formula," which would require in all schools compulsory teaching in three languages: the regional language and English, with Hindi for the non-Hindi states and another Indian language for the Hindi-speaking states. The northern Hindi advocates demanded that the South adopt Hindi in its curriculum as compulsory, but they themselves refused to adopt the three-language formula, feeling Hindi alone was sufficient.

Nehru's assurance had eased the fears of Tamil Nadu, but on Republic Day, January 26, 1965, in pursuance of the constitution, Hindi became the official language of India. In the two months of anti-Hindi demonstrations and riots that followed in Tamil Nadu, more than sixty people were killed in police firings, and unofficial reports placed the number of deaths as high as three hundred. Two young men poured gasoline upon their bodies and immolated themselves in protest. Hindi books were burned, and Hindi signs in railway stations were defaced or ripped down. All colleges and high schools in the state were closed, and student demonstrations gave way to mob violence. An uneasy peace was restored only with regiments of armed police and soldiers.[24]

The DMK, self-appointed spokesman for the Tamil cause, demanded that all fourteen regional languages be the "official languages of the respective states with English as the link language between the States and the Centre." Despite pro-Hindi agitation in the North the Government came forward with an amendment to the Official Languages Act, giving statutory form to Nehru's assurances. While the three-language formula is today official policy, it is honored in breach. Tamil Nadu has specifically eliminated Hindi from the school curriculum, and the Hindi heartland of North India remains almost wholly monolingual. English remains, for the most part, the language of the central government, but as a "link" it is increasingly tenuous.

In order to counter divisive tendencies among the linguistic states the States Reorganization Act established five zonal councils to promote cooperation and coordination of policies. Each council consists of the Union Home Minister, acting as chairman, the chief ministers of the states within the zone, and two other ministers from each state nominated by the governor. The councils have only an advisory capacity, and the results of their activities have been less than impressive. There has been some success in hydroelectric power development, but only the Southern Zonal Council has effectively served to coordinate state economic and social policies, notably in the matter of linguistic minorities.

Reorganization gave the states a political identity congruent with their culture and language.

24 See Robert L. Hardgrave, Jr., "The Riots in Tamilnad: Problems and Prospects of India's Language Crisis," *Asian Survey*, Vol. 5 (August 1965), pp. 399–407.

[It] brought State politics closer to the people, and made it easier for traditional leaders and influential regional groups to capture control or, at least, exercise much influence over the use of power. . . . Thus, in a sense, reorganization made State politics more democratic, but less western in style. It meant, for one thing, that State politics would be increasingly conducted in the regional language rather than English; thus power was now open to others than the small English-speaking elite.[25]

States Reorganization provided the framework for expanded participation. It made the people more accessible to political mobilization and, at the same time, provided them with increased institutional access for the articulation of demands—but demands that have often reflected the parochialism of region and language.

State Government

Each of the states reproduces in miniature the structure and organization of the Union government.

The Governor

In his relationship to the Chief Minister and the state council of ministers and to the state legislative assembly, the Governor holds a constitutional position much like that of the President at the Center. He is appointed by the President for a term of five years, and by convention the state ministry is consulted to assure his acceptability. The Governor is usually from another state, free from local political commitments and, presumably, able to view the problems of Union-state relations with detachment and objectivity.[26]

Like the President the Governor holds the formal executive power. Although this power is in fact exercised by the council of ministers, the governor has important discretionary powers to perform as agent of the central government. The decision as to what lies within his discretion is solely his own. The Governor formally appoints the Chief Minister. If no clear majority is returned to the state assembly, the Governor may exercise his discretion in the selection of a leader who can form a stable ministry, and while the confidence of the assembly is required, the Governor's role may be critical.

The 1967 elections highlighted this role and brought the position of the governor into controversy. Five states were without clear majorities

[25] Duncan B. Forrester, "Electoral Politics and Social Change," *Economic and Political Weekly*, special number (July 1968), p. 1083.
[26] M. V. Pylee, *Constitutional Government in India* (Bombay: Asia Publishing House, 1965), p. 513.

after the election, and in other states subsequent liquidity of support, with the defection of members to the opposition in floor-crossings, brought on instability that gave Governors considerable room to act. In the states without clear majorities Governors had to assess which of the competing coalitions could marshal majority support for a ministry; in the other states they had to determine whether the ministry retained the confidence of the assembly and, if not, whether a new ministry could be formed. If no government can be found, a state may then be brought under President's Rule. The Governor, as agent of the Union, then assumes the emergency powers of administration. Since the 1967 election the process has become a familiar one. What was once an extraordinary measure of Central intervention is now almost a regular occurrence.

In addition to emergency powers the Governor also has certain legislative powers, including the power to promulgate ordinances. Every bill passed by the assembly goes to him for assent. Most bills are government sponsored, and refusal to assent would bring him into conflict with the state ministry, but he is empowered to return any bill except a money bill to the assembly for its reconsideration. If, in his opinion, a bill threatens the position of the high court, he may reserve it for the assent of the President.

The Chief Minister

The Chief Minister occupies a position in the state comparable to that of the Prime Minister at the Center. He is appointed by the Governor but is responsible with his ministry to the popularly elected legislative assembly. Until 1967 the number of ministers in each state averaged about a dozen. In the process of ministry formation after the 1967 elections, however, the ministries were greatly expanded as additional posts were offered to counter opposition attempts to lure members into defection through the promise of ministerial positions in new governments.

The Legislative Assembly and the Legislative Council

The constitution provides that in each state there shall be a Legislative Assembly (Vidhan Sabha). Eight states also have a second chamber, the Legislative Council (Vidhan Parishad). The assembly is directly elected for a five-year term, with a membership of not more than five hundred or fewer than sixty. In order to maintain uniformity in the population represented, the constituencies are reapportioned with each election in accordance with the census. If the Anglo-Indian community is not represented in the assembly, the constitution empowers the governor to nominate an appropriate number of Anglo-Indians as members.

In those states with a bicameral legislature the upper house, the

Legislative Council, is selected by a combination of direct election, indirect election, and nomination, with a total membership not more than
one-third of the number in the Legislative Assembly but not fewer than
forty. The council is not subject to dissolution, and like the Rajya
Sabha, it renews one-third of its membership every two years. Unlike
the Rajya Sabha, however, the upper house of the states exercises what
in fact is an advisory role alone. At most, it can delay the passage of a
bill and has been attacked as a "costly ornamental luxury."

Members of the Legislative Assembly

Members of the state legislative assemblies command positions of
increasing importance, for it is the assembly rather than Parliament that
is the legislative unit closest to the people. Likewise, assembly elections
are viewed within the states as far more critical than parliamentary
elections. The social character of the assembly differs considerably from
that of Parliament in reflecting generally lower levels of education and
westernization. The MLA is highly astute politically, however, and it is
through him that the masses make their most effective contact with
the elite. Reflecting an increasing parochialization as local bosses, adept
in the arenas of traditional village politics, rise to positions of state
power, the legislative assemblies are the focal point of modern and
traditional political styles. The successful MLA is likely to combine
the styles in his role as a political broker. What the voters want in an
ideal MLA might well approximate the villagers' ideal described by
F. G. Bailey in his study of Orissa:

> Their MLA is not the representative of a party with a policy
> which commends itself to them, not even a representative who
> will watch over their interests when policies are being framed,
> but rather a man who will intervene in the implementation of
> policy, and in the ordinary day-to-day administration. He is there
> to divert the benefits in the direction of his constituents, to help
> individuals to get what they want out of the Administration, and
> to give them a hand when they get into trouble with officials.
> This is the meaning which the ordinary villager—and some of
> their MLAs—attach to the phrase "serving the people."[27]

With each election, the assemblies have become more nearly representative of the people, with members drawn from increasingly varied
backgrounds. In Tamil Nadu, for example, the first assembly (1952–57)
was dominated by a highly educated, westernized, English-speaking
elite—middle-class lawyers, landlords, and a variety of hereditary notables.[28] Through the creation of a unilingual Tamil state, States Re-

---

[27] *Politics and Social Change: Orissa in 1959* (Berkeley: University of California
Press, 1963), p. 25.
[28] Duncan B. Forrester, "State Legislators in Madras," *Journal of Commonwealth
Political Studies*, Vol. 7 (March 1969), p. 37.

organization increased the number of opportunities for mobilization and participation and encouraged more traditional and less well-educated leaders to enter the government. Knowledge of English was no longer essential. Sufficient education to be an effective intermediary between the government and the people was necessary, but increasingly the MLAs lacked an adequate education for effective policy-making and came to rely more heavily on the bureaucratic structure. The "legislative life" of the MLA is secondary to his role as political broker. "The average MLA comes into his own not on the floor of the Assembly but in helping his constituents to get places in college, permits, licenses, and jobs. It is this kind of work that occupies most of his time, and this that pays the greatest electoral dividends."[29]

The legislative assembly in Tamil Nadu, as in the rest of India, has increasingly come under rural dominance. Most MLAs have strong ties to their constituencies, and it is through the MLAs that localism has come to dominate state politics. Under the Congress, localism carried with it the dominance of the wealthiest sectors of rural society. Landowners and leaders of the traditionally dominant agricultural castes came into prominence through the political machine. Many of these men had remained aloof during the nationalist movement, and only after independence, both to protect themselves and to take advantage of new opportunities to augment their power, did they enter the political arena. The English-educated veterans of the struggle for independence were thus displaced in the assembly by those who were committed to the defense of vested interests and the politics of the pork barrel. Duncan B. Forrester sees their struggle for the spoils of office as the pathway to their own defeat, for political competition has brought larger numbers into political life, made them politically conscious and sensitive to the power of the vote. In 1967 the Tamil Nadu electorate reacted and brought in a new assembly composed of a new generation of state political leaders—in general, better educated, more urbanized, less wealthy, less caste conscious, and more radical than the bosses they pushed out.[30] Tamil Nadu, if anticipating a more general displacement of the network of local bosses throughout India, is not typical. In most states, rural landed interests retain their hold over assembly majorities—both Congress and non-Congress—resisting the emergence of new claimants for the limited resources available. Few states, if any, have developed the institutional and resource capacity to accommodate expanded participation and new and varied demands.

Local Government

The system of local government in India today retains a fundamental continuity with the past. Its hierarchical structure was built by the

[29] *Ibid.*, p. 39.
[30] *Ibid.*, pp. 51–52.

British on the foundations of Mogul administration and has been refined by independent India to suit the needs of a developing society.

The Local Administrative Hierarchy

The major unit of local administration is the district. There are 365 districts in India, varying in size and population from state to state and often within a state. The average area of a district, however, is about 3,200 square miles, with a population of 1,300,000.[31]

Under the British, a single district officer, commonly referred to as the collector, was charged with keeping the peace, collecting revenue, and administering justice in each district. With the combined roles of magistrate, collector, and judge, he represented the highest quality of the Indian Civil Service. For most Indian villagers the "Collector Sahib" was in fact *the* government. Subordinate to the collector were the district superintendent of police and the chief engineer. In the latter years of the nineteenth century, specialized departments for education, agriculture, and health were established, their district field representatives coordinated by the collector. Today, following the constitutional directive principle that "the state shall take steps to separate the Judiciary from the Executive in the public services,"[32] most states now have a district judge, in no way subordinate to the collector. The collector continues to be the most important government official in local administration, however. As the government has taken increased initiative in rural development and social welfare, his responsibilities have been greatly enlarged, and he carries an almost overwhelming workload. At the same time, his role has become increasingly ill defined as both power and responsibility in local government have been decentralized.

The collector is appointed by the state government from the Indian Administrative Service or the State Civil Service. As an agent of the state the collector is responsible for all government action in the district. His powers are extensive and, to some extent, discretionary. The Bombay Revenue Department Manual specifies, for example, that "nothing can or should pass in the District of which the Collector should not keep himself informed."[33] He must frequently be on tour, accessible to all villagers and responsive to their needs. The daily visitors to his office may include wealthy businessmen, influential politicians, or a delegation of illiterate villagers. They come to seek favor, to register a complaint, or simply to make their presence known.[34]

In the structure of local administration, the district is divided into *taluqs* (or *tehsils*). The taluq, usually comprising from two hundred to

---

[31] *The Changing Role of the District Officer* (New Delhi: Indian Institute of Public Administration, 1961), p. ix.

[32] Constitution of India, Article 50.

[33] Quoted in David C. Potter, *Government in Rural India* (London: London School of Economics and Political Science, 1964), p. 68.

[34] Potter, *Government in Rural India*, p. 71.

six hundred villages, is headed by a *taluqdar*, who is responsible for the supervision of land records and the collection of revenue. The government representative in the village is the *patwari*, "the eyes and ears of the Collector." Although no longer the power today he was in the colonial period, the patwari, or "village accountant," is still "the general busybody of government."[35] He is primarily concerned with land records, however, and thus he has a position of power with an opportunity for graft that is often difficult to resist. Traditionally the village is also served by a headman, whose position is hereditary, and by a policeman, really a watchman.

Village Government: Panchayati Raj

In the centuries before British rule the village communities, while subject to periodic visitation by tax collectors, were left to govern themselves through a council of elders, the traditional *panchayat*, meaning literally "council of five." The panchayats declined under the British raj, however, as a result of improved communications, increased mobility, and a centralized administration that emphasized the individual in society and not the elders of the village. By the mid-nineteenth century the panchayats had ceased to be of real importance. At that point, however, the British sought to revitalize the institutions of local self-government. Lord Ripon declared that it was "our weakness and our calamity" that "we have not been able to give to India the benefits and blessings of free institutions." In pursuance of his Resolution of 1882, elected district boards were established to give representation and practical experience in self-government to the Indian people. The district boards (which were retained for a period after independence) were given responsibility for public works, health, and education. There were also some attempts to revive panchayats on a statutory basis as popularly elected bodies. In villages where the older, unofficial panchayats of elders still existed, these new bodies were frequently constituted as parallel panchayats, giving official recognition to matters that had been decided informally by the traditional leadership.

During the independence movement, the panchayats of ancient times were eulogized as democratic "little republics." Gandhi sought to recapture that ideal in a revitalization of village life, but for many, like Dr. B. R. Ambedkar, the village was "a sink of localism, a den of ignorance, narrow-mindedness, and communalism." According to Nehru the Congress had "never considered" the Gandhian view of society, "much less adopted it."[36] At the Constituent Assembly a Gandhian constitution was offered, based on the principle of economic and politi-

---

[35] E. N. Mangat Rai, *Civil Administration in the Punjab*, Occasional Papers in International Affairs, No. 7 (Cambridge, Mass.: Harvard University Center for International Affairs, 1963), p. 13.

[36] Jawaharlal Nehru, *A Bunch of Old Letters* (Bombay: Asia Publishing House, 1960), p. 509.

cal decentralization. The village panchayat was to be the basic unit in a hierarchy of indirectly elected bodies. A national panchayat at the top was to be responsible for such matters as currency and defense.[37] The assembly did not accept the Gandhian proposal. Stability, unity, and economic progress demanded a more centralized government, but the constitution directed the states "to organize village panchayats and to endow them with such powers and authority as may be necessary to enable them to function as units of self-government."[38] The aim was to foster democratic participation, to involve villagers in the development effort, and to ease the administrative burden on the states. Institutions of local self-government were to be both instruments of economic development and social change and agents of community mobilization. They were intended to stimulate participation and provide channels for meaningful political expression.

During the First Five-Year Plan the Center emphasized the importance of local authorities in community development, but little was done. The Second Plan called specifically for a "well-organized democratic structure of administration within the district"[39] in order to evoke popular initiative and participation. The Mehta Report recommended that the old district boards be replaced by a three-tiered system of local self-government with each tier linked by indirect election. In 1958 the Government asked each state to evolve a system of *panchayati raj*, suited to its own needs, that followed the broad outlines of the Mehta Report.[40]

Panchayati raj is now in operation throughout most of India alongside and in coordination with the Community Development Program.[41] Although there is some variation in structure the first system established, that of Rajasthan, provided a pattern of organization. The panchayat is the basic unit and may represent one or several villages. It is a body of twelve to fifteen members that includes a chairman elected by the entire panchayat electorate, eight to ten members from wards within the panchayat (one elected from each ward), and three or four members co-opted to represent women and Scheduled Castes and Tribes. All the chairmen elected to panchayats within a block area constitute the second tier, the *panchayati samiti*. Additional members are also co-opted to insure representation of special interests and to bring in administrative expertise. The average samiti has forty-two members, of whom eight

---

[37] Granville Austin, *The Indian Constitution* (New York: Oxford University Press, 1966), p. 39.

[38] Constitution of India, Article 40.

[39] *Second Five Year Plan: Summary* (New Delhi: Government of India, Planning Commission, 1956), p. 62.

[40] See *Report of the Team for the Study of Community Projects and National Extension Service*, Balvantray Mehta, Chairman, 3 vols. (New Delhi: Government of India, Committee on Plan Projects, 1957).

[41] Panchayati Raj has not been implemented in Madhya Pradesh, Kerala, Jammu and Kashmir, or Nagaland.

are co-opted. A chairman is elected from among the members. Members of the legislative assembly are associate members of the samitis in their constituency, and the block development officer acts as chief executive of the body. The *zila parishad* is the third tier and is congruent with the district. Its members include the chairmen of all samitis in the district; the members of the Rajya Sabha, the Lok Sabha, and the state legislative assembly elected from the district; and the president of the Central Co-operative Bank. Additional members may be co-opted, and the collector, ex officio, attends as a nonvoting member.[42]

As the process of decision-making is brought closer to the people through panchayati raj, it becomes more susceptible to local pressure. Patterns of traditional dominance, through caste and land ownership, may be institutionalized with "democratic" sanction, as the economically dependent villagers are pressured or intimidated into supporting the leaders' candidates. This development is particularly serious when it serves to elevate traditional village leaders to higher levels of power through indirect election. It has also been feared that the dependence of samiti and zila parishad leaders upon local voters, the result of the decentralization of power, may subject them to pressures from traditional village leadership to weaken the social content of government policy. Panchayati raj has brought an infusion of traditional elements into Indian political life, but the system has also provided a vehicle for the emergence of a new leadership at the local level. David C. Potter, in his study of Rajasthan, finds that panchayat members tend to be prosperous landowning agriculturalists or village merchants, comparatively young, educated, and, at least in Rajasthan, "progressive in outlook." The samiti and parishad chairmen represent a generally higher level of education and a wider range of political contacts.[43]

Dominated by short-term goals and a consumer orientation, panchayati raj has not notably advanced community development, but it has, for all its limitations, transformed the Indian political culture. Village panchayat elections were originally decided by a show of hands, a method that provided easy targets for recrimination, but secret ballots are now used. Competitive elections have politicized the villages. At the time of the local panchayat elections campaign flags fly from the most disheveled huts and all available wall space proclaims the candidacy of the political aspirants. The development resources available to the panchayats, particularly at the critical samiti level, have made the elections serious business.

With seeming unawareness of traditional conflict, some political observers have warned that "the traditional balance in the village may be upset leading to disharmony in the even tenor of rural life." Uneducated men may be elected who can be manipulated by the forces of

---

[42] Potter, *Government in Rural India*, pp. 48–52.
[43] *Ibid.*, pp. 53–56.

extremism. Electoral competition, they argue, will encourage factionalism and caste conflict. "In fact, the new elective process seems to entrench caste even more rigidly and post-election wrangles are likely to operate on purely caste lines."[44] Competition, however, may serve to make the dominant caste more genuinely responsive to the lower castes, for in panchayat elections, factions must inevitably seek the support of lower castes and harijans.

The Mehta Report contended that "one of the banes of democratic village administration . . . has been the intensification of factions and feuds" and that "the system of electoral contests at the village level has often added to these."[45] The traditional panchayat had reached decisions through a sense of the meeting, continuing discussion until a consensus was reached. This consensus admittedly reflected the interests of the dominant caste, but it represented an ideal of unanimity, not the factious rule of a numerical majority. To stem the growth of conflict at the village level, state governments have sought to encourage consensus politics, and at least one state has offered special awards to panchayats with at least 80 percent of their members unanimously elected.

The Gandhian vision of a "partyless democracy" held by former socialist leader Jayaprakash Narayan is shared by many for the village level, and parties are in fact officially prohibited in panchayat elections. Factions clearly operate, but the lack of party competition reduces the possibility of holding one group accountable and ignores the functions of social conflict. Competition may serve to keep the incumbents responsive to the electorate, for they can always be replaced; it may open new channels of access for participation and leadership; and it may stimulate development as groups vie with one another to expand their bases of support. "The nostalgia for traditional village consensus," Susanne H. Rudolph writes, "is neither morally consistent nor practical if at the same time change in the material and moral order of the village is thought desirable." Village consensus reflected a belief in one right answer, but "what was self-evident to the fathers is becoming one alternative among many to the sons. Prescription minimizes conflict; freedom enhances it."[46]

The system of panchayati raj was created to enhance the institutional capacity of local government for economic development and to expand democratic participation in rural areas. The two were to advance together as participation was channeled into the work of community development. Mobilization was to provide the lifeblood of rural uplift. Participation bred conflict, however, stimulating intense competition

---

[44] Ram K. Vepa, "Changing Pattern of Panchayat Raj in Andhra Pradesh," *Indian Journal of Public Administration*, Vol. 10 (October–December 1964), p. 700.

[45] The Mehta Report, p. 18.

[46] "Consensus and Conflict in Indian Politics," *World Politics*, Vol. 12 (April 1961), p. 396.

for development resources. The possibilities for consensus were undermined as traditional village factions were reinforced or displaced by new factional divisions allied with competing political parties at the constituency, district, and state levels. The democracy of panchayati raj has politicized the Indian village, but expanded participation and a heightened political consciousness have created demands to which the institutions can no longer fully respond. Aspirations and demands outnumber the limited resources available. With new power in their hands but without the means of securing the promise of a better life, the poor and the landless of Indian rural society grow increasingly restless.

Urban Government

India is overwhelmingly rural, but according to the 1971 census, 20 percent of India's population lives in towns and cities of over 10,000 and a sizable portion of these people are concentrated in the major metropolitan areas. There are 147 cities with a population of more than 100,000. Madras has a population of about 2,500,000; Delhi, 3,600,000; Bombay, 6,000,000; and Greater Calcutta, 7,000,000. The larger cities are governed by municipal corporations, composed of a popularly elected council and a president or mayor, elected from within the council. A commissioner, appointed by the state government, is the chief executive, and the state may supersede the municipal corporation if it is deemed incapable of maintaining order and effective government. Smaller towns are governed by municipal committees or boards.[47] City government is responsible for the safety, health, and education of its citizens. It is charged with the maintenance of sanitation facilities, streets and bridges, parks and public facilities—responsibilities that it is increasingly unable to meet effectively.

The weakness of urban government in India is related in substantial part to the fact that the key to formal power is at the state level, external to the city. As Rodney Jones has argued, "The narrow scope of municipal government limits the service and patronage opportunities of municipal politicians to build durable political constituencies or to organize loyal clienteles. Governmental functions and services that impinge most continuously and vitally on the bulk of the urban population are not directly accessible to municipal politicians."[48] The bureaucratic linkages to the state level, however, are mediated by group ties and informal channels of access. The centrality of state politicians and administrators in urban policy has not negated the importance of municipal government as an arena of political participation. Municipal

---

[47] The distinction between "larger" cities and "smaller" towns is not uniform but varies considerably from state to state.

[48] "Linkage Analysis of Indian Urban Politics," *Economic and Political Weekly*, Vol. 7 (June 17, 1972), p. 1198. See also *Urban Politics in India: Area, Power, and Policy in a Penetrated System* (Berkeley: University of California Press, 1974).

councilors may become vigorous agents of interest articulation for citizen demands, and although their formal powers may be limited, they can and do successfully marshall personal resources for the exertion of influence.[49] "At a minimum," Donald Rosenthal writes, "the urban politician serves an important function in Indian society by helping to integrate the diverse populations of Indian cities into a working political order responsive to popular pressures and then employs his leverage to democratize an often formalistic administrative process. Maximally, municipal political actors—and particularly the more influential local politicians—are able to influence not only the actions of municipal authorities but those decisions made for the locality by state and national authorities."[50]

It is within the city that tradition is most severely challenged by rapid change and a heterogeneity of values and behavior. The cities are the locus of new economic and cultural values, of new social roles and action patterns. The availability of mass communications and the density of urban populations have facilitated the mobilization of city-dwellers for political action. India's cities have been centers of opposition and political unrest. Demonstrations, strikes, and riots have become daily occurrences as demands rise beyond the government's capacity to respond. The city may offer rural migrants a chance for a better life, but for the middle classes, committed to an urban life that can no longer satisfy their basic needs, it nourishes explosive frustrations. Municipal governments, stagnant and lacking adequate authority and finance, cannot begin to meet the problems before them. The state governments, responsive to the rural base of their support, have been unwilling to assume the burden of the deepening urban crisis. A high and accelerating level of political participation and a low and static level of institutionalization pose the problem of political development in stark form.

[49] See, for example, Roderick Church's discussion in "Authority and Influence in Indian Municipal Politics: Administrators and Councillors in Lucknow," *Asian Survey*, Vol. 13 (April 1973), pp. 421–38.

[50] "Symposium on Indian Urban Politics: Introduction," *Asian Survey*, Vol. 13 (April 1973), pp. 384–85.

RECOMMENDED READING

Chanda, Asok, *Federalism in India*. London: George Allen & Unwin, 1965.
    An analysis of Union-state relations by a distinguished Indian civil servant.

Das Gupta, Jyotirindra, *Language Conflict and National Development: Group Politics and National Language Policy in India*. Berkeley: University of California Press, 1970.
    A study of language rivalry and national integration.

Franda, Marcus F., *West Bengal and the Federalizing Process in India.*
Princeton, N.J.: Princeton University Press, 1968.
> Case studies from West Bengal that serve to illuminate the wider problems of
> the federal relationship throughout India.

Harrison, Selig S., *India: The Most Dangerous Decades.* Princeton, N.J.:
Princeton University Press, 1960.
> Posing the problem of India's continued viability as a nation, the volume
> examines the stresses imposed by the "fissiparous tendencies" of linguistic re-
> gionalism, caste, and political extremism.

Jones, Rodney W., *Urban Politics in India: Area, Power, and Policy in a
Penetrated System.* Berkeley: University of California Press, 1974.
> An analysis of municipal government as affected by bureaucratic and po-
> litical linkages to the state level.

Leonard, T. J., "Federalism in India," in William S. Livingon, ed., *Federalism in the Commonwealth: A Bibliographic Commentary.* London:
Cassell, 1963.
> A lengthy bibliographic essay on modern India; while taking federalism as its
> focus, it ranges widely and is probably the best and most complete source of
> its kind on Indian political history.

Maddick, Henry, *Panchayati Raj: A Study of Rural Local Government in
India.* London: Longmans, Green, 1970.
> A detailed account of panchayati raj, its development and operation.

Maheshwari, S. R., *Local Government in India.* New Delhi: Orient Longman, 1971.
> Traces the history of local government and examines the structure and func-
> tion of both rural and urban institutions.

Menon, V. P., *The Story of the Integration of the Indian States.* Bombay:
Orient Longmans, 1956.
> An account of the merging of the princely states with the former provinces
> of British India into a single nation of India, written by a man who played an
> instrumental part in the events, Sardar Patel's lieutenant, the ICS secretary
> to the newly created Ministry of States.

Nayar, Baldev Raj, *National Communication and Language Policy in India.*
New York: Praeger, 1969.
> An evaluation of the impact of Government language policy.

Potter, David C., *Government in Rural India.* London: London School of
Economics and Political Science, 1964.
> A concise description of contemporary district administration.

Rai, E. N. Mangat, *Civil Administration in the Punjab.* Occasional Papers
in International Affairs, No. 7. Cambridge, Mass.: Harvard University
Center for International Affairs, 1963.
> An examination of the structure and operation of district administration in
> an Indian state.

Retzlaff, Ralph H., *Village Government in India.* Bombay: Asia Publishing
House, 1962.
> A case study of rural government and the operation of the panchayat in an
> Uttar Pradesh village.

Rosenthal, Donald B., *The Limited Elite: Politics and Government in Two Indian Cities.* Chicago: University of Chicago Press, 1970.
    A study of urban politics in the municipal corporations of Agra and Poona.

Rosenthal, Donald B., ed., *Essays on Indian Politics.* Delhi: Thompson Press (forthcoming).
    Studies in municipal government and urban politics.

Weiner, Myron, ed., *State Politics in India.* Princeton, N.J.: Princeton University Press, 1968.
    A comparative study of eight Indian states, with particular concern for patterns of political participation, integration, party systems, and governmental performance.

V

ARENAS OF CONFLICT: GROUPS IN INDIAN POLITICS

No political system can satisfy all the demands of all its members all the time. Its response to public pressure is calculated in accordance with the political capital that backs various demands—numbers, wealth, prestige, or violence. The legitimacy of a particular demand, that is, its congruence with basic values in the society, is a major factor in political response. More important still is the access afforded demands in general, which is of critical importance in the development of a stable and responsive political system. If resources are limited demands may far outrun the capacity of the government to respond. Rational economic planning may conflict with the exigencies of democratic response, forcing decision-makers to consider demands as such illegitimate and to argue that the compulsions of a backward society require restriction of political access and democratic competition. Competition, from this view, serves only to stimulate the formation of demands as parties bid for support and thus to raise the level of frustration.

In India there is a basic distrust of politics as a struggle for power, reflecting the traditional view that those who seek power are suspect.

"Each man must accept his own *dharma* (duty) and perform his duty well. . . . Authority is acceptable, but to struggle for a position of authority is not."[1] W. H. Morris-Jones has written of a "paradoxical or ambivalent attitude to authority. Authority in India appears to be subject at once to much more abusive criticism and much more effusive adulation than one is accustomed to elsewhere."[2] Leaders, ideally, are to be above politics. Gandhi, for example, was not a formal member of the Congress. Dr. Rammanohar Lohia never joined the Samyukta Socialist Party, of which he was leader, and Jayaprakash Narayan renounced party politics altogether to follow in the steps of Vinoba Bhave, the "walking saint," whose *bhoodan*, or land-gift, movement calls for self-sacrifice and "polity without power." Asoka Mehta has argued that "development, in our backward country, depends on the acceptance of equality, austerity and hard work." In his view "a broad based government holding power on a long-term tenure—in effect not in law" would be the ideal replacement for the "frequent changes in government that parliamentary democracy assumes."[3] There is a fundamental tension, however, between modern democratic values and the nostalgia for consensus, whether it is in the name of tradition or rationality. The expectation that politicians are to wear a saintly mantle of self-sacrifice and the realization that they are all too often the victims of human foibles have bred a general cynicism about political life.

The Role of Interest Groups in Indian Political Development

As wider sectors of Indian society have been politicized through the expansion, dispersion, and democratization of power, larger numbers of people have been drawn into the political system. Brash and rustic political bosses have replaced the Western-educated leaders of the nationalist movement. Political life at state and local levels—and increasingly at the national level—is directed by a new leadership, with roots in the villages and sensitivity to factional and caste loyalties and to emerging class interests. The credentials of the new leadership are instrumental, not sacrificial; government and party are something to be used.[4]

Although the new entrants into politics may often operate in a traditional mode, the political issues are by no means traditional. "There is nothing traditional about demands for more schools, roads, wells, fer-

---

[1] Myron Weiner, "Struggle Against Power: Notes on Indian Political Behavior," in *Political Change in South Asia* (Calcutta: Mukhopadyay, 1963), p. 156.

[2] *Parliament in India* (London: Longmans, Green, 1957), p. 34.

[3] Quoted in Susanne H. Rudolph, "Consensus and Conflict in Indian Politics," *World Politics*, Vol. 12 (April 1961), pp. 395–96.

[4] Myron Weiner, "India's Two Political Cultures," in Lucian Pye and Sidney Verba, eds., *Political Culture and Political Development* (Princeton, N.J.: Princeton University Press, 1965), p. 212.

tilizers, and jobs."[5] Traditional structures and patterns of behavior may be resilient and adaptive to new and changing environments, becoming, for example, channels of interest articulation and instruments of political pressure. The distinction between tradition and modernity blurs as, in dialectical relationship, they "infiltrate and transform each other."[6] In this process, politics has become more meaningful to the mass electorate, potentially more responsive to its demands. But as politics has become more vernacular, it has been decried by those suspicious of group pressure as pandering to the irrationalities of casteism, communalism, and regionalism and to narrow and special interests. Interest groups, as agents of political demands, are seen as disruptive of order and consensus. The quest for stability, however, may be the precursor of repressive order.

Interest groups in India are a form of linkage and a means of communication between the masses and the elite. They provide channels of access for expanding participation, and their institutionalization is a critical element in the development of a responsive political system, for they are barometers of the political climate by which decision-makers can make and assess policy. "The interest group absorbs the raw demands of its members, collates them, sometimes adulterates them in the interests of the majority, and finally articulates them in a form whereby they may be acted upon at the appropriate place within the society."[7] While the interest group makes demands upon society for the benefit of its members, it also serves to restrain them.

Interest groups not only act as agents of interest articulation, they also increase the political consciousness and participation of their membership—democratic achievements, although they may strain the responsive capacity of the system. In addition, interest groups may be reservoirs of political leadership. Most important perhaps, interest groups are a vehicle for social integration. Bringing individuals from ascriptive relationships into new and modern associations for the expression of common interests, they may bridge the gap not only between the mass and the elite but between traditional divisions within the society as a whole. Interest groups may thus serve as agents of both vertical and horizontal integration. Even interest groups that have reinforced existing cleavages in Indian society, such as caste associations, have frequently been the catalyst for change, opening the community to increasingly differentiated interests and cross-cutting ties. The problem for India, as for most developing societies, has not been in having too many strong interest groups but in having too few.

In India interest groups have been slow to develop, but while they

---

[5] *Ibid.*, p. 241.
[6] Lloyd I. and Susanne H. Rudolph, *The Modernity of Tradition* (Chicago: University of Chicago Press, 1967), p. 3.
[7] Bruce H. Millen, *The Political Role of Labor in Developing Countries* (Washington, D.C.: The Brookings Institution, 1963), p. 40.

now number in the thousands, they are disparate and weak. They have been unable to accommodate and channel rapidly expanding participation and the emergence of new groups to political consciousness. Under the British those individuals and groups commanding traditional sources of power exerted pressure at the local administrative level. Those without power had little access to the administration, and from a position of powerlessness they regarded the Government as an extractive force to be avoided whenever possible. Most mass organizations developed from the activities of the nationalist movement, and even in the years since independence, most interest groups have been connected with political parties, more agents of mobilization than of interest articulation; opposition parties have utilized various front organizations in mass action to rally popular support and augment party strength, and the Congress has sought to co-opt group support through mass organizations and to harness their potential into development activities. The Congress party itself has been an important link between local groups and state governments, acting as a middleman in applying pressure on the state administrative apparatus; in states where the Congress is in power the administration has proved sensitive to such pressure. Through the response of the local Congress machine, with its access to administration and patronage, the party has slowed the development of autonomous interest groups. Indeed, Congress party factions have served as agents of particular interests. The party's source of power has come increasingly to be associated with rural landed interests, with those who are in effect political brokers, astute in the manipulation of both traditional and modern political styles. The landless and the poor, so long as they remain invisible, may be eulogized and conveniently ignored.

Most Indians have a low sense of political efficacy. In their opinion, government officials are generally distant, unresponsive, and corrupt. Officials, on the other hand, regard interest-group activity with distrust. Rational policy formation, they argue, should be unaffected by their narrow demands. Consequently, group pressure in India has been directed toward influencing the administration and implementation of policy rather than its formation. Its greatest success has been achieved in forestalling certain government actions and in modifying policy rather than in initiating it. It is at the state and local administrative levels that officials have been particularly responsive to such pressure, and it has been the landed interests who have been most adept in applying it; land-reform legislation may be quietly forgotten as development funds are channeled into the hands most capable of utilizing them, the landed middle peasantry. Those who have nothing are unlikely to reap the benefits of government action, for they lack the resources of immediate political capital. In the long run, however, once mobilized, their numbers will be overpowering.

In the name of rationality and the public interest, decision-makers have often turned deaf ears to the demands of interest groups. Because the Government is unresponsive, groups resort to mass demonstrations, hartals, strikes, and civil disobedience to force government action. This in turn only confirms the official image that the groups are irresponsible and that such mass activity is against the national interest. The Government does respond to such action, however; the political capital to which it has proved most sensitive is violence. Various legal measures, such as the Preventive Detention Act and the emergency provisions in the constitution, have been enacted to restrain political activity that threatens public order. The line between activities that do threaten public order and those that do not may be thin, since group politics itself is regarded with suspicion. Gandhian techniques of civil disobedience have been used by disaffected groups against the Congress Government, an unfair and perverted use of satyagraha in the eyes of the Congress, but mass political activity has often been violent. Disorder seems vindicated by success. "Only when public order is endangered by a mass movement is the government willing to make a concession," Myron Weiner writes, "not because they consider the demand legitimate, but because they then recognize the strength of the group making the demand and its capacity for destructiveness. Thus, the Government often alternates between unresponsiveness to the demands of large but peaceful groups and total concession to groups that press their demands violently."[8] The capitulation of the Government to the demands for States Reorganization only in the wake of widespread rioting and the reevaluation of official language policy after the agitation in Tamil Nadu in 1965 are classic examples of the efficacy of violence. That mass actions have succeeded so frequently has given them a certain legitimacy.

The relationship between order and responsiveness lies at the heart of the development process. In India the solution has too often been a declamation of radical intent followed by conservative inaction, reflecting the power of interests upon which Congress political support has rested. The plea for a "bargaining culture" of pluralism only brings to the surface what is already a political reality: the Government will be responsive to those groups with effective political resources. The masses may well be ignored, at least until they become dangerously restless. Stability becomes the highest value.

The creation of an effective infrastructure of democratic linkage between the masses and the political elite may serve initially to draw the conservative, rural leadership into the political system. Through this process the Congress state machines came to power. When this new base of power emerged, the system became responsive to the political capital that it commanded, but in a capillary process, penetration that

<hr />

8 *The Politics of Scarcity* (Chicago: University of Chicago Press, 1962), p. 201.

brings traditional leaders to wider prominence inevitably mobilizes the "under mass." In place of unimplemented reform, revolution may be the order of things.

Caste

The mantle of Indian civilization covers divisions and conflicts of region, language, caste, tribe, and religion. The "fissiparous tendencies" of regionalism and communalism have posed a serious threat to the creation of an Indian political community and a viable democratic system. In the process of economic change and social mobilization, India's increasingly participant communities[9] have grown more politically self-conscious, and this self-consciousness has deepened existing cleavages.

Though decried as a reversion to "tribalism" the increasingly prominent role played by community associations in political life, for all the problems it presents, may reflect an extension of the particularistic and ascriptive ties of primordial sentiment to wider horizons of identity. The development of primordial sentiment into a cultural nationalism—at the level of the linguistic region or within a religious or caste community—may be regarded with horror by those who see it as the seed of separation or destruction. But it may in fact be an effective vehicle for the transference of loyalty to the larger political community, a channel of linkage between the masses and the elite, between traditional behavior and modern democratic processes.

The caste association, representing the adaptive response of caste to modern social, economic, and political changes, reveals the potential "modernity of tradition." Combining the traditional and the modern, the caste association is a voluntary association with a formal membership of perhaps only a few thousand drawn from the ascriptive reservoir of the community as a whole. As various caste communities have sought social uplift and economic advancement, they have organized to secure more effective political access.[10] The caste association, Lloyd I. and Susanne H. Rudolph have written, "provides the channels of communication and bases of leadership and organization which enable those still submerged in the traditional society and culture to transcend the technical political literacy which would otherwise handicap their ability to participate in democratic politics."[11] The meaning of caste itself has

---

[9] In India, *community* usually refers to a racial, caste, linguistic, or religious group rather than to a locality, as in the United States.

[10] Among the largest and most successful caste associations is that of the Nadar community. See Robert L. Hardgrave, Jr., *The Nadars of Tamilnad: The Political Culture of a Community in Change* (Berkeley: University of California Press, 1969).

[11] "The Political Role of India's Caste Associations," *Pacific Affairs*, Vol. 33 (March 1960), pp. 5–6.

changed in the encounter between tradition and modernity. "By creating conditions in which a caste's significance and power is beginning to depend on its numbers rather than its ritual and social status, and by encouraging egalitarian aspirations among its members, the caste association is exerting a liberating influence."[12] In writing of Kerala, Marxist leader E. M. S. Namboodiripad argues that the caste association was "the first form in which the peasant masses rose in struggle against feudalism."[13] As he rightly suggests, however, such associations consolidate community separatism and must be transcended if the peasantry is to be organized as a class.

With secular aspirations after a "casteless" society, the Congress leadership, joined by most leaders of the opposition, has viewed the demands of community associations as illegitimate. Although each of the major parties has spawned a variety of affiliated mass organizations —labor, agrarian, youth—to mobilize political support, they have for the most part sought to avoid the appearance of intimate association with any particular community. Close identification between the party and one caste, for example, might seriously affect the party's ability to aggregate wide support, for in few constituencies, much less an entire district or state, does one caste so predominate as to command a majority. But the parties have been ready in practice to secure support wherever and however available and in each election have courted various communities. Politicians and political scientists alike speak of the "Ezhava vote" or the "Jat bloc," just as in the United States people often talk of the black, Irish, or Italian vote.[14]

The process by which an atomized and divided community gains consciousness and unity, entering the political system as a major actor, is a familiar one in the broader process of political behavior. The unity of such blocs is situational and temporal, however, varying from constituency to constituency and from time to time. Community associations are themselves the agent of increasing internal differentiation. As the association secures its goals, the social and economic gaps within the community widen, at the same time dispersing political support. The association thus becomes the agent of its own destruction, for in the process of differentiation individuals are subjected to the cross-cutting ties of a multiplicity of interests and associations. In the process of political development, as the structures of society change under the impact of social mobilization, the old clusters of social, economic, and psychological commitments weaken, and individuals become available

---

[12] *Ibid.*, p. 9. See also Rudolph and Rudolph, *The Modernity of Tradition.*

[13] *Kerala: Yesterday, Today and Tomorrow* (Calcutta: National Book Agency, 1967), p. 115.

[14] Survey data suggest widespread perception among the Indian public that "caste provides an extensive basis for mobilizing support in politics and elections." See Bashiruddin Ahmed, "Caste and Electoral Politics," *Asian Survey*, Vol. 10 (November 1970), pp. 979–92.

for new patterns of socialization and behavior.[15] If the social structure and political life of modern India is increasingly characterized by a class orientation, it reflects a movement toward a more open stratification system rather than the simple replacement of class for caste.[16] Caste has by no means ceased to be an important factor in determining political behavior, but it is only one of many variables that affect the individual voter's decision.

Communalism

The specter of communalism has been omnipresent in Indian political life, a threat to unity and to the secular ideal of the constitution. With the memories of partition still bitterly nurtured, Hindu-Muslim tensions easily ignite rioting. In 1969 Gujarat became the scene of a communal bloodbath, the worst since partition, leaving more than one thousand dead (mostly Muslims) and thousands of others homeless.[17] Each year, several hundred incidents of communal violence are officially reported. Most involve no more than a village dispute arising over a Hindu procession near a mosque, but such incidents, however minor in themselves, have frequently turned into major riots. In 1974, the most serious communal riot in Delhi since partition began as a brawl outside a cinema house and ended in widespread arson and ten deaths.

HINDU COMMUNALISM

Muslim communalism contributed to the partition of India in 1947, but today it is communalism in the name of the Hindu majority that poses the major challenge to the secular state. Rooted in the nineteenth-century Hindu revivalism of the Arya Samaj and the extremism of Tilak, Hindu communalism today is most prominently represented by the Bharatiya Jana Sangh, a political party with the trappings of secularism, which is examined in the next chapter. The foundations of the Jana Sangh are to be found in the more explicitly communal movements of the Hindu Mahasabha, the Ram Rajya Parishad, and the Rashtriya Swayamsevak Sangh.

The Hindu Mahasabha was founded in reaction to the Muslim League, but in its early years the organization was obscured by the Congress party, with which most of its members were associated. The Lucknow Pact of 1916 and the ascendancy of the Moderates within the

---

[15] Karl Deutsch, "Social Mobilization and Political Development," *American Political Science Review*, Vol. 55 (September 1961), p. 494.

[16] For a discussion of the process of differentiation within caste and the emergence of class segments that form the basis for new interests and associations, see Robert L. Hardgrave, Jr., "Caste: Fission and Fusion," *Economic and Political Weekly*, Vol. 3, special number (July 1968), pp. 1065–70.

[17] For a superb analysis of the riot, see Ghanshyam Shah, "Communal Riots in Gujarat: Report of a Preliminary Investigation," *Economic and Political Weekly*, annual number (January 1970), pp. 187–200.

Congress alienated many of the Hindu extremists, however, and under the leadership of V. D. Savarkar, an admirer of Tilak and, like him, a Chitpavan Brahmin from Maharashtra, the Mahasabha parted with the Congress in a call to "Hinduize all politics and militarize Hinduism." Reform fused with revivalism in opposition to untouchability and caste inequality. To overcome the fragmentation of sect, caste, and language, the Mahasabha launched the *sanghatan* movement for the unification, integration, and consolidation of Hindu *rashtra*, the Hindu nation. The movement sought to reclaim those who had left the Hindu fold and to reassert the fundamental "Hinduness" of the Indian people. The Hindu Mahasabha has regarded the creation of Pakistan as the "vivisection" of Mother India and has sought reunification by force if necessary. Toward its goal of "Hindu Raj in Bharat," the Mahasabha platform includes a hard stand toward Pakistan, compulsory military training, a total ban on cow slaughter, repeal of all "anti-Hindu legislation," and a vague policy of "Hindu socialism."[18]

The Ram Rajya Parishad, founded in 1948, is the most orthodox of the Hindu communal parties. The strength of the party, which is supported by conservative landlords, has been almost entirely limited to Rajasthan. The party seeks to resurrect the Divine Kingdom of Rama and return the people to rule by dharma.[19] In both the 1967 and 1971 parliamentary elections, neither the RRP nor the Hindu Mahasabha gained a single seat.

The Rashtriya Swayamsevak Sangh was founded as a paramilitary organization in 1925 by Dr. Keshav Hedgewar. He was succeeded on his death in 1940 by M. S. Golwalkar ("Guruji"), under whom the RSS grew rapidly. The RSS claims to be a movement directed toward achieving the cultural and spiritual regeneration of the Hindu nation through a disciplined vanguard that represents the ideal model of Hindu society. The movement has drawn its support principally from urban regions of North India, where it has attracted wide support among students and the lower middle classes. RSS volunteers, uniformed in brown shirts, engage in an intensive program of ideological discussion, physical training, and military discipline. In January 1948, Gandhi was assassinated by a Hindu fanatic who had been associated with both the Mahasabha and the RSS. In the face of an explosive public reaction, the Hindu Mahasabha, under the leadership of Dr. S. P. Mookerjee, who had succeeded Savarkar as president in 1943, suspended political activity. The RSS was banned by the Government. Only with the agreement of the RSS to renounce political activity and to publish a constitution was the ban lifted more than one year later.[20]

---

18 Donald E. Smith, *India as a Secular State* (Princeton: Princeton University Press, 1963), pp. 455–64.
19 *Ibid.*, p. 464.
20 See Walter Andersen, "The Rashtriya Swayamsevak Sangh," Parts I–IV, *Economic and Political Weekly*, Vol. 7 (1972), pp. 589–97, 633–40, 673–82, and 724–27.

The RSS continues to be active within the "cultural" sphere, but in the struggle for a Hindu nation, it has been joined by a multiplicity of Hindu communal organizations. Their efforts, for example, have been directed against the Hindu Code Bill (reforming Hindu marriage and inheritance practices) and cow slaughter. In 1966 a procession of some 100,000, led by Hindu holy men, saffron-robed *rishis*, and naked, ash-covered *sadhus*, marched to the Parliament building in New Delhi to present demands for a ban on cow slaughter. (In the confusion, rowdies overturned cars and buses and attacked the residence of Congress president Kamaraj only minutes after his hasty escape.) [21] More recently Hindu anxieties have been stirred by the Government's family planning program. Although 83 percent of the population is Hindu, communalists see Hindu dominance endangered by the higher rate of population growth among Muslims and Christians.

MUSLIM COMMUNALISM

The Muslims of India, although a minority of only 11 percent, number more than 65 million—making India the third most populous Muslim nation in the world, after Indonesia and Bangladesh. India's Muslims, however, are themselves heterogeneous. As they are culturally varied (distinguished, for example, by language and custom among the Urdu-speaking Muslims of North India and Andhra, the Malayalee-speaking Mappillas of Kerala, and the Tamil-speaking Labbais of Tamil Nadu), so are they divided on religion and politics. They range from Islamic fundamentalists to secular Congressmen and Communists.

In the years immediately following partition India's remaining Muslim population assumed a position of low visibility. Those who were politically active were primarily in the Congress, but Muslims found themselves a minority community in all but a few constituencies in Kerala and West Bengal and, of course, in Kashmir, where 68 percent of the population is Muslim. Outside of these few Muslim-majority areas, Muslim candidates, on the Congress ticket, for example, played down their religious identity lest they raise Hindu ire and insure themselves defeat.

Muslim communalism has been represented, most notably, by the Jamaat-e-Islami and by the reactivated Muslim League in its various manifestations.

The revivalist Jamaat-e-Islami claims to be a cultural organization with an open membership, but like its Hindu counterpart, the RSS, it is purely communal. Moreover, like the RSS, it has a paramilitary character, and since the 1969 Gujarat riots, the Jamaat's activities have intensified. Along with the Jamiat-ul-Ulema, it is the representative of Muslim orthodoxy, and its demands embrace a wide range of measures

[21] Norman D. Palmer, "India's Fourth General Elections," *Asian Survey*, Vol. 7 (May 1967), pp. 278–79.

for the protection of the Muslim community, such as the preservation of Muslim personal law, compulsory religious instruction in Islam for Muslim children, the censorship of publications—particularly school textbooks—so as to eradicate materials repugnant to Muslim belief, and the prohibition of alcoholic beverages.[22]

The major political organization of Indian Muslims has been the Muslim League. With the departure of most North Indian Muslim leaders for Pakistan in 1947, the League became almost wholly a party of the South. Under the leadership of the late M. Mohammed Ismail of Madras the party survived challenge and split. In opposition to the splinter All-India Muslim League, which extended support to the Congress, Ismail's Indian Union Muslim League has pursued a strategy of coalition with opposition parties against Congress.[23] In Tamil Nadu the League allied with the DMK, but in Kerala, where the Muslim League commanded a pivotal position as a member of the Communist-led coalition ministry, the League made uneasy truce with its Congress senior partner. The position of the Muslim League in Kerala, the only state where it has substantial electoral strength, has been undermined by a party split, but the League has become increasingly active in North India. In reaction to the Gujarat riots and the growth of the RSS and the Jana Sangh, Muslims are awakening politically and proclaiming allegiance to a variety of local parties. The League is attempting to revive an all-India organization, although its efforts in the North are being challenged by a rival party, the Muslim Majlis, supported by the Jamaat-e-Islami.[24]

The Muslim League has sought the protection of the community primarily through nonreligious demands, including that for the preservation of the Urdu language (Arabic in Kerala), expanded economic opportunities for Muslims and an end to discriminatory hiring practices, and the reservation of seats for Muslims proportionate to their population in colleges, government employment, and in Parliament and the state assemblies.[25] Most ominously for Indian secularism the League is again raising the cry for separate electorates.

Election law clearly declares any appeal based on language, caste, or religion to be illegal. Religious communities, however, have historically been the object of political appeal. It was the Muslim League, advancing its claim to be the sole representative of the Muslim people, that successfully challenged the secular Congress in securing partition of

---

[22] Theodore P. Wright, Jr., "The Effectiveness of Muslim Representation in India," in Donald E. Smith, ed., *South Asian Politics and Religion* (Princeton: Princeton University Press, 1966), pp. 105–06.

[23] Theodore P. Wright, Jr., "The Muslim League in South India Since Independence: A Study in Minority Group Political Strategies," *American Political Science Review*, Vol. 60 (September 1966), pp. 579–99.

[24] For a discussion of the League revival, see *Link*, July 22, 1973, pp. 14–19.

[25] Wright, "The Effectiveness of Muslim Representation in India," pp. 106–07.

India and the formation of the Islamic state of Pakistan. The Muslims of India today are self-conscious and frequently respond to political appeals as a group. In constituencies where their numbers are significant they may constitute a major base of local power to be courted by all parties. In Kerala a revived Muslim League continues to claim their political loyalty. Christians, although by no means united politically or religiously, are in certain areas sufficiently numerous to exercise a powerful political force. In Kerala, where they number about a quarter of the population, they have been the main support of the Congress, and the pulpit has frequently served as a rostrum for political exhortation. The *gurdwaras* of the Punjab have served as bases for the political activity of the Akali Dal. Eighty percent of India's people are Hindu, and although the Jana Sangh may cautiously phrase its public appeals in secular terms, Hindu communalism is a potent factor in Indian politics, and the nostalgia for Bharat (Hindu India) is a dynamic element of nationalist feeling readily exploited by the traditional right.

The Untouchables

The Constitution of India abolishes untouchability and further specifies that no citizen shall on grounds of religion, race, caste, sex, or place of birth be subjected to any disability or restriction with regard to places of public use or accommodation. There are some eighty million "ex-untouchables," or Scheduled Castes as they are officially termed.[26] Although the constitution abolishes untouchability, and the Untouchability (Offenses) Act tightened and extended the provision, the Scheduled Castes continue to suffer discrimination. Many find protection in the anonymity of the city, but 90 percent of the untouchables live in villages, and here many disabilities remain enforced by custom. The position of the Scheduled Caste members in society is characterized by two mutually reinforcing factors: the stigma of pollution and material deprivation.[27]

The government has sought to respond to this situation through a system of protective discrimination. On the assumption that there was a one-to-one correlation between the ritual status of a caste and the material condition of its members, specific castes were designated to receive special favor in education, government employment, and political representation. These benefits were granted to the Scheduled Castes, the

[26] The term "Scheduled Caste" was adopted in 1935, when the lowest ranking Hindu castes were listed in a "schedule" appended to the Government of India Act for purposes of special safeguards and benefits. Lelah Dushkin, "Scheduled Caste Politics," in J. Michael Mahar, ed., *The Untouchables in Contemporary India* (Tucson: University of Arizona Press, 1972), p. 166.

[27] André Béteille, "Pollution and Poverty," in Mahar, ed., *The Untouchables in Contemporary India*, p. 414.

aboriginal Scheduled Tribes,[28] and an open-ended category, "Other Backward Classes." Eager to avail themselves of government favor, virtually every caste in India sought "Other Backward" classification, and in 1963, the Central Government and many states began to impose economic conditions in addition to caste criteria for benefits.

The system has been controversial. Many caste Hindus, particularly Brahmins, who have been denied government employment or entrance into universities feel that they have been victims of reverse discrimination. The reservation of benefits for the Scheduled Castes has also given rise to the charge that it has built in a vested interest in backwardness and has served to perpetuate some of the very evils against which the government has fought. To receive benefits one must virtually wear a badge of untouchability. But all untouchables have not benefited equally. There has emerged what Lelah Dushkin identifies as a "new class," those who have benefited from scholarships, reserved seats in higher education, and, above all, government jobs. "With the operation of the system over the years, the gap between those more fortunate ones and the rest of the Untouchables seems to have widened."[29] Another major criticism has been that the system is primarily a tool of those who control it, a means by which the Congress party can dominate and control "a minority which might otherwise have proved troublesome."[30] Protective discrimination, particularly the arrangements for government jobs, is thus seen as "an efficient and inexpensive mechanism for social control."[31]

Of all the areas of government benefits to the Scheduled Castes and Tribes, one of the most important has been the reservation of seats in Parliament and the state assemblies in proportion to their population. There are now 117 reserved seats in the Lok Sabha and a total of 837 in the assemblies. The concession was to end in 1970, but by the twenty-third amendment to the constitution it has been extended for ten years. The reservation of seats has given the untouchables a powerful voice, and in many state governments since 1967 they have held the balance of power. At the Center, between the 1969 Congress split and the 1971 parliamentary elections, Scheduled Caste MPs commanded sufficient numbers to bring down the Government. It was during this period that Jagjivan Ram, leader of the Scheduled Caste Congressmen in Parliament, was elected President of the Congress party, the second untouch-

[28] In 1971, the Scheduled Tribes, or "Adivasis," numbered about thirty-eight million. For a discussion of the transition of the tribes into the Hindu fold and the wider economic system, see André Béteille, "The Future of the Backward Classes: The Competing Demands of Status and Power," in Philip Mason, ed., *India and Ceylon: Unity and Diversity* (New York: Oxford University Press, 1967), p. 102.

[29] Dushkin, "Scheduled Caste Politics," p. 212.

[30] *Ibid.*, p. 165.

[31] *Ibid.*, p. 217.

able to hold that position. And in 1971 an important part of Indira Gandhi's electoral support came from the Scheduled Castes.

The reserved seats guarantee representation. Although members of the Scheduled Castes and Tribes may run for general seats, they do so infrequently and victories are rare. During the first two elections a system of double-member (and in some cases triple-member) constituencies was used in areas where Scheduled Castes or Tribes were numerous. Constituencies were drawn twice the normal size and were allowed to return two members, one of whom had to be of a Scheduled Caste. In 1962 the system was abolished in favor of simple reserved constituencies in which all voters make their selection among the candidates from the Scheduled Castes. Because the untouchables are a minority in all but a very few constituencies, it is normally caste Hindus who decide the elections in reserved constituencies. Scheduled Caste candidates consequently have tended to assume a low political profile. Scheduled Caste MPs and MLAs, most of whom are Congressmen, tend to concentrate their efforts on matters relating to protective discrimination. Few have taken a strong position against the continuing disabilities that most of their fellows suffer.

Dr. Ambedkar, leader of the Scheduled Castes until his death in 1956, had sought to weld the untouchables into a separate organization for political action.[32] He led the conversion of more than three million untouchables to Buddhism, but the Republican Party, which he founded in 1942 as the Scheduled Caste Federation, has had minimal success. A disgruntled faction of the party, however, has in the formation of the Dalit Panthers given the untouchables new militancy. The word *dalit* means "the oppressed" in Marathi and is used in an explicitly caste context. The Panthers have come primarily from among urban youth, educated and unemployed. It is in the villages, however, that the greatest changes are underway. Traditional agrarian relationships have yielded to the uncertain wages of the market economy; religiously sanctioned inequalities are now challenged by education, mass communications, and the power of the vote; and a consciousness of poverty and deprivation nurtures increasing discontent. The untouchable landless laborers, so long the political captives of the Congress party, listen now with responsive ears to the appeals of the socialists and the Marxists who promise them land and liberation.

Peasants

Agrarian interests in India have been expressed primarily through landlord and zamindari influence at the local and state levels. The peasants, or *kisan*, lacking the effective resources of money and organization, have carried little weight in shaping legislation. Even when

[32] See Eleanor Zelliot, "Gandhi and Ambedkar—A Study in Leadership," in Mahar, ed., *The Untouchables in Contemporary India*, pp. 69–95.

policy has been directed to their benefit, it has often been frustrated in its implementation at the local level by landed interests. Each of the major parties has adjunct peasant organizations, but they are designed more to mobilize support than to articulate interest. The All-India Kisan Sabha, founded in 1936 as a federation of state peasant movements, began as a Congress front but quickly came under Communist control. The Congress today has its own peasant organization, but the party has proved ineffective in representing the interests of tenants and landless laborers, for at the local level the Congress is controlled by those who would be most hurt by land-reform legislation.[33] Ceilings on land holdings frequently remain unenforced, for the state governments are unwilling to alienate their base of support among the middle peasants and petty landlords. Peasant agitation, such as the "land grab" movements of the early 1970s, has been sporadic and uncoordinated, but in favoring the interests of the landlords the Indian Government may simply be laying the foundations for future peasant unrest.

There have been a number of peasant revolts in India. In this century the Telengana uprising in Hyderabad State was one of the most dramatic and ill fated. It began with sporadic outbreaks in 1946, and by 1948, despite the Nizam's campaign of suppression, the movement, led by the Communist party, claimed to have "liberated" some 2,500 villages by turning out landlords and their agents and establishing communes. Support came primarily from poor peasants and landless laborers. In the area under Communist control, during the period of the movement's greatest strength, rents were suspended, debts were canceled, and land was redistributed among the landless. In September 1948 Indian troops took over the state and moved against the Communists in Telengana. The leadership of the movement was jailed, and the Communist party was outlawed in the state. The movement was officially called off by a CPI directive in 1951, beginning a new phase in Communist strategy.[34]

During this same period, a similar Communist-led agrarian uprising began in Thanjavur (Tanjore). In this area, the rice-bowl of Tamil Nadu, land is concentrated largely in the hands of Brahmin landlords, and the land is worked by landless laborers, 80 percent of whom are Scheduled Caste. The revolt in the 1950s briefly exposed discontent, but in the mid-1960s, the kisan movement in Thanjavur took on new life. Strikes and increasing pressure from the movement, under the direction of Communist cadre, succeeded in winning improved wages and guarantees from the landowners, but the inequities of the land system have

---

[33] Weiner, *The Politics of Scarcity*, p. 131.

[34] The twenty-fifth anniversary of the Telengana revolt stimulated a reexamination of the nature and significance of the struggle. See Mohan Ram, "The Telengana Peasant Armed Struggle, 1946–51," *Economic and Political Weekly*, Vol. 8 (June 9, 1973), pp. 1025–32; and P. Sundarayya, *Telengana People's Struggle and Its Lessons* (Calcutta: Communist Party of India (Marxist), 1972).

been accentuated by the intensive development efforts of the district. "In Thanjavur," writes Francine Frankel, "the increasing polarization between the landless and the large landowners is all the more bitter—and explosive—because the new cleavage now being drawn on the basis of class largely coincides with the traditional division rooted in caste."[35]

In 1967, agricultural tenants of Naxalbari in the strategic hill district of Darjeeling in West Bengal began to occupy forcibly the lands they tilled. As the handful of peasants in Naxalbari sought to secure their position against the landlords, Radio Peking proclaimed the area a "red district" and lauded the heroic effort to create a "liberated base" from which to wage a protracted revolutionary struggle. The Indian government reacted with alarm to what it viewed as Chinese infiltration in the sensitive border region, and the rebellion was put down in short order. Naxalbari was to become the rallying cry for armed revolution, and from this uprising, Indian Maoists took on the name "Naxalites."[36]

More substantial than Naxalbari was the peasant struggle in the Andhra hills of the Srikakulam district. Concentrated in the eight-hundred-square mile Girijan tribal agency tract, Communist-led Girijan guerrilla bands—armed with spears, bows and arrows, axes, and captured guns—began in 1968 to engage in clashes with landlords and police. The peasant struggle attracted college youth and seasoned party cadre, but although Srikakulam was hailed by Peking as a victory for Maoist tactics in India, the movement was suppressed by the end of the following year.[37]

Beyond Thanjavur, Naxalbari, and Srikakulam there are other pockets of militant agrarian unrest. In Kerala the Marxists have mobilized poor peasants and landless laborers through the kisan sabhas. In West Bengal members of the kisan movement in 1969 forcibly occupied some 150,000 acres, with the tacit support of the United Front government, although sporadic violence, political murders, and the absence of police intervention led moderate elements of the Government to denounce the breakdown of law and order in the state. The movement's intensity was spurred by the competition of the various wings of the Communist movement to gain control of kisan leadership.

Most peasants and laborers remain silent and unorganized, but an awakened consciousness, intensified by the "new agricultural strategy," has brought restlessness to India's agrarian poor. In the words of a Government of India report, the new strategy has been "geared to goals

---

[35] *India's Green Revolution: Economic Gains and Political Costs* (Princeton: Princeton University Press, 1971), p. 118.

[36] See Sankar Ghosh, *The Disinherited State: A Study of West Bengal, 1967–1970* (Calcutta: Orient Longmans, 1971), pp. 97–114; and Marcus F. Franda, *Radical Politics in West Bengal* (Cambridge: M. I. T. Press, 1971), pp. 149–81.

[37] See Mohan Ram, *Maoism in India* (Delhi: Vikas, 1971), pp. 106–36; and Bhabani Sen Gupta, *Communism in Indian Politics* (New York: Columbia University Press, 1972), pp. 329–46.

of production, with secondary regard to social implications."[38] "Unless the Green Revolution is accompanied by a revolution based on social justice," Home Minister Y. B. Chavan warned, "I am afraid the Green Revolution may not remain green."[39]

Trade Unions

Labor unions in India, as in most developing countries, have been highly political. Reflecting the central role of the state in labor relations, union demands for better working conditions and higher wages are directed less frequently toward management than toward the Government. Government tribunals for binding arbitration as well as wide ministerial discretion have made the Government the critical focus of pressure. With both labor and management dependent on Government intervention, collective bargaining is virtually nonexistent, and the Government has come to bear the brunt of all dissatisfaction. Government labor policy has been guided, for the most part unsuccessfully, by an effort to reduce the number of strikes and lockouts; the particular demands of labor or management are subordinated to the goals of national economic development.

During the nationalist movement, many unions were agents of political mobilization; their activities were subordinated to party priorities. After independence the labor movement fragmented, and the unions aligned themselves with India's major parties. The All-India Trade Union Congress (AITUC) had fallen under Communist control. A new Congress-oriented federation, the Indian National Trade Union Congress (INTUC), was organized with Government blessings. The Socialists organized the Hind Mazdoor Sabha (HMS), and non-Communist Marxists established the United Trade Union Congress (UTUC). Today there are some seventeen thousand registered unions in India, representing a little more than five million workers. Of these, about twenty-six hundred unions are affiliated with one of the four federations. Members have little loyalty toward the unions, frequently switch affiliation, and often join more than one. A person may join INTUC to take advantage of administrative privileges enjoyed by the Congress federation and at the same time may side with the Communist AITUC in protest against a broad range of social, political, and economic issues.[40]

In contrast to other unions, INTUC has taken a position of moderation, believing that "the interests of workers can best be satisfied by national growth, and national growth depends upon strong government and a strong Congress party."[41] In the service of stability and economic

---

[38] "The Causes and Nature of Current Agrarian Tensions," (Ministry of Home Affairs, Research and Policy Division, 1969), mimeographed, p. 3.

[39] Quoted in *Link*, January 18, 1970, p. 13.

[40] Millen, *The Political Role of Labor*, p. 23.

[41] Weiner, *The Politics of Scarcity*, pp. 78–79n.

growth the union has become more an agent of discipline than one of interest articulation. Its close ties with Congress and the Government have reduced INTUC's effectiveness in presenting labor demands, often to the advantage of more militant unions. It has been argued in defense of the Congress-INTUC alignment that INTUC has served as a counterweight to conservative elements within the Congress, but the unions have in fact had little influence over Congress policy. In the selection of candidates, for example, the Congress has generally disregarded INTUC recommendations.

The trade unions' lack of autonomy is revealed in their "outside" leadership of middle-class intellectuals and politicians. Weiner attributes the pattern of outside leadership to a variety of possible factors: need for command of English and special legal and administrative skills; early involvement of politicians in union organization to win support for the nationalist struggle; lack of adequate financing; status considerations; and in some industries, linguistic and ethnic gaps between the workers and management or Government.[42] The union may provide a channel for the leader's personal political advancement, for it may be the instrument by which political ends only indirectly related to labor problems are sought. But frequently pressure has come from the rank and file of the union on the leadership to field candidates. In a study of the Textile Workers' Union of Coimbatore in Tamil Nadu, an affiliate of the Hind Mazdoor Sabha, E. A. Ramaswamy found that the members viewed the union and party (the PSP) as "inextricably intertwined." Political loyalties frequently arose out of prolonged union membership, and a nucleus of politically committed members provided a ready source of campaign support and a militant base for demonstrations and strikes.[43]

Strikes each year take an increasing number of workers off the job. From 1951, with yearly fluctuation, the number of industrial disputes has more than doubled. In 1972 there were 2,912 disputes, involving 1,593,333 workers and a loss of 17,921,344 man days.[44] Toward the mid-1970s, as labor unrest deepened, the government took an increasingly hard stance against the unions. In 1974 the strike by the two million workers belonging to the All-India Railwaymen's Federation threatened to cripple the nation economically. The Prime Minister refused to negotiate the demands for a doubling of wages; the army was moved in to man key rail installations; some 6,000 labor leaders, including Socialist Party chairman George Fernandes, were immediately arrested; and in the course of the strike, the most serious India has confronted, more

---

[42] *Ibid.*, p. 91. See also V. B. Karnik, *Indian Trade Unions: A Survey*, 2nd ed. (Bombay: Manaktalas, 1966).

[43] "Politics and Organized Labor in India," *Asian Survey*, Vol. 13 (October 1973), pp. 914–28.

[44] *India: A Reference Annual* 1974 (New Delhi: Government of India, Ministry of Information and Broadcasting, 1974), p. 312.

than 30,000 workers and union activists were jailed. After twenty days the strike was abandoned, and from the cells the union leaders called upon the workers to return to their jobs.

Union militancy frequently descends to sabotage or coercion, as in the *gherao*, the physical encirclement of the managerial staff to secure "quick justice."[45] Excessive and wholly unrealistic demands arise in part from low levels of commitment to industrial occupations on the one hand and from millennial aspirations on the other. Trade unions have not been effective agents of interest articulation. Because of the ready labor supply from the ranks of the unemployed, the labor movement has been weak and unable to bargain effectively. There are always new recruits available, anxious to work at any wage.[46] "Unions are poorly organized, membership turnover is great, dues-paying is limited to a few and is irregular, and union activities are limited to strikes, demonstrations, and election work. Only rarely," Weiner writes, "does a union provide services for its members. Rival unionism is rampant, unions are led by outsiders, and control of unions is often in the hands of political parties seeking to use them for their own ends."[47]

Business

India has committed itself to the development of a socialist pattern of society, but if it is officially socialist, it is in practice overwhelmingly private. Some 85 percent of India's gross product is generated by the private sector, more even than in the United States.[48] The private sector, however, has long been an object of suspicion and distrust, reflecting traditional hostility to the business communities. Most of the modern business and industrial conglomerates are owned by families of the traditional trading communities—Gujarati Vaisyas, Parsis, Chettiars, Jains, and Marwaris. The public image of the business classes, infected by practices of usury, false weights, and quick profits, has not improved with the rumor of undeclared "black money," the revelation of scandal, or the notorious concentration of economic power in the hands of large industrial combines. The Monopolies Inquiry Commission reported in 1965 that the modern industrial sector of business in India was dominated by 75 managing agencies, which controlled almost half of the nation's nongovernmental, nonbanking assets.[49] Of these business

---

45 See Natish R. De and Suresh Srivastava, "Gheraos in West Bengal," *Economic and Political Weekly*, Vol. 2 (1967), pp. 2015–22, 2062–68, 2099–2104, 2167–76; and Natish R. De, "Gherao as a Technique for Social Intervention," *Economic and Political Weekly*, Vol. 5, annual number (January 1970), pp. 201–08.

46 Karnik, *Indian Trade Unions*, p. 302.

47 *The Politics of Scarcity*, p. 93.

48 Wilfred Malenbaum, "Politics and Indian Business: The Economic Setting," *Asian Survey*, Vol. 11 (September 1971), p. 843.

49 *Report of the Monopolies Inquiry Commission, 1965* (New Delhi: Government of India, 1965), pp. 119–22.

houses, the top 37 were predominantly controlled by the traditional communities—with the Marwaris and Parsis leading the field. The House of Tata (Parsi), headquartered in Bombay, ranked first, with 53 companies and assets of almost one billion dollars. The House of Birla (Marwari), based in Calcutta, followed, with 151 companies and assets of nearly three-quarters of a billion dollars.[50]

The Indian business community is represented by a multiplicity of associations. These include trade and industrial associations, employer associations, and chambers of commerce. Some are regional; some, like the Marwari (now Bharat) Chamber of Commerce in Bengal, represent particular communities. The activities of the various associations, as well as individual firms, are coordinated by three major national federations: the All-India Manufacturers Organization (AIMO) represents medium-sized industry, primarily in Bombay; the Associated Chambers of Commerce and Industry of India (Assocham) represents foreign British capital; and the Federation of Indian Chambers of Commerce and Industry (FICCI), "first in size, prestige, and influence among the apex organizations," is broadly representative of major industrial and trading interests.[51] With association constituents as well as individual firm members the Federation represents some 100,000 firms employing over five million workers.[52] For all its size, however, FICCI involves less than 1 percent of all private businessmen in India,[53] but even among those it does represent, to the neglect of small and medium trade and industrial interests, the Federation is dominated by big business. The six largest houses (all based in Calcutta, and five Marwari) provide a third of FICCI's total membership. Birla House alone commands 25 percent of the votes at the annual meeting.[54]

The major targets of FICCI in its effort to influence public policy have been the Prime Minister, the Cabinet, and the upper echelons of the bureaucracy. By custom the Prime Minister addresses the Federation's annual meeting in what, in effect, is a dialogue between Government and business. The Federation has gained representation on nearly one hundred Government commissions, committees, and councils, and through its secretariat, maintains continuous contact with various ministers and the bureaucracy. The Federation has also established a parliamentary office for liaison with Members of Parliament.[55]

FICCI has stood back from direct involvement in politics, but it has sought aid from government and protection for industry, while pro-

[50] Stanley A. Kochanek, *Business and Politics in India* (Berkeley: University of California Press, 1974), pp. 96, 338–39.
[51] Stanley A. Kochanek, "The Federation of Indian Chambers of Commerce and Industy and Indian Politics," *Asian Survey*, Vol. 11 (September 1971), p. 869.
[52] Kochanek, *Business and Politics in India*, p. 170.
[53] Malenbaum, "Politics and Indian Business: The Economic Setting," p. 847.
[54] Kochanek, *Business and Politics in India*, pp. 174–75.
[55] Kochanek, "The Federation of Indian Chambers of Commerce and Industry and Indian Politics," pp. 873–78.

testing regulation, control, and the jungle of licensing procedures. Accepting an expanding public sector it nevertheless has remained apprehensive about nationalization. The Federation members have for the most part followed the lead of G.D. Birla in casting their lot—however reluctantly—with the ruling party in order to secure direct channels of access to the Government. Birla argues, moreover, that a weakened Congress can only bring political instability, labor unrest, and a strengthened Communist movement.

The Tatas, standing aloof from FICCI, urge a more active role of political opposition for Indian business. They have sought to educate the public and Parliament to the cause of a capitalist economy through the Forum of Free Enterprise and to cleanse the tarnished image of the private sector through the Fair Trade Practices Association. The Tatas also have been major supporters of the Swatantra Party. In his study of business and politics in India, Stanley Kochanek found that "although the vast majority of the industrialists shared pro-Swatantra sentiments, they divided sharply over the advisability of supporting it. . . . Business in India is torn between alignments of ideological purity and alignments of convenience, between holding on to what they have left of influence with the ruling Congress party and switching allegiance to some party whose clearcut sympathy with private sector ambitions would promise easy access and certain influence at some future date."[56]

It is through informal personal contact that businessmen, as individuals and through chambers, most frequently gain access to government, and by which they have achieved what Dandekar has called the "private understanding between the ruling party and big business."[57] The Birlas, for example, have commanded a position of such power as to give them a strong voice in the selection of the Finance Minister. Contact between government and business is facilitated by traditional ties of community, family, and personal friendship, and often at the lower levels of the bureaucracy by the flow of bakshish, a bribe for the performance of administrative duty, serving to expedite, for example, an application for a permit or a license. Contributions to the Congress party may also serve to facilitate political access, and the Congress, as the party in power, has frequently extracted "contributions" from businesses dependent upon Government favor, a process all too familiar in the American context.

Although business pressure has sought to shape and modify policy formation, this pressure has been exerted more often by individual businessmen than by organized lobbies, and most frequently it has been used to bend the administration and implementation of policy rather than to form it. Much of its activity has, for this reason, been focused at the level of the states—particularly in those states responsive to its

---

[56] Kochanek, *Business and Politics in India*, pp. 39–40.
[57] V. M. Dandekar, "Next Steps on the Socialist Path," *Economic and Political Weekly*, Vol. 7, special number (August 1972), p. 1557.

interests. Business, however, has not been able to influence substantially the shape and direction of public policy in India. Kochanek contends that "business has never succeeded in blocking or even modifying a major redistributive policy in India." It may be able to delay an objectionable policy, but it "has not yet been able to convert its considerable economic power into truly effective political power." Kochanek argues that "the extent of business influence in India is exaggerated by its enemies and understated by its friends."[58]

> Business in India has considerable political capital and resources to draw upon, and because it has been able to mobilize at least a portion of these resources, it has become the best organized interest group in the country. It is the only group in India capable of sustained action and continuous day-to-day contact with both the Parliament and ranking heads of government. Nevertheless, although business enjoys a high level of access to government decision-makers, its ability to convert this capital into influence is substantially held in check by a variety of internal organizational and external systemic restraints.[59]

The influence of business is restrained by a hostile political culture that sets the parameters within which the business community may act, but it is checked as well by a vacillating yet official commitment to create a socialist society, predicated on economic and distributive justice, and by the constraints of a planned economy.

The Princes

Bejeweled maharajahs will always be a part of the romantic image of India, but they are an expensive anachronism in a modern democratic state. At the time of independence and princely accession, petty princes were simply given lump-sum payments, but 284 princes and their heirs were to receive in perpetuity an annual privy purse. As guaranteed by the constitution—the price paid for the bloodless transition from princely to republican rule in the integration of states—the purses, tax-free, ranged from as little as 192 rupees per year to the more than one million rupees received by six former rulers.[60] Accompanying the purses were a multiplicity of privileges, from such things as special license plates and flags to exemption from various taxes.

Soon after independence, in 1949, a number of princes founded the

---

[58] Kochanek, *Business and Politics in India*, pp. 321–33.
[59] *Ibid.*, p. 323.
[60] Several, including all those over one million rupees, were to be reduced with succession. See William L. Richter, "Princes in Indian Politics," *Economic and Political Weekly*, Vol. 6 (February 27, 1971), p. 538. For a general account of the princes in modern India and their fall, see D. R. Mankekar, *Accession to Extinction: The Story of Indian Princes* (Delhi: Vikas, 1974).

Ganatantra Parishad party, which in 1962 was merged with Swatantra. But the Congress itself—at least until the party split in 1969—
had the largest claim on princely support. In the 1960s the princes
had begun to play an increasingly prominent role in Indian politics,
particularly in the states of Orissa, Bihar, Rajasthan, Gujarat, and
Madhya Pradesh. Some, like the Maharani of Jaipur, who campaigned
in a helicopter, captured the fancy of the international press. In the
Fourth Lok Sabha (1967–71), there were nineteen former rulers. Nine
belonged to Congress, five to Swatantra, one to the Jana Sangh, and
two were independents. In the Fifth Lok Sabha, elected in 1971, there
were sixteen princes—four in Congress, two in the Congress (O), three
in Swatantra, four in the Jana Sangh, and three independents.[61]

The decline in princely representation in the Congress no doubt reflected a less hospitable environment. In 1967 the Congress, in an effort
to cast itself in a more radical image, proposed to abolish princely
privileges and privy purses. The princes organized a Concord of States
in defense of purse and privilege, but it was not until 1970 that Prime
Minister Indira Gandhi introduced the abolition bill in Parliament. The
legislation was in the form of an amendment to the constitution and as
such required a two-thirds vote in each house of Parliament. The bill
secured the requisite majority in the Lok Sabha, but in the Rajya Sabha
it failed by one vote. A Presidential Order was then issued "derecogniz-
ing" all princes. The princes challenged the order, and in a divided
opinion the Supreme Court held that the President had exceeded his
authority and that the princes were still entitled to the privileges and
purses that they had previously received. It was on this issue, among
others, that Mrs. Gandhi successfully sought her electoral mandate in
1971. With an overwhelming majority behind her in Parliament, the
Prime Minister reintroduced the abolition bill, which passed both
houses by a massive vote and was enacted as the twenty-sixth amendment. The princes were no more.

The Military

In a large part of the developing world the military has played a
prominent role in political life. With coups, both bloodless and violent,
few new nations have been free of military intervention. The Indian
army has remained remarkably nonpolitical, however. The explanation
does not lie in the character of the military, for with essentially the
same traditions, organization, and social background, the Pakistani
army seized power under General Ayub Khan. The most important
causes of military intervention are political and are to be located in the
availability of meaningful channels of political access and of institutions for mediating and resolving conflict. If the political system is
unable to respond to increasing participation and escalating demands

[61] *Link*, August 1, 1971, pp. 12–15.

and at the same time maintain order, the military, cohesive and bureau-cratized, may step in.

The Indian army, numbering more than 800,000—the fourth largest in the world—has a proud and romantic tradition, regimental color, and Sandhurst tastes. Morale, having suffered from the humiliation of the Chinese invasion, was bolstered by the heroism of Indian soldiers in the twenty-two-day war with Pakistan in 1965 and by the stunning victory six years later in the liberation of Bangladesh. Indian defense expenditure declined from 1950 to 1961, then rose rapidly in response to the Chinese threat, and has since maintained an overall average of approximately 20 percent of total government expenditures, or about 4 percent of the Gross National Product—considerably below the world average of 7 percent.[62] In India, as elsewhere, however, defense expenditures are often hidden in a variety of budgetary allocations. Military expenditure may thus be considerably larger than official figures indicate. In addition, India has received considerable military assistance from the Soviet Union. The defense establishment has gained a powerful position in bidding for scarce resources within the public sector, but as yet the military has not sought greater leverage in political life.

Even if the army were to overcome its tradition of restraint, a coup would require the concerted action of the five regional commands—no easy task. That the President might in a governmental crisis declare a state of emergency and invite military intervention is more plausible. Political democracy in India, Lloyd I. and Susanne H. Rudolph warn, is by no means secure: "The authoritarian character created by the traditional family, the attraction of cultural fundamentalism to the urbanized lower middle classes, and the appeal of order, discipline and efficiency to the professional classes, now marginal features of Indian political life, are susceptible of mobilization by military leadership under the right circumstances."[63]

Students

If the vast majority of India's people is politically inarticulate and uncoordinated, students are loudly vocal, but they too lack direction and coherence. The nationalist movement gave students an active role in mass agitation, beginning with the noncooperation movement in 1920 and reaching a height with the Quit India movement in 1942. When the All-Indian Student Federation, founded in 1936, came under Communist domination, the Students' Congress captured student loyalties in the continuing struggle against the British. After independence, however, the Gandhian program of constructive work held little attraction for the politicized student population. The student movement had lost

[62] See K. Subrahmanyam, "Indian Defence Expenditure in Global Perspective," *Economic and Political Weekly*, Vol. 8 (June 30, 1973), pp. 1155–58.

[63] "Generals and Politicians in India," *Pacific Affairs*, Vol. 37 (Spring 1964), p. 7.

"its sense of militant unity and ideological purpose. . . . The nationalist fervor of the preindependence period has been replaced by generally unorganized and sporadic agitation usually aimed at specific grievances."[64] Student activism is a reaction to increasing frustrations caused by unresponsive university authorities and an uncertain economic future.

Even more than in the West, the university degree in India is the passport to a "good job," but perhaps more often, it is the route to educated unemployment. With more than two million students registered in some 3,500 colleges and universities—more than six times the number of students at independence—there are far more graduates each year than positions available. Rather than suffer the humiliation of taking a position beneath their newly acquired status, many simply join the expanding ranks of the unemployed.

But if India has a plethora of college graduates, there is a paucity of those capable of handling India's most pressing developmental problems. Graduate students in foreign universities frequently never return, becoming statistics of the "brain drain." The largest number of students pour into already overcrowded arts colleges, only to pull their declining standards still lower. A rigid administrative structure, a Victorian syllabus, and the dread comprehensive final examinations have made the Indian university an impersonal experience. Since the vast majority of today's students enter from rural backgrounds, with often only a rudimentary knowledge of English, the continued use of English as the medium of instruction in many universities is both a farce and a tragedy. Although colleges are increasingly shifting to the regional vernacular, the chasm between the majority of the students and the privileged few with an English-language-lower-school background remains wide. Those who have a command of English take the coveted positions in the IAS, go on to graduate or professional studies, or enter business. Many of the others settle for the dubious distinction of a "B.A. (Failed)," which at least is evidence of having attended college.

In such an atmosphere "student indiscipline" has been endemic. Defined loosely, the term includes any activity that interferes with the normal process of education. There are broadly four types of such activity:[65] (1) "Demands by students upon university authorities." Students have opposed fee increases or have demanded easier entrance requirements to colleges. (2) "Student demands upon non-university authorities on issues of special concern." Tram-fare controversies have attracted student activists, as have increases in the price of cinema

[64] Philip G. Altbach, "Student Politics and Higher Education in India," *Daedalus*, No. 97 (Winter 1968), p. 260.

[65] The typology is that of Myron Weiner. See *The Politics of Scarcity*, pp. 172–73. Also see Lloyd I. Rudolph, Susanne H. Rudolph, and Karuna Ahmed, "Student Politics and National Politics in India," *Economic and Political Weekly*, Vol. 6, special number (July 1971), pp. 1655–68; and Lloyd I. and Susanne H. Rudolph, eds., *Education and Politics in India* (Cambridge: Harvard University Press, 1972).

tickets. Both incidents have triggered rioting. (3) "Sporadic, generally unorganized outbursts by students only vaguely associated with concrete demands." Students in Calcutta, for example, threw over the tables at an examination they considered too stiff, initiating a riot that closed the university. (4) "Activities associated with larger political movements in the areas surrounding the school, college, or university." Examples of such activities include the participation of Tamil students in linguistic agitation and student involvement in the Telengana and Andhra state-hood movements and in the Naxalite movements in West Bengal and Andhra. Most dramatic has been the student role in bringing down the governments of Orissa in 1964 and Gujarat in 1974. With rising prices, food scarcities, and unresolved political grievances, matters in Gujarat had been tense for months. Student discontent was initially focused on increased hostel charges, but with the formation of the student "Society of Reconstruction," the agitation widened. Sarvodaya leader Jayaprakash Narayan, emerging from his political retirement, called upon the students to assume leadership of the statewide Gujarat Bandh in January 1974. The unprecedented agitation that followed gave rise to widespread violence, resulting in fifty deaths. One month later the Congress Government resigned and President's Rule was declared.

The Indian government has attributed student unrest to "loss of leadership by teachers, growth of economic difficulties, general loss of idealism, absence of social life, a sense of fear and insecurity and un-happy living conditions."[66] "Indiscipline" has included the Gandhian technique of satyagraha, as well as strikes, destruction of property, physical attacks on university personnel, and even self-immolation. Widespread rioting and police firings have occurred, and disturbances have closed Indian universities for weeks at a time. At one point in 1972, half of India's colleges were closed for one reason or another. Student unrest has increased yearly, with deepening violence. Political parties have tried to exploit it, but few have succeeded. Only the DMK and the Jana Sangh have successfully launched student movements, and students have played important roles in their processions, demonstrations, and electoral efforts.

The Gandhians

Only hours before his death, Gandhi drafted a resolution—often called his "last will and testament"—in which he called upon the Congress to renounce politics and to transform itself into a people's service society. While they may have looked to Gandhi for guidance, few Congressmen were willing to follow his path. One man fully prepared to follow the footsteps of the Mahatma was Vinoba Bhave. Born in 1895,

---

[66] Indian Ministry of Education, *Education in Universities in India, 1951–52*, quoted in Weiner, *The Politics of Scarcity*, p. 171.

he had been quietly involved in the "constructive work" of the nationalist movement when, in 1940, Gandhi selected him to be the first *satyagrahi* in the Quit India movement. After Gandhi's death, Vinoba in 1951 went into the Telengana countryside, then in a state of rebellion, to bring the message of nonviolence. It was there that he conceived of *Bhoodan*, "land gift." Vinoba, "India's walking saint" as he came to be called, began the journey that has since taken him thousands of miles through India's villages. In each village, appealing to the landlords' sense of trusteeship, Vinoba asked for a gift of one-sixth of their land for redistribution among the poor and landless. In 1954 *Gramdan*, "village gift," was begun, involving the institution of community rather than individual ownership of land. "It became evident," Jayaprakash Narayan later wrote, "that Bhoodan had within it the germ of total agrarian revolution."[67] What Vinoba sought was a "moral revolution." "Our work," he wrote, "consists in changing the present social order from the very root." Amidst references to the Gita and to Hindu mythology, Vinoba argued that "all land, all property, and all wealth should belong to society."[68] He sought a threefold revolution—in people's hearts, in their lives, and in their social structure. His vision was of *Sarvodaya*, "the welfare of all." Sarvodaya emphasized service, nonviolence, noncompetitiveness, and a political and economic decentralization focused on the village. All were to have equal rights to land and property, with no distinctions made in wages.[69]

In the Bhoodan movement Vinoba received millions of acres for redistribution. Some few acres were given to the landless, but more often than not, once Vinoba had gone on to the next village, the promised lands remained in the hands of their owners. Bhoodan, which had been so widely hailed in the 1950s, is now recognized as largely a failure. But Sarvodaya remains a potent force in India's political culture, largely through the personality of Jayaprakash Narayan. In 1954 Narayan, socialist leader and the man many believed to be Nehru's political heir, renounced "party-and-power politics" and dedicated his life to Sarvodaya, which he understood to be "people's socialism." "The party system, so it appears to me," he wrote, "was seeking to reduce the people to the position of sheep whose only function of sovereignty would be to choose periodically the shepherds who took after their welfare! This to me did not spell freedom—the freedom, the swaraj, for which . . . the people of this country had fought."[70] To the conflict orientation of his own earlier Marxism, Narayan sought a Gandhian

---

[67] "From Socialism to Sarvodaya," in Bimla Prasad, ed., *Socialism, Sarvodaya and Democracy* (Bombay: Asia Publishing House, 1964), p. 167.

[68] Vinoba Bhave, *The Principles and Philosophy of the Bhoodan Yagna* (Tanjore: Sarvodaya Prachuralaya, 1955), pp. 1–3.

[69] Mariam Sharma and Jagdish P. Sharma, "Hinduism, Sarvodaya, and Social Change," in Donald E. Smith, ed., *Religion and Political Modernization* (New Haven: Yale University Press, 1974), p. 238.

[70] Narayan, "From Socialism to Sarvodaya," p. 158.

alternative. He sought the reconstruction of society based on equality, freedom, brotherhood, and peace.

In 1974, as India's political and economic situation became increasingly serious, Narayan began to speak out more vehemently, and in the Gujarat agitation, J. P., as he is called, came out of his self-imposed political retirement. Hardly had the Gujarat Ministry fallen than discontent in Bihar, Narayan's home state, erupted into widespread agitation. In Patna, the state capital, half a million people marched in procession under the leadership of Jayaprakash Narayan to present the Governor with two million signatures in support of the demand for dissolution of the Bihar legislative assembly. Narayan, supported by individual members of the Jana Sangh, Swatantra, and Samyukta Socialist Party, called upon assembly members to resign, for students to boycott classes, and for the people to refuse to pay taxes. With charges of corruption and proposals for a change in the electoral system so as to institute proportional representation, Narayan launched satyagraha against the Government of the state.

The Scope and Character of Group Activity in India

A developed group infrastructure acts not merely to facilitate the articulation of demands and to provide linkage between the masses and the elite. In providing meaningful access to the political decision-makers, it gives order to expanding participation and focuses disparate demands so that they may more readily be acted upon. Indian interest groups, however, have a low level of institutionalization. Viewed with suspicion, their activities are generally seen as illegitimate, and for many people this opinion is confirmed by their recourse to violence in the face of governmental unresponsiveness.

The tempo of violence has increased yearly in India. The Government of India officially defines a riot as involving five or more people. The category, which includes brawls, gives little indication of the intensity or seriousness of the dispute, and, obviously, the statistics do not record "official violence"—police repression, lathi charges, police firings. Thousands of riots are recorded each year. In India's eight largest cities, their number increased four times from 581 in 1961 to 2,319 in 1970. The city of Ahmedabad, scene of the worse communal riot since partition, has had a fifteenfold increase in the number of recorded incidents of violence arising out of protest demonstrations, processions, strikes, bandhs, and riots. By 1973 the city witnessed such an incident on an average of once every four days.[71]

---

[71] Ghanshyam Shah, "Anatomy of Urban Riots: Ahmedabad 1973," *Economic and Political Weekly*, Vol. 9, annual number (February 1974), p. 233. See also David H. Bayley, *The Police and Political Development in India* (Princeton: Princeton University Press, 1969), p. 249.

Interest groups, in a process of political mobilization, both stimulate and structure participation. Weiner has argued that "the greatest protection against the demands of powerful community groups is the multiplication of community and non-community associations." When the number of associations increases, "the possibility that any single community will dominate a state government is likely to decrease. As more caste and tribal groups, trade unions, and peasant associations emerge, those who wish to win power will have to turn to the interests of communities other than their own."[72] A "bargaining culture" may emerge at the expense of the wider public interests, however, as India's limited resources may be dissipated in trade-offs and "logrolling" between contending and self-interested groups. But who is to determine the "public interest"? What classes are to be served? This is the classic and fundamental dilemma of democracy—one starkly posed in the context of India's struggle for economic development and social justice.

The existing class structure of India poses a serious challenge to economic growth with social justice. The alleged conflict between growth and justice is an expression of the more fundamental contradiction in the underlying structural arrangements of social relations. India is fragmented by virtually every known societal division, but while the Indian masses are beginning to respond to political appeals in terms of class interest, they have no consciousness of class. Class remains an objective category imposed analytically on the heterogeneity of India's contending groups. But in objective terms it is possible to ask which are the classes for whose benefit state power is exercised as indicated by the overall direction of state policy. In an inquiry into the class character of state power in India, a Marxist symposium concluded that it "is really shared by the landlords and the industrial bourgeoisie, especially under the leadership of monopoly capitalists."[73] The assessment of the Communist Party of India is perhaps more accurate: the state in India is the instrument of class rule of the national bourgeoisie as a whole, in which the big bourgeoisie and landlords hold powerful influence.[74]

Fundamentally, as Baldev Raj Nayar writes,

> the levers of political and state power have rested in the hands of what may broadly be termed the "middle sectors" of economic and social life in both urban and rural areas—the educated and professional groups, town merchants and small businessmen in the urban areas; and the middle peasantry or kulaks in the villages.

[72] Weiner, *The Politics of Scarcity*, pp. 70–72.
[73] "Conclusions of the All-India Conference on the Class Character of State Power," *Social Scientist*, Vol. 2 (August 1973), p. 80.
[74] "Programme of the Communist Party of India," in *Documents Adopted by the Eighth Congress of the Communist Party of India, Patna, 7–15 February 1968*, p. 297.

Numbering perhaps two hundred million or more, they command a position of relative privilege in a nation of poverty and economic backwardness.

> The source of power of these middle sectors lies in the strategic combination of considerable population size with extensive economic resources and significant social status, as against the greater economic power but small numbers of the upper business and land owning classes and the large numbers but economic destitution of the lower classes. Socialism to the middle sectors has meant, apart from what may fairly be described as tokenism toward the scheduled castes, the bringing down of the upper classes to their own level, but no redistribution or levelling down below that level. Democracy has served these classes well in this regard by facilitating the conversion of economic privilege and numerical strength into political power while at the same time giving it an aura of genuine legitimacy.

"The middle sectors have given support to the political regime in the past because it has been responsive to their interests," but they are vulnerable and confront an environment of political and economic uncertainty. In defense of their fragile position, "they have been the major block of redistribution in behalf of the underprivileged classes."[75] In competition for scarce resources, confronted by uncontrolled inflation and commodity shortages, the middle sectors, increasingly disaffected from the political system that has so long sustained them, are now challenged from below by newly politicized classes.

Comparatively few of India's newly mobilized political participants are involved in organized interest-group life. Formal memberships, if impressive in absolute terms, are inconsequential in relation to the mass of India's vast population. Five million labor-union members, one hundred thousand or so student activists, a handful of formal members in agrarian associations are unlikely to command much political capital. These associations and interest groups nevertheless represent the yet-unorganized millions who with mass communications and party competition for their votes can be stirred to political consciousness. Their group identity is now only beginning to take form. The Scheduled Castes, for example, who number some eighty million, are just awakening to their potential power as a political bloc, and though geographically dispersed, they are likely to command increasing weight in the electoral calculus.

Political mobilization has extended the identity horizon of the Indian masses in widening participation and involvement, but interest groups have been unable to provide the institutional channels of access to

[75] Baldev Raj Nayar, "Political Mobilization in a Market Polity: Goals, Capabilities and Performance in India," in Robert I. Crane, ed., *Political Mobilization in South Asia* (forthcoming).

structure and order what Weiner has called the "emergent mass political culture."[76] Political parties, notably the Congress, have assumed this critical role.

[76] Weiner, "India's Two Political Cultures," p. 199.

RECOMMENDED READING

Altbach, Philip, ed., *Turmoil and Transition: Higher Education and Student Politics in India*. New York: Basic Books, 1968.
    An examination by seven social scientists of the problem of student unrest.

* Bondurant, Joan V., *Conquest of Violence*. Berkeley: University of California Press, 1965.
    A sympathetic study of satyagraha and Gandhian political theory.

Brass, Paul R., *Language, Religion and Politics in North India*. New York: Cambridge University Press, 1974.
    The politics of language and its association with religious identity in a multilingual, multiethnic area.

* Gough, Kathleen, and Sharma, Hari P., eds., *Imperialism and Revolution in South Asia*. New York: Monthly Review Press, 1973.
    A Marxist symposium of Maoist perspective, ranging from the polemical to incisive analyses of the revolutionary situation in South Asia.

Hardgrave, Robert L., Jr., *The Nadars of Tamilnad: The Political Culture of a Community in Change*. Berkeley: University of California Press, 1969.
    An analysis of the relationship between social structure and political behavior within a changing caste community in South India.

* Isaacs, Harold C., *India's Ex-Untouchables*. New York: John Day, 1965.
    An inquiry into the changing conditions of India's untouchable community.

Karnik, V. B., *Indian Trade Unions: A Survey*. Bombay: Manaktalas, 1966.
    A comprehensive study of the development of trade unions in India, their problems and prospects.

Kochanek, Stanley A., *Business and Politics in India*. Berkeley: University of California Press, 1974.
    One of the best studies yet written on any aspect of Indian politics.

Kothari, Rajni, ed., *Caste in Indian Politics*. New Delhi: Orient Longmans, 1970.
    Nine case studies of the interaction between caste and politics within the context of social change.

Lynch, Owen M., *The Politics of Untouchability: Social Mobility and Social Change in a City of India*. New York: Columbia University Press, 1969.
    A study of the Jatav caste of Agra.

* Mahar, J. Michael, ed., *The Untouchables in Contemporary India*. Tucson: University of Arizona Press, 1972.
    A superb collection of papers focusing on social and political change among the Scheduled Castes.

* Available in a paperback edition.

Mankekar, D. R., *Accession to Extinction: The Story of Indian Princes*. Delhi: Vikas, 1974.
> Portrays the twenty-five-year struggle of the princes to retain purse and privilege and their final defeat.

* Mason, Philip, ed., *India and Ceylon: Unity and Diversity*. New York: Oxford University Press, 1967.
> A fine collection of essays dealing with five areas of social tension: linguistic and regional division, and differences of tribe, caste, religion, and education.

Park, Richard L., and Tinker, Irene, eds., *Leadership and Political Institutions in India*. Princeton, N.J.: Princeton University Press, 1960.
> A major collection of essays dealing wtih varied aspects of Indian political life.

*Rudolph, Lloyd I., and Susanne H., *The Modernity of Tradition*. Chicago: University of Chicago Press, 1967.
> A study of the ways in which tradition and modernity penetrate one another in a dialectical relationship. The dynamic of tradition is explored in the context of caste associations, the personality of Gandhi, and the Indian legal tradition.

Rudolph, Susanne H., "Consensus and Conflict in Indian Politics." *World Politics*, Vol. 12 (April 1961), pp. 385–99.
> An insightful analysis of the role of consensus in traditional Indian society and its implications for democratic politics.

Shils, Edward, *The Intellectual Between Tradition and Modernity: The Indian Situation*, Supplement I, *Comparative Studies in Society and History*. The Hague: Mouton, 1961.
> An exploration of the varied aspects of the Indian intellectual as an individual between two worlds.

* Smith, Donald E., ed., *South Asian Politics and Religion*. Princeton, N.J.: Princeton University Press, 1966.
> A collection of essays on the diversity of India's religions and their impact on politics.

Srinivas, M. N., *Caste in Modern India and Other Essays*. Bombay: Asia Publishing House, 1962.
> A penetrating analysis of politics and social change in India.

* Weiner, Myron, "India's Two Political Cultures," in Lucian Pye and Sidney Verba, eds., *Political Culture and Political Development*. Princeton, N.J.: Princeton University Press, 1965.
> A discussion of Indian political life in terms of its elite culture and the emerging mass participant culture.

————, *The Politics of Scarcity*. Chicago: University of Chicago Press, 1962.
> An analysis of group politics in India and the political response to the pressure of demands. One of the best studies yet on Indian politics.

* Available in a paperback edition.

VI

THE PARTY SYSTEM

Dᴜʀɪɴɢ ᴛʜᴇ ᴘᴀꜱᴛ ᴅᴇᴄᴀᴅᴇ ᴛʜᴇ ᴄʜᴀʀᴀᴄᴛᴇʀ ᴏꜰ ᴛʜᴇ ᴘᴀʀᴛʏ ꜱʏꜱᴛᴇᴍ ɪɴ India has fundamentally changed. In 1967 Congress suffered the shock of massive defeats. While in the states, coalition governments followed each other in rapid succession, the Congress party was racked with factional conflict, climaxed in 1969 by a formal split. For the first time, the Government no longer commanded an absolute majority in Parliament. The split in the Congress was mirrored in the contradictions and confusion of the parties in opposition. For all the talk of a general polarization and realignment in Indian politics, there were deep divisions in ideology, temperament, and social base on both the left and right. In the parliamentary elections in 1971 and in the assembly elections in 1972 the Congress of Indira Gandhi secured unprecedented majorities, but the very nature of the mandate was tenuous, to be withdrawn at the displeasure of an electorate with high expectations and an unwillingness to accept excuses for unfulfilled promises.

The Congress Party

In India before 1967, and the party split two years later, the critical arena of political competition was the Congress "system" of one-party dominance.[1] This system, which operated effectively in India until the mid-1960s, was a competitive one, but one in which the single party of consensus occupied a dominant, central position. In this system the dominant Congress party, itself factionally divided, was both sensitive and responsive to the margin of pressure; the opposition did not constitute an alternative to the ruling party but functioned from the periphery in the form of parties of pressure. In such a system, the role of the opposition parties, writes Rajni Kothari,

> is to constantly pressurize, criticize, censure and influence it by influencing opinion and interests inside the margin and, above all, exert a latent threat that if the ruling group strays away too far from the balance of effective public opinion, and if the factional system within it is not mobilized to restore the balance, it will be displaced from power by the opposition groups.[2]

The one-party dominance system has two prominent characteristics. "There is plurality within the dominant party which makes it more representative, provides flexibility, and sustains internal competition. At the same time, it is prepared to absorb groups and movements from outside the party and thus prevent other parties from gaining strength."[3]

The breakdown of the Congress "system" was rooted in its own dynamics—the internal contradictions within the party.

The Factional Character of the Congress

Within the Congress, in the years of dominance, factions interacted in "a continuous process of pressure, adjustment and accommodation" to provide a built-in opposition.[4] The party retained the character of the nationalist movement in seeking to balance and accommodate social and ideological diversity within an all-embracing, representative structure. During the struggle for independence, the Congress party, as the

---

[1] The party system in India has been characterized in this way by Rajni Kothari, "The Congress 'System' in India," in *Party Systems and Election Studies,* Occasional Papers of the Center for Developing Societies, No. 1 (Bombay: Allied Publishers, 1967), pp. 1–18; by W. H. Morris-Jones, "Parliament and Dominant Party: Indian Experience," in *Parliamentary Affairs,* Vol. 17 (Summer 1964), pp. 296–307; and by Gopal Krishna, "One Party Dominance—Developments and Trends" in *Party Systems and Electoral Studies,* pp. 19–98.

[2] "The Congress 'System' in India," p. 3.

[3] *Ibid.,* p. 6.

[4] Rajni Kothari, "Party System," *Economic Weekly* (June 3, 1961), p. 849.

vehicle of the nationalist movement, brought together an eclectic body of individuals and groups in united opposition to the British raj. Claiming sole legitimacy as the nationalist party, the Congress sought to resolve or avoid internal conflict, balance interests, and blur ideological distinctions in its search for consensus.[5] Within its ranks, however, in factions and internal parties, were the roots of opposition. Organized groups emerged from the Congress umbrella as distinct parties, but each left within the Congress an ideologically congruent faction. Thus each of the opposition parties—the Jana Sangh, Swatantra, the Socialists, and the Communists—retained access to the Congress that provided it with an influence disproportionate to its size.

The responsiveness of the Congress to these pressures was revealed in the flexibility and contradictions of its programs and practices. The Congress sustained itself by undermining the opposition, taking over their programs, conceding basic issues, and co-opting their leadership. At the national level, the Congress stole the thunder of the Praja Socialist Party through its 1955 resolution in support of a socialist pattern of society. In the states the Congress became the voice of regionalism in order to undercut the growth of separatism. At the local level the party relaxed its policy of land reform to win support from the landlords and keep Swatantra at a distance. At the top the Congress party has repeatedly denounced casteism as a reversion to a tribal mentality, but at the bottom, the Congress, like the Jana Sangh and even the Communists, anchored its organization among the dominant castes.

In consolidating its power after independence the Congress sought to achieve a national consensus through the accommodation and absorption of dominant social elements that had kept aloof from the nationalist movement. Traditional caste and village leaders, landlords, and businessmen made their way into the Congress.

> In its effort to win, Congress adapts itself to the local power structure. It recruits from among those who have local power and influence. . . . The result is a political system with considerable tension between a government concerned with modernizing the society and economy and a party seeking to adapt itself to the local environment in order to win elections.[6]

With the resources of government power and patronage the Congress attracted careerists, who sought to gain support by appealing to the parochial loyalties of language, caste, and community. "The composite character of the party was preserved," writes Gopal Krishna, "indeed made more heterogeneous by promiscuous accommodation of divergent elements, whose commitments to the new consensus created around the objectives of economic development, socialism and democracy remained

---

[5] Krishna, "One Party Dominance," p. 26.
[6] Myron Weiner, *Party Building in a New Nation* (Chicago: University of Chicago Press, 1967), p. 15.

superficial."[7] Paul R. Brass concurs: "The Congress Party has chosen to make adjustments and accommodations, to interact with rather than transform the traditional order. In India modernization is not a one-way process; political institutions modernize the society while the society traditionalizes institutions."[8]

As the party penetrated society it was influenced by it. Political mobilization served to stimulate a new consciousness and solidarity. As a channel of communication and integration providing effective vertical linkage, the party drew increasing numbers into political participation. In a capillary effect they infused the party with a new leadership, regional in the base of its support, more traditional in the idiom of its political behavior. Political consciousness was activated faster than the integrative process, however, and as a result group identity was often emphasized at the expense of the national community. As the new electorate, caste-conscious and parochial in orientation, was drawn into a more participant political life, the Congress and the opposition parties sought to win their support through the tactics of the American political machine—patronage, favors, promises, and bargains. As the electorate was politicized, the parties were traditionalized. The parties became "mediating agencies between the largely traditional and politically diffuse electorate and the modern state system with its emphasis on citizenship, purposive direction of public policy and political integration."[9]

Although all parties served to induct the new citizens into the political culture, the Congress, as the dominant party, was the critical channel of linkage between the elite and the masses. Gandhi had attempted to bring the Congress directly to the masses, but it was the development of the party organization, with its roots in tradition, that consolidated the Congress and made politics both comprehensible and meaningful to Indian peasants. In the process, however, the Congress became an advocate of much that it had opposed, encouraging both sectionalism and integration, preaching socialism, and sustaining the *status quo*.

Brass, in his study of the Congress in Uttar Pradesh, describes the internal life of the party in terms of factional conflict. The conflict is not ideological but personal; it is characterized by shifting political coalitions. "Alliances develop and splits and defections occur wholly because of the mutual convenience and temporarily shared power-political interests of the group leaders." The groups are "loose coalitions of local, district faction leaders, tied together at the state level partly by personal bonds of friendship, partly by caste loyalties, and most of all by political interest."[10] Although there seem to be no persistent conflicts, Brass argues, there is in each faction a relatively solid inner core, bound to-

[7] "One Party Dominance," p. 29.
[8] *Factional Politics in an Indian State: The Congress Party in Uttar Pradesh* (Berkeley: University of California Press, 1966), p. 2.
[9] Krishna, "One Party Dominance," p. 32.
[10] *Factional Politics in an Indian State*, pp. 54–55.

gether in personal loyalty to the leader and divided from other factions by deep personal enmities. Factional conflict is rooted at the district level, and factional systems are largely autonomous, arising out of conditions and personalities peculiar to the district. This served to compartmentalize conflict, to quarantine discontent, and to make discontent more manageable.

Factionalism in the party is closely related to factionalism in the villages, since traditional village factions increasingly seek to ally themselves with a party group. The factional character of the Congress served to accommodate local conflict and to internalize it. If the Congress were unable to tolerate factions, opposition parties would secure the support of one of the two factions in each village—as in certain regions they are now beginning to do. Highly institutionalized, the factional system within the Congress, at least until 1967, was able "to sustain popular support in the midst of intense intra-party conflict."[11]

Although factionalism often leads to paralysis at the level of local government, it may also perform certain integrative functions. The faction, as a vertical structure of power, cuts across caste and class divisions and is based on a combination of other traditional loyalties and individual interests. "All faction leaders seek cross-caste alliances, for it is political power they desire and not merely the advancement of the claims of their own communities."[12] Factional conflict also broadens the base of participation within the party as each faction competes for wider group support. By drawing in new caste and religious groups, for example, factions have politicized them in secular terms.[13]

Factionalism, however, may also lead to a form of *immobilisme*, as each faction holds the other in check. The factional character of the Congress has meant that the chief opposition to the Government has frequently come from within the Congress itself. Conflict between the governmental and organizational wings of the party virtually constituted a two-party system but one hardly designed for coherent and effective policy. With minimum response to the problems of economic inequality and social injustice, the Congress system was governed by conflict avoidance and the politics of patronage.

The Organization of the Congress

Under Gandhi the Congress organization, shown in Figure 6–1, was structured as a parallel government, extending down to the village level. Except for the fact that Congress provincial units were organized along linguistic lines, this structure corresponded to administrative boundaries, such as that of the district, not to electoral constituencies.

---

11 Weiner, *Party Building in a New Nation*, pp. 159–160.
12 Brass, *Factional Politics in an Indian State*, p. 236.
13 *Ibid.*, p. 242.

FIGURE 6-1

THE FORMAL ORGANIZATIONAL STRUCTURE OF THE CONGRESS

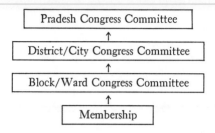

After independence the system was retained, with parallel party and government structure from top to bottom.

There are two types of party membership: primary, requiring the acceptance of Congress objectives and the payment of twenty-five paise dues annually; and active, requiring the wearing of khadi (a homespun cloth), abstinence, opposition to untouchability and communalism, participation in constructive work, and payment of one rupee dues annually. All members within a block (or ward) elect the block (or ward) Congress committee, corresponding to the samiti or development block. The district (or city) Congress committee consists of elected, ex officio, and co-opted members so as to be generally representative of various factions and groups within the party. The pradesh (or provincial) Congress committee is similarly constituted and is the locus of Congress power within each state.[14] The Congress is the only party with a permanent organization in every state. The organizational character of the opposition parties has varied with time and from party to party, but their organization tends to be patterned after that of the Congress.

The Congress organization is coordinated through a pyramidal decision-making structure, shown in Figure 6–2, with the Working Committee and the president at the apex.

The Social Base of the Congress

The Congress is the only genuinely all-India party, not merely in terms of its geographic distribution but in terms of its capacity to appeal to virtually all sections of society. By almost any variable—social, economic, demographic—the base of the Congress support is the most heterogeneous and differentiated of any political party in India. As the "party of consensus," the Congress reflects the social structure of its support. In a profile of the Congress based on a survey of the Indian

[14] For specifics of Congress field organization, see Stanley A. Kochanek, *The Congress Party of India* (Princeton, N.J.: Princeton University Press, 1968), pp. 452–53.

FIGURE 6–2

THE NATIONAL DECISION-MAKING STRUCTURE OF THE CONGRESS

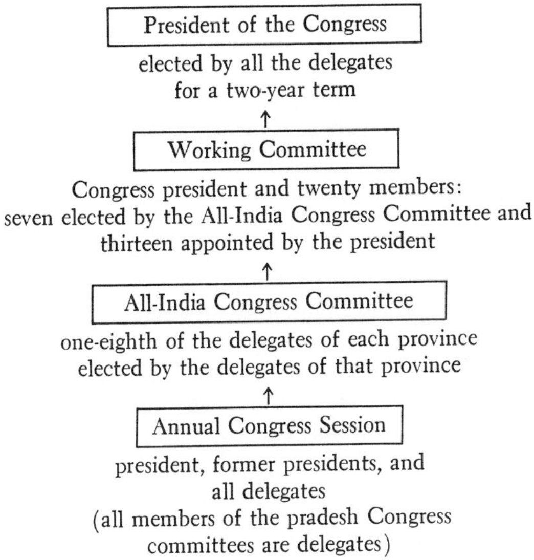

President of the Congress

elected by all the delegates
for a two-year term

↑

Working Committee

Congress president and twenty members:
seven elected by the All-India Congress Committee and
thirteen appointed by the president

↑

All-India Congress Committee

one-eighth of the delegates of each province
elected by the delegates of that province

↑

Annual Congress Session

president, former presidents, and
all delegates
(all members of the pradesh Congress
committees are delegates)

SOURCE: Stanley A. Kochanek, *The Congress Party of India* (Princeton, N.J.: Princeton University Press, 1968), p. xxii.

electorate in 1967, D. L. Sheth emphasizes the broadly aggregative character of the party, but concludes that there are certain segments of the population that lend their support disproportionately to Congress:

> Its supporters consist more of the middle-aged and old voters and less of the young voters; it has a slightly higher proportion of illiterates than highly educated voters; more rural supporters than urban supporters. Its occupational and caste base is fairly diversified, with slightly greater support from middle caste groups and Muslims. Its economic base is also very broad-based, with slightly less support from higher income groups. The party's support is almost equally spread over the various groups of landholders.[15]

The Relationship of the Congress and the Government

Stanley A. Kochanek, in a study of Congress organization, describes the evolution of party-Government relations and the transformation of inner party structure as passing through three stages. The conflict be-

[15] "Profiles of Party Support in 1967," *Economic and Political Weekly*, Vol. 6, annual number (January 1971), p. 284.

tween the two wings of the Congress reached its height and "resolution" in 1969 in the formal party split.

"THE PERIOD OF TRANSITION"

The period of transition, 1945–51, "was marked by conflict between the party and the Government and by disorder and confusion at the executive level of the party organization as the Congress sought to adapt a nationalist movement to a political party."[16] When he resigned as Congress president to head the interim government, Nehru took the top echelon of the party's leadership with him into the Cabinet. During the independence struggle the high command of the party had strongly asserted the supremacy of the organization, but with swaraj the leadership abandoned the organization for the responsibilities of public office. They had won honor through their activities in the nationalist movement, and office was their reward. The political center of gravity shifted from the party to the Government, but J. B. Kripalani, the new Congress president, insisted that Government decisions be made only in consultation with the Congress president and the Working Committee. Unwilling to oversee the subordination of the party, Kripalani resigned and later left the Congress altogether.

The decisive confrontation came with the election of the conservative P. Tandon as Congress president, which placed the organization in the hands of the right wing of the party. But when the conservatives sought to consolidate their position, the death of Patel deprived them of their major patron and protector. Nehru then assumed a more prominent role in party affairs, and with the first general elections approaching, he sought to wrest control of the organization from the right wing. Threatening to resign from the Working Committee, Nehru forced Tandon to step down in his favor. In 1951 Nehru was elected president, thus bringing the party and Government under the control of a single leader. His emergence as undisputed leader of the Congress "confirmed the pre-eminent role of the Prime Minister and reinforced the boundaries of the office of Congress president, which had been revealed once more as limited strictly to organizational affairs with no special responsibility for policy-making."[17]

"THE PERIOD OF CENTRALIZATION AND CONVERGENCE"

Nehru's assumption of the Congress presidency marked the beginning of the period of centralization and convergence, 1951–63. His three-year joint tenure restored harmony between the party and the Government, but at the party's expense. The Government was responsible not to the party but to Parliament and the electorate. To hold the Prime Minister accountable to the party, Nehru argued, would reduce parliamentary democracy to a "mockery"; the party might "broadly affect"

[16] Kochanek, *The Congress Party*, p. xxiii.
[17] *Ibid.*, p. 53.

policy or "push it in this direction or that," but responsibility for decision-making lay with the Government.[18] In 1954 Nehru turned over the organization to a succession of "captive" party presidents who carried his personal endorsement—U. N. Dhebar, Indira Gandhi, Sanjiva Reddy, and D. Sanjivayya. Their dependence on the Prime Minister precluded any effective challenge to his leadership, and while some independent action was possible—for example, Mrs. Gandhi played an important role in bringing down the Communist ministry in Kerala in 1959—the Congress president was frequently described in this period as "a glorified office boy of the Congress central government headed by the prime minister."[19]

Under Nehru the Working Committee was brought under the dominance of the parliamentary wing, the most powerful chief ministers and important Central Cabinet ministers forming the core of its membership. It

> came to play an important role in providing policy leadership to the party organization, in coordinating party-government relations, and in accommodating the conflicting demands of Congress leaders representing the broadening base of the party. The Working Committee became the sounding board by which the Prime Minister could test the acceptability of new policies as well as an important feedback mechanism by which to assess the reactions of party and state leaders.[20]

In the period of transition the Working Committee had virtually no control over the state governments, but Nehru sought to use the committee for the direction of state Congress ministries. The Working Committee became the agent of arbitration, conciliation, and mediation in an effort to achieve a new national consensus on the Congress economic program. Divergent factions were drawn under the Congress umbrella through persuasion, reconciliation, and accommodation. In the process, however, as power devolved to leaders at the state level, Dhebar warned of the dangers of bossism, entrenchment, and indiscipline.[21]

While the Congress at the national level was made subordinate to the Government, and political reality receded in the face of a complacent and romantic ideology, the lower levels of the party organization were gradually captured by a new generation of politicians. These men were brokers who, in understanding both traditional society and machine techniques, provided the channels of linkage between the villages and the modern political system. The party organization became the vehicle for their own advancement, the agent of upward mobility for an aspiring new leadership. For some, the movement into the party

[18] *Ibid.*, p. 57.
[19] Frank Moraes, *India Today* (New York: Macmillan, 1960), p. 98.
[20] Kochanek, *The Congress Party*, p. 307.
[21] *Ibid.*, p. 64.

organization was from an established base of traditional influence within their village or samiti. For others, politics was a vocation. K. Kamaraj Nadar, for example, rose from the bottom of the party organization to secure control of the Tamilnad Congress Committee. In the states the new leadership gained control of the organization, challenged the old order, and took over the government, its power and patronage. Kamaraj, boss of the Congress in Tamil Nadu, ousted Rajagopalachari as Chief Minister. C. B. Gupta in Uttar Pradesh, Chavan in Maharashtra, and Patnaik in Orissa were all organization men who, with the party machinery in their hands, took control of their state governments and came to wield considerable power at the national level.

"THE PERIOD OF DIVERGENCE"

The changes evidenced in the states made their appearance at the national level in 1963 with the introduction of the Kamaraj Plan. This opened what Kochanek has called the period of divergence. Kamaraj proposed "that leading Congressmen who are in Government should voluntarily relinquish their ministerial posts and offer themselves for full-time organizational work."[22] All chief ministers and Central Cabinet ministers submitted their resignations. The decision as to which resignations to accept was left to Nehru. Six chief ministers, including Kamaraj, and six Cabinet ministers were asked to take up organizational work. The Kamaraj Plan was generally regarded as a device to get rid of Morarji Desai, considered conservative and rigid, but its more significant consequence was the induction of state party bosses into positions of power at the national level, with Kamaraj at the helm of the organization as new Congress president. The plan "restored" the prestige and power of the central organization, which had been virtually eclipsed under the dominance of Nehru.[23]

The Congress and the Politics of Succession to the Prime Ministership

Following the Kamaraj Plan in 1963, in an effort to deny Desai the Congress presidency and to isolate him further from power, a group of powerful state leaders (Kamaraj, Atulya Ghosh from West Bengal, Sanjiva Reddy from Andhra, S. Nijalingappa from Karnataka, and S. K. Patil from Bombay), informally organized as "the Syndicate," united behind Kamaraj as the man most likely to provide stable and effective party leadership. In January 1964 Nehru suffered a stroke. G. L. Nanda and T. T. Krishnamachari, the senior ministers, assumed responsibility for those areas normally handled by the Prime Minister. The question "After Nehru, who?" was now raised more poignantly than ever before. Lal Bahadur Shastri, who had left the Cabinet under

[22] Quoted in Kochanek, *The Congress Party*, pp. 78–79.
[23] Kothari, "The Congress 'System' in India," p. 16.

the Kamaraj Plan, was now brought back as Minister without Portfolio. With Nehru's blessing and the powerful support of the Syndicate, Shastri occupied a strategic position. Four months later, on May 27, 1964, Nehru was dead. Home Minister Nanda was designated to act as Prime Minister until the Congress Parliamentary Party, composed of all Congress MPs, could elect a successor.

Although Shastri held majority support within the CPP, Desai sought to prevent Shastri's election. Maneuvering for a unanimous election, Kamaraj called a meeting of an enlarged Congress Working Committee. The forty-two-member body, which Michael Brecher has called "the Grand Council of the Republic,"[24] included the regular members of the Working Committee, the chief ministers, the leaders of the Congress party in Parliament, senior Cabinet ministers, and invited members such as Krishna Menon. The election was to be held two days later and the Congress president was authorized to "ascertain the consensus of opinion on the question of the choice of Leader of the Congress Party in Parliament and tender his advice accordingly."[25] In the next forty-eight hours, Kamaraj consulted all the chief ministers, the members of the Working Committee, and many members of the CPP. Shastri's election was assured, and in response to overwhelming pressure, Morarji Desai agreed to second Shastri's nomination to secure his unanimous election.[26] An example of party discipline, the Congress effort to avoid a contest reflected a search for consensus that not only is traditional in Indian political culture but was characteristic of the party's struggle against the British when it could not afford an open split in its ranks.

Desai had had the support of a diverse coalition—the traditional right wing, business elements, harijans, and, in addition, disaffected leftists led by Krishna Menon. Shastri, on the other hand, was backed by the leaders of the South and the non-Hindi states of Maharashtra and West Bengal; moreover, as a native of Uttar Pradesh he represented the Hindi heartland, despite the fact that the major leaders of this region were for Desai. The Syndicate played the critical role in coalescing the diverse interests behind Shastri and in securing consensus. According to Michael Brecher,

> the outcome was determined by peaceful competition among various interest groups. The decisive factor was the clear majority for Shastri in the three key institutional groups, the Working Committee, the state party machines, and in the CPP, superimposed on the relatively inarticulate but known choice of Shastri by the mass public.[27]

[24] *Nehru's Mantle: The Politics of Succession in India* (New York: Praeger, 1966), p. 61.
[25] Quoted in Kochanek, *The Congress Party*, p. 89.
[26] For an analysis of the succession, see Brecher, *Nehru's Mantle.*
[27] *Nehru's Mantle*, p. 88.

The Syndicate gave political form to that national preference.

The succession served also to reveal the shift in political gravity toward the states. The state party organizations occupied a pivotal position —in the role of the Chief Ministers in the decisions of "the Grand Council of the Republic" and in their control over blocs of votes within the Congress Parliamentary Party.[28]

In January 1966, less than two years after he had taken office, Shastri died, just hours after having signed a truce with Pakistan at Tashkent. Faced with the second succession, Kamaraj no longer commanded the position of strength from which he had directed the events following Nehru's death. The Syndicate had lost its cohesion: "The politics of unanimity" had given way "to the politics of overt conflict."[29] Kamaraj sought to weld a consensus behind Indira Gandhi by means of massive pressure conveyed indirectly through the Chief Ministers. The Syndicate had no choice but to go along. Kamaraj had again emerged as "king-maker," but the process had been more difficult. Morarji Desai, against the advice of his colleagues, pressed for an open contest. He would not step down in favor of another as he had done in 1964. In a vote, the first contested election for leadership, Mrs. Gandhi overwhelmed Desai, 355 to 169. The successions revealed the capacity of the Congress to absorb conflict, but at the same time exposed deep division within the party.

The ascendancy of Kamaraj indicated a revitalized party, and his role in engineering the two successions underscored the more prominent position the party sought in the post-Nehru years. The party presidency was certainly enhanced, but "while it is impossible not to recognize that Kamaraj added new stature and authority to the Congress presidency, played an influential role in policy-making, and enjoyed considerable autonomy in organizational affairs, it is also clear that his position was in many ways subordinate to that of the Prime Minister."[30] Indira Gandhi was not going to allow herself to become the puppet of the Syndicate, and her relations with Kamaraj became increasingly cool.

The struggle for succession revealed not merely the power of the party but, even more critically, the pivotal position of the state Congress organizations. The result was a polycentric system of decision-making in which power was dispersed among several competing but overlapping groups: the Working Committee, the chief ministers, the Cabinet, and the Congress party in Parliament. With the national leadership split, the Working Committee could no longer effectively play its mediating role. Dominant factions in the states sought to consolidate their positions. Dissident state factions, "feeling isolated from power within the party because of the inability of the central leadership to intervene to

[28] *Ibid.*, p. 72.
[29] *Ibid.*, p. 205.
[30] Kochanek, *The Congress Party*, p. 93.

protect them," defected from the party.[31] The dilemma confronting the Congress was basic: "To dominate, Congress must accommodate; yet accommodation encourages incoherence which destroys the capacity to dominate."[32] The more autonomous the Congress party in each state became, with its effectiveness derived from local resources, the more vulnerable it was to displacement by regional opposition parties operating from the same sources of strength.

The defeats sustained by the Congress in the 1967 elections again opened conflict over party leadership and control of the new Government. The Congress was in disarray, with dissension and defections on all sides. The electoral reverses, however, "had generated tremendous pressures for a consensus on the leadership issue in order to avoid a schism in the already weakened party."[33] Kamaraj, despite his own defeat at the polls, achieved a bargain settlement by which Mrs. Gandhi was unanimously reelected Prime Minister, while Desai was appointed Deputy Prime Minister. Reinforcing the consensus, Nijalingappa, Chief Minister of Karnataka, was chosen the new Congress president. Mrs. Gandhi, freed of the pressures of the old state bosses by their election defeats, emerged with new strength.

Crisis and Split

The 1969 presidential election increased the tension between the Government and the organizational wings of the party to the point of open conflict and initiated the four-month crisis that split the eighty-four-year-old Indian National Congress.[34] Challenging the Syndicate, Indira Gandhi sought to reestablish securely the dominance of the Prime Minister within the party. To gain the initiative Mrs. Gandhi sent a note of "stray thoughts" to the Working Committee urging a more aggressive stance toward economic policy—nationalization of major commercial banks, effective implementation of land reforms, ceilings on urban income and property, and curbs on industrial monopolies. The Syndicate, lacking ideological cohesiveness, was divided in its reaction. In alliance with Desai, however, the Syndicate was determined to retain its hold over the party and to secure the Congress presidential nomination for its own man, Sanjiva Reddy, Speaker of the Lok Sabha, in opposition to Mrs. Gandhi's preference for V.V. Giri, the seventy-four-year-old Acting President.[35]

[31] *Ibid.*, p. 315.
[32] W. H. Morris-Jones, "Dominance and Dissent," *Government and Opposition*, Vol. 1 (July–September 1966), p. 460.
[33] Kochanek, *The Congress Party*, p. 412.
[34] For a detailed account of the events leading up to and surrounding the schism, see Robert L. Hardgrave, Jr., "The Congress in India: Crisis and Split," *Asian Survey*, Vol. 10 (March 1970), pp. 256–62.
[35] By custom the nomination is made by the eight-member Central Parliamentary Board elected by the AICC.

When Reddy was nominated by Congress, V. V. Giri entered the presidential contest as an independent. He resigned as Acting President and, in accordance with the constitution, was replaced by the Chief Justice of India, M. Hidayatullah. In a vigorous campaign, Giri drew the support of the Samyukta Socialist Party, the DMK, the Muslim League, the two wings of the Communist party, and almost all elements of the United Front governments of Kerala and West Bengal. Swatantra, Jana Sangh, and the Bharatiya Kranti Dal of Uttar Pradesh jointly put forward former Finance Minister C. D. Deshmukh as their candidate. The Praja Socialists sat the fence between Giri and Deshmukh.

Within the Congress the Prime Minister sought to retain the initiative. She relieved Morarji Desai of his Finance portfolio, deepening the wedge between the two groups, and to save his "self-respect," Desai resigned as Deputy Prime Minister. Indira Gandhi then announced the nationalization of fourteen major commercial banks. The purpose of nationalization, she said, was to provide more equitable access to bank credit, particularly for small farmers and artisans. The banks, holding some 70 percent of the country's total bank assets, were largely in the hands of a few dominant business families, the Birlas, Tatas, Dalmias, and Jains. Nationalization involved the expenditure of little political capital and reaped widespread support for the Prime Minister. She called the action "only the beginning of a bitter struggle between the common people and the vested interests in the country."[36]

Although she had signed Reddy's nomination papers, Mrs. Gandhi had yet to come out clearly in favor of the party's conservative nominee. Indeed, there was speculation that Reddy would try to use the untested powers of the Presidency against the Prime Minister, if not to unseat her altogether. Whereas Reddy's election at first seemed assured with the Congress holding 52 percent of the votes, increasing rumors of defections to Giri caused considerable unease among Syndicate members. Within one week of the election, party president Nijalingappa issued a whip instructing all Congress MPs and MLAs to vote for Reddy and requested Mrs. Gandhi to make an immediate statement of support for the Congress nominee. The Prime Minister, leader of the Parliamentary Party, refused to issue a whip for Reddy, and her supporters called for a "free vote" of conscience in the election. More than half of the Congress MPs indicated their favor for a free vote; some publicly tore up the whip notice. Support for Giri was now in the open.

Fifteen candidates, with three leading contenders, stood for the election, held on August 16. Neither Reddy nor Giri achieved a majority on the first count; the second preferences of the Deshmukh ballots were then tabulated. On the second count, Giri was declared elected.

Greeted with tremendous popular enthusiasm, Giri's election left the Syndicate in disarray and opened an intraparty struggle cast in an

[36] *Hindu* (Madras), August 5, 1969.

ideological mold. The Syndicate was fundamentally nonideological, but conservative in temper and tied to a base of support among landed and big business interests. Indira Gandhi, if committed to socialism, had among her followers some of highly questionable ideological credentials. The Chief Ministers, most of whom had aligned with her, had never been particularly eager to implement a socialist policy of land reform and risk the alienation of their landed source of money and votes. Their assessment of Congress prospects, however, prompted an inclination to move slightly to the left and a recognition that long-professed Congress policies if left unimplemented would leave Congressmen behind at the polls at the next election.

In November 1969 the Congress was torn apart after four months of intraparty conflict. The truncated leadership of the party organization, isolating itself from the will of the majority, expelled Prime Minister Indira Gandhi, daughter of Nehru. The Syndicated-dominated Working Committee instructed the Congress Parliamentary Party to elect a new leader, but by an overwhelming majority, the CPP reaffirmed support for the leadership of Mrs. Gandhi. Syndicate supporters in Parliament, meeting separately at the residence of Morarji Desai, formed a rival Congress Parliamentary Party. Against the 65 Congressmen in opposition in the Lok Sabha, the Prime Minister held the support of 226, but her Government no longer commanded an absolute majority. The Congress had split; the verdict would be pronounced at the polls. In the centenary year of Mahatma Gandhi's birth, two Congress parties fought for the tattered standard of the nationalist movement.

The "Indira Wave"—Swell and Decline

Calling elections in March 1971, a year before the Fourth Lok Sabha would have completed its full term, Indira Gandhi made a direct appeal to the Indian voters. In the first parliamentary election "de-linked" from state assembly contests, she sought to raise national issues, but the major issue was the Prime Minister herself. In a campaign pledged to eliminate poverty, the new Congress won a sweeping victory with a two-thirds majority of the seats in Parliament.

Indira Gandhi, however, was not yet able to pursue a program of economic transformation. On March 25, 1971, the force of the Pakistani army came down upon the people of East Bengal, and in the next nine months, ten million refugees poured from East Pakistan into India, creating a situation that for India was economically, socially, and politically unacceptable. It was imperative that the refugees return to their homes in East Bengal. While the Bengali guerrillas of the Mukti Bahini, in their struggle for independence, would in all likelihood have succeeded, only India's military intervention could have provided the leverage to insure the return of these refugees, most of whom were Hindu and might well not be welcomed back. Moreover, hundreds of thousands of Bengalis had already been killed, and in the Indian judg-ment a prolongation of Pakistani rule in Bengal could only bring a greater loss of life. With these considerations, in December 1971 the Indian army crossed the border into East Bengal, and with the fall of Dacca two weeks later, the State of Bangladesh came into being.

India was euphoric over its victory. Humiliated militarily, broken as a nation, Pakistan no longer challenged Indian hegemony in the sub-continent. A new opportunity for stability and development was seen on the horizon of Pax India. Ebullient with success, Prime Minister Indira Gandhi now sought to secure her strength in the Indian states, and in March 1972 elections were held for the legislative assemblies in all but four states. Almost across the board the results brought a land-slide victory. The new Congress captured more than 70 percent of the assembly seats. Confirming the mandate of the 1971 parliamentary elections, Congress control in the states now gave Indira Gandhi un-precedented power. Freed from the interference of the old Syndicate bosses, freed from the vulnerability of reliance on allied parties, the Prime Minister now appeared to be in a position to implement her pledge to the people, to fulfill their demands for social justice and to meet their expectations of economic betterment. The "Indira wave" had overcome the powers of reaction. In the eyes of the people Mrs. Gandhi was no longer thwarted by an effective opposition to a program of radical economic and social transformation. Even the obstruction of the conservative Supreme Court could now be overridden by parlia-mentary majorities. The Congress could no longer offer excuses for in-action. "The country has taken her at her word," the *Hindustan Times* wrote, "and she will now have to deliver her promises."

Herein lay her Achilles' heel. The great electoral victories reflected more the weakness of the opposition than the secure power of the new Congress. Congress had won only 48 percent of the vote in the states, even though it had won 70 percent of the seats. Many of the new Congressmen were young, inexperienced, and lacking in political clout. Virtually appointed by the Center, they lacked any base of local power. The new Chief Ministers were particularly vulnerable to challenge from the power of entrenched local interests and the dominant factions of the state. Within eighteen months of the 1972 elections, six Chief Ministers had been eased out of office and President's Rule imposed in four states. In relying heavily on personal charisma and populist politics, Indira Gandhi destroyed the boss-structure of the old Congress, but she did not replace it with an effective structure linking the Center with the local party units. "Moreover, the tendency to concentrate power at one centre," write Joshi and Desai, "reduced tolerance of factional com-petition and the decline in the autonomy of state party structures have led to a weak and attenuated party and lack of stable loyalty struc-tures."[37]

[37] Ram Joshi and Kirtidev Desai, "The Opposition: Problems and Prospects," *Economic and Political Weekly*, Vol. 8 (October 20, 1973), pp. 1913–22.

Despite the party split, the new Congress was still under an umbrella of highly disparate interests. The ideological polarization so many had foreseen never took place, and the conservatives by no means had lost leverage on the Prime Minister or on the Congress Working Committee. In the period after the 1971 elections Congressmen who had followed the Syndicate bosses sought to save themselves from political oblivion by returning to the Congress fold, and Indira Gandhi herself opened negotiations with Kamaraj to secure an electoral understanding in Tamil Nadu against the DMK—discussions that many saw as leading to Kamaraj's possible reentry into the Congress or even to a reunited party.

But whatever political constraints may have been imposed on the Congress in implementing the program of garibi hatao, the fundamental constraint was economic scarcity. "We do not have all the time in the world," Indira Gandhi said soon after the 1972 state elections. "Maybe we have only three or four years to show concrete results. If we fail, whether because of the mistakes of the government or business or industry, or because any one section is more concerned about their rights than those of others, we will all topple together—not any one section, but the entire country."[38]

The Socialist Parties

The Indian socialist parties are the direct descendants of the Congress Socialist Party, founded in 1934 in response to Congress failure to pursue a more revolutionary policy. The Socialists sought to gain control of the Congress, within which they had organized, through a process of gradual displacement of right-wing leaders by the "composite leadership" of the left. They failed to build sufficient numerical strength to challenge Congress leadership, however, and although the Socialists gained a position of influence during the Quit India movement, their strength was soon dissipated by their resignation from the Congress Working Committee and refusal to participate in the Constituent Assembly or to accept seats in Nehru's Cabinet.[39]

Nehru and an increasingly sympathetic Gandhi wanted to accommodate the Socialist leaders, but the Patel group blocked further Socialist incursions into party leadership, and following Gandhi's death brought a resolution by the All-India Congress Committee outlawing political parties within the Congress. At this point the Socialists, confident of their own strength, withdrew from the Congress. The new Socialist Party sought to weld an alliance of the left for "nationalism, socialism,

---

[38] Speech before the Federation of Indian Chambers of Commerce, reported in the *Times of India*, March 26, 1972.
[39] Thomas A. Rusch, "Dynamics of Socialist Leadership in India," in Richard L. Park and Irene Tinker, eds., *Leadership and Political Institutions in India* (Princeton, N.J.: Princeton University Press, 1959), p. 191.

and democracy"; it aimed to challenge the Congress through a program of Gandhian "constructive work," parliamentary activity, and nonviolent agitation—"the spade, the vote, and prison."[40]

The 1951 elections dealt the Socialists a severe blow. Although the party gained a little more than 10 percent of the vote in the parliamentary elections, it secured only 12 seats out of 489 in the Lok Sabha, making it only the third strongest party, after the Communists with 16 seats. They had grossly overestimated their own strength and had failed to foresee the splintering of opposition strength among the various parties and independent candidates.[41] In order to salvage their position, the Socialists negotiated a merger with the similarly disillusioned Kisan Mazdoor Praja Party, a collection of Congress dissidents led by Archarya J. B. Kripalani. The KMPP, which had withdrawn from the Congress on the eve of the election, was Gandhian in orientation. Its strength lay primarily in the eastern and southern states, complementing the concentration of Socialist representation in the North and West. The two parties minimized the differences between them by weakening the Socialist platform, and in 1952 formed the Praja Socialist Party. It was soon joined by a section of the Forward Bloc, a West Bengal party devoted to the political memory of Subhas Chandra Bose.

The Praja Socialist Party

The Praja Socialist Party was an uneasy but pragmatic mixture of various ideological positions. The Congress Socialists had reflected three divergent but overlapping tendencies—Marxism, democratic socialism, and Gandhism. Over the years, however, their socialism took on an increasingly Indian character. Emphasis on Gandhian notions of decentralization, nonviolence, constructive work, and the land-gift movement "turned the Socialists away from their past preoccupation with solely Western writings as the basis of their ideology."[42] Jayaprakash Narayan, an early Marxist and the most prominent of the Praja Socialist leaders, fell increasingly under Gandhian influence. In 1954, skeptical of the promise of industrialization and "progress," Narayan withdrew from active politics to dedicate his life to Bhoodan and the constructive work of Vinoba Bhave. An advocate of "partyless democracy," Narayan now worked to achieve the "people's socialism" of Sarvodaya.

Before his withdrawal, Narayan had entered discussions with Nehru about a closer relationship between the PSP and the Congress. Given the wide areas of agreement between the two parties, socialist leader Asoka Mehta argued that increased cooperation was demanded by the "political compulsions of a backward society." His argument, basically,

---

[40] *Ibid.*, pp. 200–01.

[41] *Ibid.*, p. 202.

[42] Myron Weiner, *Party Politics in India* (Princeton, N.J.: Princeton University Press, 1957), p. 30.

was that a society of scarce resources such as India cannot afford the luxury of opposition. The national conference of the PSP in 1953 rejected the Mehta thesis in favor of Dr. Rammanohar Lohia's line that the party adopt a position of "equi-distance" form both the Congress and the Communists. Tension between the two wings of the PSP increased when the Congress declared its advocacy of a socialistic pattern of society. To distinguish himself clearly from the Congress, Lohia took a more revolutionary stance. His efforts to organize a militant wing within the PSP soon led to his expulsion and the formation of a new Socialist Party.

Even after the departure of the Lohia group, the relationship of the party to the Congress remained the central issue within the PSP. Mehta continued to push for closer cooperation with the Congress, and in 1963 he accepted the deputy chairmanship of the Planning Commission. Viewing this as a step calculated to bring Congress-PSP consolidation, the PSP national executive, badly split, voted to expel Mehta from the party. With his followers, Mehta reentered the Congress, and the PSP accepted a bid from Lohia's Socialist Party for merger. In 1964 the Samyukta Socialist Party was formed. Within one year, however, disaffected PSP leaders charged the SSP with developing a personality cult around Lohia, with supporting alliances with communal and antidemocratic groups, and with fanaticism in its pro-Hindi language policy.[43] They withdrew to reestablish the PSP. In 1971, the PSP secured only two seats in the Lok Sabha elections and 1 percent of the vote. Moreover, the party was crippled by defections to Congress. In yet another attempt to achieve unity, the PSP and SSP again merged into a reconstituted Socialist Party.[44]

The Samyukta Socialist Party and the Socialist Party Reconstituted

In 1964, the Samyukta Socialist Party emerged as the leading party of democratic socialism in India. The SSP described itself as a revolutionary party for radical social change. It was committed to building socialism in the Third World. It advocated the decentralization of power in small units of direct democracy—the village, the town, and the district. The party had a pronounced egalitarian ideology: It would restrict private ownership to property, place a ceiling on all incomes, strictly limit the ownership of land and redistribute excess lands among poor peasants and landless laborers, and reserve upward of 60 percent of seats in government and education for members of the backward classes. The policy of the SSP, while emphasizing the development of regional languages, was generally associated with the advocacy of Hindi. The

---

[43] Benjamin N. Schoenfeld, "The Birth of India's Samyukta Socialist Party," *Pacific Affairs*, Vol. 38 (1965–66), p. 266.
[44] Lewis P. Fickett, Jr., "The Praja Socialist Party of India—1952–1972: A Final Assessment," *Asian Survey*, Vol. 8 (September 1973), pp. 826–32.

party vigorously opposed the continued use of English, which it regarded as an unwelcome reminder of foreign oppression and a badge of
national humiliation. Most important, it believed, English is undemocratic in perpetuating and even increasing the social and economic distance between classes.

The SSP was actively committed to the practice of civil disobedience
and used the technique of satyagraha against the Congress Government.
On the basis of limited tactical fronts, the SSP sought to unite the
opposition parties—of all positions—to bring an end to Congress rule.
The SSP electoral policy of joint fronts with a minimum program
("non-Congressism," as it was called) was vindicated in the widespread
defeats inflicted upon the Congress in the 1967 elections. In that election, support for the SSP was spotty and regional (concentrated particularly in Bihar), but it had a wide social base with enormous
potential for expansion. It was rural, disproportionately young (drawing
heavily from voters between twenty-six and thirty-five years of age), and
predominantly poor. Support came from the lowest castes, untouchables
and tribals, from illiterates, and from poor peasants and landless laborers—the classes to which the SSP had directed its strongest appeal.[45]
But the SSP's cynical participation in the 1971 anti-Congress Four
Party Alliance with the Jana Sangh, Swatantra, and the Congress (O)
tarnished the party's radical image and cut deeply into the base of
support it had established in 1967.

The party had a heterogeneous character, and much of its cohesion
was dependent on personal loyalty to Dr. Lohia. Following his death in
1967, the Samyukta Socialists were torn by factional conflict, and the
party suffered serious electoral defeats in 1971, declining from 23 seats
in the Lok Sabha in 1967 to only 3. In August the SSP merged with the
PSP to form the Socialist Party. Less than a year later, in the 1972 assembly elections, the Socialist Party won only fifty-seven seats, a decline
due less to a dramatic loss of votes than to the pattern of alliances.
The dominant Samyukta faction, led by Madhu Limaye and George
Fernandes, had favored merger with the PSP and abandonment of
"non-Congressism" in favor of alliances only with parties of the left.
The Raj Narain faction, concentrated in Uttar Pradesh where continued alliance with the Congress (O) and the Jana Sangh offered some
prospect of power, opposed merger and pushed for a continuing strategy
of "all parties against the ruling Congress." Failure to resolve the conflict culminated once again in a party split, this time with the recrea-
tion of the SSP by the Raj Narain group[46] and its subsequent merger,
in 1974, with the Bharatiya Lok Dal. (See section on Other Parties.)

---

[45] Sheth, "Profiles of Party Support in 1967," p. 285.
[46] See Paul R. Brass, "Leadership Conflict and the Disintegration of the Indian
Socialist Movement: Personal Ambition, Power, and Policy," in B. N. Pandey,
ed., *Leadership in South Asia* (forthcoming).

The Communist Parties

Since its inception in 1928 the Communist Party of India has been divided in its social character, its base of support, and its ideological stance. These divisions reflect its origins in the regional organizations of the Workers' and Peasants' party. In its early years the CPI, closely tied to the Communist Party of Great Britain, was largely under Comintern control and followed Moscow directives with dutiful twists and turns. During the 1930s the party adopted a tactic of "the united front from above" in cooperation with the nationalist movement. Entering the Congress Socialist Party, Communists soon secured leadership in the Socialist organization, particularly in the South, where they gained effective control. Expelled in 1939, they took much of the CSP membership in the South with them. The final break with the Congress came with the Nazi invasion of the Soviet Union and the CPI's call for cooperation with the British in what was deemed an anti-imperialist war. The Congress chose noncooperation, and as Congress leaders languished in jail the CPI infiltrated student, peasant, and labor organizations, expanding its membership from five thousand in 1942 to fifty-three thousand by 1946. Although the CPI effectively gained control of a number of mass organizations, its participation in the war effort, its continued attack on Gandhi, and its support for the Muslim League demand for Pakistan tainted the party as antinational and minimized its influence.

Closed out from above, the CPI adopted a tactic of "the united front from below" in alliance with workers and peasants against the Congress leadership. In 1948 P. C. Joshi was replaced as general secretary by B. T. Ranadive, with the advancement of a more militant "left" line. Under his leadership the CPI embarked on a course of revolution—with strikes, sabotage, and urban violence. Following the Russian model, Ranadive emphasized the working class as the instrument of revolution and discounted the peasant uprising in the Telengana region of Hyderabad. The Andhra Communists, however, pushed for the adoption of a Maoist line of revolution from the countryside and obtained a short-term victory for the tactic of rural insurrection with the election of Rajeshwar Rao as general secretary in 1950. The party became increasingly isolated, party membership declined, and in various states the CPI was outlawed.

During this period Nehru was denounced as a "running dog of imperialism" and the Congress, in both its foreign and its domestic policy, as the reactionary captive of capitalist and landlord elements. In the early 1950s, however, the official attitude of the Soviet Union toward the Nehru Government began to change. The CPI was officially advised to abandon its "adventurist" tactics. The policy shift was welcomed by those within the party, notably P. C. Joshi, S. A. Dange, and Ajoy Ghosh, who favored participation in the forthcoming general elections. In 1951 the revisionist line won out, with the selection of Ajoy Ghosh as general secretary of the party. Ghosh, from a centrist position, led the party toward "constitutional communism." The CPI sanctioned Indian foreign policy and extended its full support to all "progressive" policies and measures of the government.[47] Its willingness to engage in parliamentary politics and to seek alliances with parties of the left in a democratic front seemed vindicated by the success of the Kerala Communists in 1957 and the formation of the first democratically elected Communist government under E. M. S. Namboodiripad. The Amritsar thesis, drafted by the party conference in 1958, set forth the nationalist credentials of the CPI:

> The Communist Party of India strives to achieve full Democracy and Socialism by peaceful means. It considers that by developing a powerful mass movement, by winning a majority in Parliament and by backing it with mass sanctions, the working class and its allies can overcome the resistance of the forces of reaction and insure that Parliament becomes an instrument of people's will for effecting fundamental changes in the economic, social, and State structure.[48]

The Amritsar thesis only papered over fundamental tensions within the party between the right and left, between those favoring cooperation with the Congress and the "national bourgeoisie" and those advocating revolutionary struggle for the defeat of the Congress. Its relationship to the Congress in strategy and tactics posed a dilemma for the CPI. It was obliged, on the one hand, to fulfill its ideological commitment to the international Communist movement but, on the other, sought to retain a nationalist identity.[49]

The internal balance of the CPI was soon threatened. In Kerala, sparked by the Education Bill, widespread agitation was launched against the Communist government, bringing Central intervention and the proclamation of President's Rule. The left saw it as patent that the Congress would never allow serious socialist reform, but the fate of the Kerala government only served to define more clearly the polarities emerging on the Sino-Indian question. The Tibet uprising in 1959 and

---

[47] The evolution of this strategy is detailed in Victor M. Fic, *Peaceful Transition to Communism in India* (Bombay: Nachiketa Publications, 1969).

[48] Constitution of the Communist Party of India, adopted at the Extraordinary Party Congress, Amritsar, April 1958 (New Delhi: Communist Party of India, 1958), p. 4.

[49] Ralph Retzlaff, "Revisionism and Dogmatism in the Communist Party of India," in Robert A. Scalapino, ed., *The Communist Revolution in Asia* (Englewood Cliffs, N.J.: Prentice-Hall, 1965), p. 309.

the CPI's support for Chinese actions had already brought popular reaction against the party in India. The border clashes brought internal conflict into the open. Headed by S. A. Dange, a leading exponent of the right, or nationalist, faction, the national council of the CPI recognized Indian claims to all territories below the McMahon line, the border demarcation. The left regarded this as a betrayal of international proletarian unity. The positions, set in the context of increasing Sino-Soviet conflict, placed the left in what was regarded as the pro-Chinese camp.

In early 1962, as conflict deepened within the CPI, Ajoy Ghosh, the balancer, died. The factional settlement—election of Dange to the newly created post of chairman, with Namboodiripad, the centrist, as general secretary—proved fragile. In the wake of the Chinese invasion of Indian territory, as criticism of the CPI mounted, the national council resolved to condemn the Chinese action as "aggression" and to call upon the Indian people to "unite in defense of the motherland." In protest the leftists resigned from the party secretariat, and as the situation deteriorated, Namboodiripad submitted his resignation as general secretary of the party and as editor of *New Age*, the official party publication. In response to the widespread arrests of leftist Communist cadres, the CPI sought to reorganize state party units under rightist control. Their actions served only to stimulate the creation of parallel left structures outside the disciplinary organization of the CPI.

At the national council meeting in 1964 the left attempted, without success, to oust party chairman Dange. They came armed with a letter, allegedly written by Dange in 1924, in which he had offered to co-operate with the British in exchange for his release from jail. Denouncing the letter as a forgery the council refused to consider the charges. The left and center, led by Namboodiripad and Jyoti Basu, staged a walkout and appealed to the party to repudiate Dange and the "reformist" line. The split became final when all signatories to the appeal were suspended from the party. The left, organized as the Communist Party of India (Marxist), claimed to be the legitimate Communist party of India. Although there was little real evidence to link the CPM with China, the Marxists were viewed as pro-Peking, and in 1965 leading CPM members were arrested throughout India and vaguely charged with promoting "an internal revolution to synchronize with a fresh Chinese attack."[50]

The CPM favored a tactic of united front from below, of alliance with peasants and workers to defeat the Congress, which it regarded as a party of the bourgeoisie and landlord classes, dominated by the big bourgeoisie. Elections were to be used as a means to mobilize the masses;

---

[50] Home Minister Nanda, quoted in the *Hindu Weekly Review*, January 11, 1965, p. 11.

the constitution was to be used as "an instrument of struggle."[51] The Marxists sought to "break the Constitution from within."[52]

The regular CPI, closely associated with trade unionists, retained control of the official party organs and identified itself with Moscow. It sought to advance the cause of a "national democratic front" with progressive elements of the nationalist bourgeoisie in order to "complete the anti-imperialist, anti-feudal, democratic revolution."[53] Following the Congress split in 1969, the CPI gave strong, if cautious, support to Indira Gandhi. By 1974, however, the party had begun to take an increasingly critical stance toward the Congress, and its support for the railway workers in the 1974 strike served to place some distance between the CPI and the Prime Minister.

Although the Communist party has had an all-India organization, at least theoretically subject to the discipline of "democratic centralism," its structure, like that of the Congress, has been essentially regional in orientation. Neither Communist party has been able to establish a firm base in the Hindi heartland. This may be related, in part, to the Communists' devotion to the Soviet treatment of the "nationalities problem," which in India stresses the development of regional identity. Tactics have been determined more by the local situation than by directive from the top. In the general elections, state party units have frequently adopted variant tactics, for example, supporting "progressive" Congressmen in one state and opposing all Congressmen in another.

Communist support is proportionately distributed among both urban and rural areas. It is highest among low caste groups but low among Muslims and other religious minorities. Although the CPM has begun to make significant inroads among Scheduled Castes and Tribes—notably in Kerala, Andhra, and Tamil Nadu—these classes remain disproportionately in the Congress camp. Survey data reveal that predominant support for the two Communist parties "lies among the new and young voters, both illiterates and highly educated, both the middle-class professionals and white collar workers and the industrial and agricultural working class, and the 'lowest' and 'high' income groups."[54]

In the parliamentary elections, the CPI gradually increased its support from 3.30 percent in 1952 to 9.96 percent in 1962. The party split little affected the distribution of the vote, for in 1967, the CPI received 5.19 percent and the CPM, 4.21 percent. In 1971 the CPI and CPM secured 4.73 and 5.12 percent respectively. Communist support has not been evenly distributed regionally. Only in West Bengal, Kerala, and

[51] E. M. S. Namboodiripad, *The Republican Constitution in the Struggle for Socialism*, R. R. Kale Memorial Lecture (Poona: Gokhale Institute of Politics and Economics, 1968), p. 1.

[52] Joint statement of E. M. S. Namboodiripad and A. K. Gopalan, quoted in the *Hindu*, July 8, 1969.

[53] "Program of the Communist Party of India," *New Age* (January 10, 1965), p. 10.

[54] Sheth, "Profiles of Party Support in 1967," p. 285.

Andhra have Communists had a strong base of electoral support. Significantly, the CPM finds its greatest support in these areas of traditional Communist strength. In Kerala, where the two parties together polled about 33 percent of the assembly vote in 1967, the CPM secured nearly three times the support of the CPI. In West Bengal the CPM got about twice the vote of the CPI, with a combined vote of some 23 percent. In each state, the two Communist parties participated in the United Front against the Congress and dominated the subsequent coalition governments. In Kerala, Namboodiripad served as Chief Minister until 1969, when the Marxists were pushed out of the coalition and a new Government was formed under CPI leader Achutha Menon. (The Congress subsequently entered the coalition, marking the Congress' first participation in a coalition ministry and its first formal association with the CPI.) In Andhra, although both the CPI and CPM each gained about 7 percent of the vote in 1967, the two parties were engaged in bitter dispute, and the election marked the steady decline of Communist support from a high of nearly 30 percent in 1957.[55]

Although Marxist strength was concentrated primarily in three states so that it had a base of power, the two parties were close in the number of seats they gained in 1967 and again in 1971. In the 1971 parliamentary elections the CPM won 25 seats with 5.12 percent of the vote; the CPI won 23 seats with 4.73 percent. A year later, however, in the assembly elections the CPM, while holding its share of the vote, suffered a substantial loss of seats because of the pattern of party alliances —declining from the 127 seats it had held in 1967 to only 34, in contrast to the CPI's 112 seats.

Electoral success for the CPM opened the party to internal conflict, as extremists, arguing from an avowedly Maoist position, opposed participation in elections and Government in favor of armed struggle from the countryside. Soon after the elections in West Bengal, the Naxalbari uprising took place. The Marxists of the United Front Government in West Bengal were embarrassed and confused and, in containing the peasant rebellion, opened tensions within their ranks. In Bengal, Communist strength is concentrated in Calcutta, with support from the lower middle class, students, refugees, and workers. Its support in the rural areas has been minimal and the peasant revolt was regarded as adventurist.

Those supporting the uprising, the "Naxalites," found general favor from the Marxist organization in Andhra and from extremist factions within the CPM in various states. Naxalites of Kerala in late 1968 attempted to establish a base in the hills of Wynad in Malabar for the

---

[55] For analyses of the Communist movement in Kerala, West Bengal, and Andhra, see the chapters by Hardgrave, Franda, and Mohan Ram in Paul R. Brass and Marcus F. Franda, eds., *Radical Politics in South Asia* (Cambridge: M.I.T. Press, 1973). See also Franda, *Radical Politics in West Bengal* (Cambridge: M.I.T. Press, 1971).

formation of a Red Army on the Maoist model. The problem of restoring law and order lay with Namboodiripad and what the Chinese viewed as an increasingly revisionist Communist left. Various Naxalite factions came together in 1969 in the formation of a third Communist party, the Communist Party of India (Marxist-Leninist), avowedly Maoist and dedicated to revolution. Under the leadership of Charu Mazumdar, the CPI(M-L) took the lead in calling for immediate armed struggle, liberation of the countryside, and encirclement of the cities, following the Maoist formula. Naxalite solidarity soon foundered on Mazumdar's tactic of urban terrorism and annihilation of class enemies. Representing another "shade of Maoism," Nagi Reddy's Andhra Pradesh Revolutionary Communist Committee, supported armed struggle, but one based on an agrarian program and mass peasant involvement.[56]

The Communists in India, Bhabani Sen Gupta writes, confront a fundamental dilemma: they

> are pitted against a state and a political system created, devised, and evolved by the bourgeoisie to which the Communists could make little positive contribution of their own. The choice that has baffled them all these years is whether they should work within the political system and use its institutions and instruments to gradually change its qualitative character, or whether they should try to overthrow the system and replace it with another based on a radical realignment of productive relationships.
>
> The split . . . enables them to try three different tactics at the same time. The CPI tactic is to work with the progressive bourgeoisie so that eventually it can take over the system. The CPI(M) tactic is to wreck it from within. The Maoist groups intend to overthrow the system nibbling at it first in the countryside, and finally by leading an offensive front from liberated rural bases against the urban citadels of power.[57]

The Swatantra Party

The Swatantra (Freedom) Party was founded in 1959 to save India from "a pointless plunge to the left" and to protect "farm and family" against the inroads of "statism."[58] Among its founders were conserva-

---

[56] See Mohan Ram, *Maoism in India* (Delhi: Vikas, 1971), pp. 137–69. See also Marcus F. Franda, "India's Third Communist Party," *Asian Survey*, Vol. 9 (November 1969), pp. 797–817.

[57] *Communism in Indian Politics* (New York: Columbia University Press, 1972), pp. 404–05.

[58] Quoted in P. D. Devanandan and M. M. Thomas, eds., *Problems of Indian Democracy* (Bangalore: The Christian Institute for the Study of Religion and Society, 1962), p. 133.

tives, such as C. Rajagopalachari, the guiding force of the party, and former ICS member V. P. Menon, who had been Patel's lieutenant in the integration of states. A more liberal tint was provided by N. G. Ranga, leader of the Congress peasant movement in the 1930s, and M. R. Masani, who had abandoned his earlier socialist leanings to espouse free enterprise. The declared mission of the party is "to restore *dharma* to the country"—not the dharma of Hindu orthodoxy, but of the Indian business community. "In point of fact," Rajagopalachari once said, "my party is the political projection of the Forum of Free Enterprise."[59]

Since its support is derived largely from the business community and the rural establishment the party has been condemned as reactionary, but its founders were not defenders of orthodoxy or of militant Hindu nationalism. Their conservatism reflected not so much tradition as the old Moderate position within the Congress.[60] The liberalism of the party, however, in stressing the threat to freedom from the left has led the party to ignore the dangers to freedom from the right.[61] At the higher levels the party leadership has been moderate, secular, and nationalist, but at the lower levels it has frequently become the captive of reaction. In Rajasthan and Orissa, Swatantra strongholds, the party is dependent upon princes and landlords. In Rajasthan, Swatantra is led by the Maharani of Jaipur and dominated by the Rajputs. In Orissa the Ganatantra Parishad, led by princes, merged with Swatantra to form the mainstay of its support. Overall, the party's social base is overwhelmingly rural, and support has come predominantly from substantial landowners and their "clients" among low caste landless laborers. Because of its secular character, anti-Communism, and moderate stance toward Pakistan, Swatantra has also attracted some Muslim support.[62]

Howard L. Erdman describes Swatantra as "a holding company for local dissident groups" who have come together in an effort to provide effective opposition to Congress at the Center.[63] In the 1967 elections Swatantra secured forty-four seats to displace the Communists as the second largest party in the Lok Sabha. In Orissa the party emerged as the strongest in the state and took power in coalition with the dissident Jana Congress. Swatantra has entered into a variety of arrangements with the opposition, as with the DMK in Tamil Nadu, and Rajagopalachari once said he was prepared to "ally with the devil himself" in order to defeat the Congress.[64] In 1971 Swatantra was a member of the anti-Congress Four Party Alliance, but with 3.06 percent of the

[59] *Ibid.*, p. 136.
[60] Howard L. Erdman, "India's Swatantra Party," *Pacific Affairs* (Winter 1963–64), p. 399.
[61] Howard L. Erdman, *The Swatantra Party and Indian Conservatism* (Cambridge: Cambridge University Press, 1967), p. 257.
[62] Sheth, "Profiles of Party Support in 1967," p. 284.
[63] Erdman, *The Swatantra Party and Indian Conservatism*, p. 288.
[64] Quoted in *Link*, July 9, 1961.

vote, it secured only 8 seats. In the 1972 assembly elections, amidst negotiations for possible merger with the Congress(O) or the Jana Sangh, Swatantra suffered even greater losses. From the 257 seats it had won in 1967 it was reduced to a total of 15 seats. With the death of the party's founder, Rajagopalachari, later that year, Swatantra's continued existence became problematic. In 1974, following the party's decision to disband and merge into the Bharatiya Lok Dal, Swatantra split, with a faction led by Masani retaining the Swatantra name. In opposition to merger, Masani stated his belief that the movement led by Jayaprakash Narayan offered the only national alternative to Congress.

The Bharatiya Jana Sangh

At the time of Gandhi's assassination, Dr. S. P. Mookerjee, President of the Hindu Mahasabha, was a member of Nehru's Cabinet. In December 1948 he resigned from the Mahasabha when his proposal to open membership to non-Hindus was rejected. In early 1950 he resigned from the Cabinet, a leader in search of a party. The *Organiser*, a semiofficial publication of the RSS, called for a new political party, with Mookerjee clearly in view, and in 1951 Mookerjee announced the formation of the Bharatiya Jana Sangh, the people's party. The object of the party is the rebuilding of Bharat as a modern, democratic society in accordance with religious precepts. Four "fundamentals" guide the party: one country, one nation, one culture, and the rule of law.[65]

The program of the Jana Sangh is an eclectic mix of tradition and modernity. The party manifesto sets forth a wide range of policy positions, but the Sangh carries a decidedly communal flavor. The Jana Sangh denies being communal, however, and emphasizes its open membership. The ideology is of *Bharatiya*, Indian, culture, not of Hindu raj. Nevertheless, for all its "non-sectarian" claims the Jana Sangh seeks to promote national unity by "nationalizing all non-Hindus by inculcating in them the ideal of Bharatiya Culture."[66] It would guarantee equal rights and opportunities to all citizens, yet would not recognize religious minorities. Secularism, for the Jana Sangh, is simply a disguised policy of Muslim appeasement. The Sangh does not recognize the partition of

[65] Craig Baxter, "The Jana Sangh: A Brief Political History," in Donald E. Smith, ed., *South Asian Politics and Religion* (Princeton, N.J.: Princeton University Press, 1966), p. 81. See also Craig Baxter, *The Jana Sangh: A Biography of an Indian Political Party* (Philadelphia: University of Pennsylvania Press, 1969).

[66] *Manifesto and Program of the Bharatiya Jana Sangh*, 1958, quoted in Donald E. Smith, *India as a Secular State* (Princeton, N.J.: Princeton University Press, 1963), p. 471.

India and is militantly anti-Pakistan. It has supported a foreign policy of "non-involvement," but has adopted a sharply anti-Chinese stance. The Jana Sangh has lobbied for a powerful defense establishment and has espoused a strongly pronuclear position. It seeks a united India under a unitary state, with Hindi as the national language. Hindu dominance is symbolized by the party's stand for cow protection and for the promotion of Ayurvedic, or traditional, medicine.

Since it was organized in 1951 the Jana Sangh has been closely associated with the RSS. Indeed, Nehru described the party as its "illegitimate child." The RSS has served as the organizational base for the party, and the *Organiser* has served as the English-language voice of both the Jana Sangh and the RSS.

The Jana Sangh has at various times sought to weld an electoral alliance with the Mahasabha and the Ram Rajya Parishad. Their failure to cooperate, although affecting the electoral success of each, has served to draw support to the Jana Sangh from the other two communal parties, and with each election the Mahasabha and the Parishad have increasingly lost support. In its electoral strategy, the Jana Sangh has entered into a number of "local adjustments" with other opposition parties. In 1967 the Sangh, which made substantial gains in the Hindi areas, entered coalition governments in the states of Bihar, Madhya Pradesh, Uttar Pradesh, Haryana, and the Punjab (where in united opposition to the Congress it cooperated with the Akali Dal), and the party has intermittently taken control of the Delhi Council. In 1971 the Jana Sangh shared defeat with most other parties of the opposition. It declined both in the number of seats won and in its percentage of the vote. A year later, in the state elections, the Jana Sangh won less than half the number of assembly seats it had secured in 1967. Support for the Jana Sangh is restricted largely to North India and is concentrated within the Hindi heartland. Despite inroads into rural areas of Uttar Pradesh and Madhya Pradesh, it remains essentially a party of the urban-educated Hindu middle classes—professionals, small businessmen, and white-collar workers.

Serious discussions were periodically carried on over possible alliance with Swatantra. The two parties shared an essentially identical economic policy, but elements in both parties opposed cooperation. Swatantra's secular position and its stand for reconciliation with Pakistan and the Jana Sangh's demand for Hindi as the national language were mutually unpalatable.[67] The Jana Sangh, however, has had difficulty enough keeping its own organization intact. In 1973 Balraj Madhok, former president of the Jana Sangh, was expelled and formed a new party based on Gandhian principles.

[67] Baxter, "The Jana Sangh: A Brief Political History," pp. 99–100.

The Dravida Munnetra Kazhagam

The efforts to transcend narrow and parochial identification in the nation-building process in India continue to be frustrated by the "fissiparous tendencies" of regionalism. Among the strains on India's unity, one of the most dramatic has been the Tamil secessionist movement and its manifestation today in the demand for increased state autonomy by the Dravida Munnetra Kazhagam.

The DMK is the heir of the Dravidian movement, with roots in the anti-Brahmin conflict in Madras in the early years of the century.[68] After the Montagu-Chelmsford Reforms the Justice Party was organized in Madras to secure an uplift of the non-Brahmin community and to oppose the nationalist movement, which would, in its view, replace the neutral administration of the British with a Brahmin oligarchy. The Justice Party held power in Madras until 1934, when it was routed in a Congress victory. Weakened and tainted by its support of the British the party found a new dynamism in the leadership of E. V. Ramaswamy Naicker, founder of the "self-respect movement," which aimed to purge South India of Brahmin tyranny and the religion by which the Dravidian people were held in submission. In the first of his anti-Hindi campaigns, Naicker launched agitation against the Congress Government's introduction of Hindi in Madras schools. He then announced that his goal was the creation of a separate Dravidian state, Dravidasthan, and to that purpose the party was reorganized as a quasi-military organization, the Dravida Kazhagam, or Dravidian Federation.

In reaction to the elitist character of the DK, C. N. Annadurai, a young journalist and film writer, in 1949 led a breakaway faction to form the Dravida Munnetra Kazhagam, the Dravidian Progressive Federation. Whereas the DK, continuing as a reform movement, had never contested elections, the DMK combined the techniques of agitation with electoral activity. The party, although still waving the banner of Dravidasthan, became increasingly oriented to pragmatic economic issues. During the Chinese invasion the DMK rallied to the national cause, and on adoption of the antisecessionist amendment to the constitution in 1963, the party formally dropped its demand for an independent Tamil Nadu. Although the DMK failed to gain a foothold outside Tamil Nadu, the party expanded its social base within the state, appealing to non-Brahmin and Brahmin alike. Awakening Tamil nationalist sentiment the DMK demands greater state autonomy and an end to northern domination. Its platform emphasizes the ideals of a casteless and classless society (although the party leadership is so domi-

[68] See Eugene Irschick, *Politics and Social Conflict in South India: The Non-Brahmin Movement and Tamil Separatism 1916–1929* (Berkeley: University of California Press, 1969).

nated by members of the Mudaliar caste that the party is frequently referred to as the Dravida Mudaliar Kazhagam). Its economic program reflects a radical populism, calling for the creation of a socialist economy, with nationalization of banks and transport and a vigorous policy of land reform and redistribution.[69]

With each election the DMK has extended its base of strength from the urban centers deeper into rural areas. The DMK and its army of student volunteers responded to the issues of rising prices and the imposition of Hindi on an unwilling South with demonstrations and propaganda against the Congress Government. A number of Tamil film writers, directors, and actors added their glamor to the rising party, and in a simbiotic relationship with the party, the swashbuckling hero M. G. Ramachandran (M.G.R.), "idol of the masses," rose to become the most popular film star in South India.[70] In 1962 the DMK emerged as the strongest opposition party ever to challenge the entrenched Congress in Tamil Nadu, capturing 50 seats in the legislative assembly and 7 in the Lok Sabha. In 1967, leading an alliance that included both the Swatantra and the CPM, the DMK crushed the Congress in a landslide victory. The Congress suffered defeats throughout India, but the DMK was the only opposition party to secure an actual majority of seats and to form a ministry without a coalition.[71] As it gained increased support the Dravida Munnetra Kazhagam was transformed from a secessionist movement, nurtured on vague dreams of a glorious past and an impossible hope for the future, to a party of increasing political maturity and parliamentary discipline. As it was drawn into the political system, interests became more specific and were formulated as pragmatic political demands.

Annadurai, founder and leader of the DMK, died in 1969. The leadership of the party and government was taken by M. Karunanidhi, who, like his predecessor, was a film writer and director. "Anna" had already established a working relationship with the Congress ministry in New Delhi, and the DMK extended support to Mrs. Gandhi in her struggle with the Syndicate, not without considerable favor in return, which strengthened the position of the DMK over the Tamil Nadu

[69] See Robert L. Hardgrave, Jr., *The Dravidian Movement* (Bombay: Popular Prakashan, 1965), and "The Politics of Tamil Nationalism," *Pacific Affairs*, Vol. 37 (Winter 1964–65), pp. 396–411. For the DK, see Mohan Ram, "Ramaswami Naicker and the Dravidian Movement," *Economic and Political Weekly*, Vol. 9, annual number (February 1974), pp. 217–24.

[70] Robert L. Hardgrave, Jr., "Politics and the Film in Tamil Nadu: The Stars and the DMK," *Asian Survey*, Vol. 13 (March 1973), pp. 288–305; "The Celluloid God: M.G.R. and the Tamil Film," *South Asian Review*, Vol. 4 (July 1971), pp. 307–14; and, with Antony C. Neidhart, "Film and Political Consciousness in Tamil Nadu," *Economic and Political Weekly* (forthcoming).

[71] For an analysis of DMK ideology and the party's rise to power, see Marguerite Rose Barnett, "The Politics of Cultural Nationalism: The D.M.K. in Tamil Nadu, South India," unpublished doctoral dissertation, University of Chicago, 1972.

Congress led by Kamaraj. In the Tamil Nadu assembly elections in 1971, held in coordination with the Lok Sabha elections, the Congress of Indira Gandhi left the contest wholly to the DMK. The lopsided alliance soon foundered on DMK chauvinism. In the early months of 1972 Karunanidhi—challenged from within his own party by M. G. Ramachandran on charges of "dictatorial methods" and rampant corruption—voiced new demands for regional autonomy and began to tout himself as the "Mujib of Tamil Nadu." As a climax to presistent rumors of intraparty discord and impending schism, the party split, and under the leadership of M. G. R., the Anna DMK was formed, pledged to return the party to the principles of Annadurai.

The Akali Dal

The Akali Dal is both regional and communal. It is confined to the Punjab and open only to members of the Sikh community, of which it claims to be the sole representative. The Akali Dal was first organized as a reform group to bring the *gurdwaras* (the Sikh shrines) under the control of the orthodox Sikh community. Following a policy of direct action, the Akalis succeeded in 1925 in bringing the gurdwaras under the authority of a committee elected by universal adult franchise within the community. Control of the committee, with jurisdiction over hundreds of gurdwaras and their endowments and with great patronage powers, considerably strengthened the position of the Akali Dal in the Punjab. Master Tara Singh, leader of the dominant Akali faction until 1965, declared the necessity of a Sikh state to protect the gurdwaras and defend the Sikh religion. At the time of partition the Akalis had sought an independent Sikhistan, but in the agitation of the 1950s for linguistic states, the Akali demand was translated to that of a Punjabi-speaking state of Punjabi Suba.

In a bilingual settlement the Akalis made their truce with the Government and merged with the Congress at the time of the 1957 elections. In 1960, however, Master Tara Singh launched militant demonstrations for Punjabi Suba and filled the jails with Akali volunteers. Factionalism within the Akali Dal deepened with its failure to gain its demand, and a rival Akali party organized by Sant Fateh Singh won control in the gurdwara elections of 1965. Sant Fateh Singh then issued an ultimatum that the Government accept the Akali demand or he would fast for fifteen days and if still alive would immolate himself. At this point war broke out with Pakistan; Sant withdrew his threat and called upon the Sikhs to rise in defense of India. On the cessation of the war, the Congress announced its acceptance of Punjabi Suba.

For all its influence, the Akali Dal has never had wide electoral appeal, even among the Sikhs. The Akali obtained 11.9 percent of the total vote in the Punjab in 1962. In the Punjabi-speaking region, where the Sikhs numbered 55 percent of the population, it secured only 20 percent of the vote, or no more than 40 percent of the Sikh vote.[72] In the 1967 elections in Punjabi Suba, the two wings of the Akali Dal together received approximately 25 percent of the vote (with twenty-four seats secured by the Sant group and two by the Tara Singh group). In a united front with Congress dissidents, the Jana Sangh, and the Communists, the Akali Dal led the formation of a coalition government. In the 1969 mid-term elections, the Akali Dal enhanced its position, but in 1971, as a result of Akali defections to the Congress, the Punjab government fell and President's Rule was imposed. Factionally divided, the Akali Dal was vulnerable to continued defections in promise for Congress tickets. In 1972 twelve former Akali MLAs stood as Congressmen, and Indira Gandhi walked away with a substantial majority of the assembly seats.

Other Parties

There is a vast number of other parties in India—based on caste, language, religion, fine points of ideology, or simply the personality of the leader. Some are solely regional; others have all-India status, if not wide support. Among the more important are the reactivated Muslim League, active primarily in Kerala, and the Republican Party of the untouchables, who were examined in Chapter V. Indian parties continuously face schism within their ranks, and no party has spawned more new splinter parties than the Congress. Attempts to consolidate the parties of the opposition have, more often than not, simply extended the process of fission, as in the case of the Bharatiya Lok Dal (People's Party of India). The BLD was formed in 1974 by Charan Singh, leader of the Bharatiya Kranti Dal (BKD), itself a Congress splinter.

The new party was an alliance of seven parties, some caste or personal parties, and each with limited and essentially regional support: the SSP (Narain group); Swatantra; the BKD of Uttar Pradesh; the Utkal Congress of Orissa, led by Biju Patnaik; the Loktantrik Dal of Balraj Madhok; the Punjab Khetibari Zamindar Union; and the Kisan Mazdoor Party, a Harijan group of Haryana. The formation of the new party, committed to a "middle Gandhian path," was welcomed by both Acharya Kripalani and Jayaprakash Narayan. The party, however, has a position of potential strength only in Uttar Pradesh, Orissa, and perhaps Bihar, and in its formation, virtually every one of the constituent parties split over the question of merger.

[72] Baldev Raj Nayar, in Myron Weiner, ed., *State Politics in India* (Princeton, N.J.: Princeton University Press, 1967), p. 481. See also Nayar, *Minority Politics in the Punjab* (Princeton: Princeton University Press, 1966).

The Party System and Political Development in India

The emergence of increasingly vigorous opposition parties in electoral competition with the Congress has been a significant catalyst of the "participation explosion." The possibilities for victory, dramatized in the 1967 elections and enhanced by the economic crisis and political disillusionment that supplanted the "Indira wave" of the early 1970s, have accelerated party efforts to mobilize new bases of support and to aggregate a range of varied interests. The opposition, at least in coalition, provides a meaningful alternative to Congress rule in many states, but it has yet to achieve cohesion at the Center. The opposition parties are fragmented and for the most part weak, but while the Congress retains overwhelming dominance, the stability of the "one-party dominant system" has been effectively challenged.

India's parties, Congress and non-Congress, have been instruments for the stimulation of political consciousness and expanded participation. As agents of induction into the political system the parties have given organization and structure to participation, in a dual process of vertical and horizontal integration. Parties provide the institutional means of initiating, sustaining, and accelerating change and of absorbing the impact of that change. The Congress defeats at the hand of the opposition and the Congress split seriously challenged the political *status quo*, but the economic crisis of the 1970s poses an even more serious threat to India's democratic political system. The system of one-party dominance has come to an end, and if the political horizon affords a prospect of unstable coalition government in the states and, potentially, at the Center, it brings with this threat also the possibility of a Government more genuinely responsive to the people.

RECOMMENDED READING

Baxter, Craig, *The Jana Sangh: A Biography of an Indian Political Party.* Philadelphia: University of Pennsylvania Press, 1969.
  A study of the origins and history of the quasi-communal Hindu party.

Bhatia, Krishnan, *Indira: A Biography of Prime Minister Gandhi.* New York: Praeger, 1974.
  The first major biography of India's leader.

Bhatkal, Ramdas G., *Political Alternatives in India.* Bombay: Popular Prakashan, 1967.
  Profiles of seven major parties written by their leaders.

Brass, Paul R., *Factional Politics in an Indian State: The Congress Party in Uttar Pradesh*. Berkeley: University of California Press, 1966.
    An analysis of party organization at the local and district levels and of the impact of internal factionalism on party effectiveness.

――――, and Franda, Marcus F., eds., *Radical Politics in South Asia*. Cambridge: M.I.T. Press, 1973.
    A comparative study of regional radical movements, with an incisive introductory essay by Brass.

Burger, Angela S., *Opposition in a Dominant Party System*. Berkeley, University of California Press, 1969.
    An examination of the Jana Sangh, the Praja Socialist Party, and Socialist Party in Uttar Pradesh.

Erdman, Howard L., *The Swatantra Party and Indian Conservatism*. Cambridge: Cambridge University Press, 1967.
    A study of the origin, social base, doctrines, and political organization of the Swatantra Party.

Franda, Marcus F., *Radical Politics in West Bengal*. Cambridge: M.I.T. Press, 1971.
    A lucid analysis of what often seems the hopeless confusion of Bengal politics. An important study of revolution in suspended gestation.

Hardgrave, Robert L., Jr., *The Dravidian Movement*. Bombay: Popular Prakashan, 1965.
    An analysis of the politics of Tamil nationalism, from the non-Brahmin movement to the rise of the Dravida Munnetra Kazhagam.

Kochanek, Stanley A., *The Congress Party of India*. Princeton, N.J.: Princeton University Press, 1968.
    Focuses on the development of the party at the national level in the years since independence, the changing role of the Congress president and the Working Committee, and their relationship to the Prime Minister and the Government.

Kothari, Rajni, ed., *Party Systems and Election Studies*. Occasional Papers of the Center for Developing Societies, No. 1. Bombay: Allied Publishers, 1967.
    A collection of essays by some of India's most astute political scientists. Of particular importance are the essays on the system of one-party dominance.

Nayar, Baldev Raj, *Minority Politics in the Punjab*. Princeton, N.J.: Princeton University Press, 1966.
    A detailed study of the Akali Dal and the Sikh demand for Punjabi Suba.

Overstreet, Gene D., and Windmiller, Marshall, *Communism in India*. Berkeley: University of California Press, 1959.
    Still the most complete study of the Communist movement in India, its history, organization, and leadership.

Ram, Mohan, *Indian Communism: Split Within a Split*. Delhi: Vikas, 1969.
    An examination of the development of Maoist perspective in the Indian Communist movement.

――――, *Maoism in India*. Delhi: Vikas, 1971.
    An analysis of divergent tactical lines within the Maoist movement in India, with particular attention to the Naxalbari and Srikakulam struggles.

* Sen Gupta, Bhabani, *Communism in Indian Politics*. New York: Columbia University Press, 1972.
    A study of the Communist movement in the political context of India today.

Sisson, Richard, *The Congress Party in Rajasthan: Political Integration and Institution Building in an Indian State*. Berkeley: University of California Press, 1972.
    A detailed examination of the history, organization, and operation of the Congress in a former princely region.

Weiner, Myron, *Party Building in a New Nation*. Chicago: University of Chicago Press, 1967.
    An analysis of the Indian National Congress through case studies of the party in five districts, with a focus on the problems of adaptation and development.

————, *Party Politics in India*. Princeton, N.J.: Princeton University Press, 1957.
    An examination of the relationship between parties through the cases of the Socialists, the Hindu communalists, and the Marxist left parties.

* Available in a paperback edition.

VII

ELECTIONS AND POLITICAL BEHAVIOR

THE 1967 ELECTIONS RADICALLY CHANGED THE POLITICAL MAP OF INDIA.
They marked the emergence of a new political era in India—more participant, less stable. The campaign had been conducted "in an atmosphere
of frustration, despondency, uncertainty, and recurrent—almost con-
tinual—agitation."[1] Rising prices, food scarcities, near famine in Bihar,
strikes, and mass agitations had contributed to a situation of such seeming gravity that some observers were exceedingly pessimistic about
India's future as a democracy. The election results were dramatic: the
Congress failed to secure majorities in eight states, and its majority at
the Center was reduced to a narrow margin of 54 percent. In Tamil
Nadu the Dravida Munnetra Kazhagam won 138 out of 234 assembly
seats. Congress secured only 49. In Kerala the Congress won only 9 of
the 133 seats, not even enough to form a recognized opposition party.
The Communist-led United Front victory was decisive, bringing Namboodiripad to power again, eight years after the imposition of President's

[1] Norman D. Palmer, "India's Fourth General Elections," *Asian Survey*, Vol. 7
(May 1967), p. 277.

TABLE 7–1

THE DISTRIBUTION OF CANDIDATES, SEATS, AND VOTES
IN LOK SABHA ELECTIONS, 1952–71

Parties	Number of candidates	Number of seats won	% of seats	% of votes
1952				
Congress	472	364	74.4	45.00
CPI	49	16	3.3	3.30
Socialist Party	256	12	2.5	10.60
Kisan Mazdoor Praja Party	145	9	1.8	5.80
Hindu Mahasabha	31	4	0.8	0.95
Jana Sangh	93	3	0.6	3.10
Ram Rajya Parishad	55	3	0.6	2.03
Republican Party	27	2	0.4	2.36
Other parties	215	35	7.2	11.10
Independents	521	41	8.4	15.80
Total	1,864	489		
1957				
Congress	490	371	75.1	47.78
CPI	108	27	5.4	8.92
Praja Socialist Party (SP and KMPP)	189	19	3.8	10.41
Jana Sangh	130	4	0.8	5.93
Republican Party	19	4	0.8	1.50
Hindu Mahasabha	19	1	0.2	0.86
Ram Rajya Parishad	15	—	—	0.38
Other parties	73	29	5.9	4.81
Independents	475	39	7.9	19.39
Total	1,518	494		
1962				
Congress	488	361	73.1	46.02
CPI	137	29	5.9	9.96
Swatantra	172	18	3.6	6.80
Jana Sangh	198	14	2.8	6.44
Praja Socialist Party	166	12	2.4	6.84
DMK (Tamil Nadu only)	18	7	1.4	2.02
Socialist Party	107	6	1.2	2.49
Republican Party	69	3	0.6	2.78
Ram Rajya Parishad	35	2	0.4	0.55
Hindu Mahasabha	32	1	0.2	0.44
Other parties	64	14	2.9	4.31
Independents	497	27	5.5	12.27
Total	1,983	494		

TABLE 7-1 (*Continued*)

Parties	Number of candidates	Number of seats won	% of seats	% of votes
1967				
Congress	516	283	54.42	40.73
Swatantra	179	44	8.46	8.68
Jana Sangh	250	35	6.73	9.41
DMK (Tamil Nadu only)*	25	25	4.80	3.90
CPI	109	23	4.42	5.19
Samyukta Socialist Party	122	23	4.42	4.92
CPM	59	19	3.65	4.21
Praja Socialist Party	109	13	2.50	3.06
Republican Party	70	1	0.19	2.48
Other parties	65	19	3.65	3.67
Independents	865	35	6.73	13.75
Total	2,369	520		
1971				
Congress	441	352	67.95	43.68
CPM	85	25	4.82	5.12
CPI	87	23	4.44	4.73
DMK (Tamil Nadu only) †	24	23	4.44	3.83
Jana Sangh	157	22	4.24	7.35
Congress(O)	238	16	3.08	10.42
Swatantra	59	8	1.54	3.06
Samyukta Socialist Party	93	3	0.57	2.42
Praja Socialist Party	63	2	0.38	1.04
Other parties	403	30	5.84	9.99
Independents	1,134	14	2.70	8.36
Total	2,784	518		

* Percentage of vote in Tamil Nadu alone was 35.78.
† Percentage of vote in Tamil Nadu alone was 33.94.
SOURCES: Adapted from W. H. Morris-Jones, *Government and Politics in India* (London: Hutchinson, 1966), pp. 163–66, and from the Indian Election Commission, *Report on the Fourth General Elections in India*, Vol. 1 (New Delhi: Government Press, 1968), pp. 94–95; and *Report of the Fifth General Election to the House of the People in India*, 1971, Vol. 2, Statistical (New Delhi: Election Commission of India, 1973).

Rule had ended his first government. In Orissa, Swatantra emerged as the largest party, with 49 of 140 seats, and formed a ministry with its allies. United Front governments were formed in the Punjab, Bihar, and West Bengal. The Congress entered into shaky coalitions in Haryana, Uttar Pradesh, and Madhya Pradesh, and in Rajasthan the Congress succeeded in forming a government only after an inauspicious period of President's Rule that was imposed immediately after the election.

The voters brought down from power not only the Congress party but some of its most prominent leaders. Congress president Kamaraj was defeated in his own home town by a DMK student leader. Congress bosses Atulya Ghosh of Bengal and S. K. Patil of Bombay were defeated. Nine Union ministers, four chief ministers, and numerous state ministers were defeated. The losses were not wholly confined to Congress. Acharya Kripalani, Krishna Menon, and N. G. Ranga, all long on the Indian political scene, were also defeated. Most subsequently found their way back to the Lok Sabha in by-elections.

The elections were interpreted both as a swing to the right and as a swing to the left. In fact, however, the pattern of Congress defeats was highly idiosyncratic, related to the peculiarities of each state, with no consistency in the direction of opposition sentiments. In the Lok Sabha, Swatantra gained 20 seats to become the largest opposition group, with 44 members. It emerged as the largest single party in Orissa and as the main opposition in Andhra, Gujarat, and Rajasthan. The Jana Sangh, which made gains throughout North India, increased its strength in the Lok Sabha from 14 to 35 seats, captured control of the Delhi Municipal Corporation, and became the main non-Congress party in three states: Haryana, Madhya Pradesh, and Uttar Pradesh. The Samyukta Socialist Party doubled its strength and emerged as the major non-Congress party in Bihar. The combined vote of the two Communist parties remained close to that of 1962, and their seats in both the Lok Sabha and in the state assemblies were substantially increased. The CPM became the largest party in Kerala and the major non-Congress party in West Bengal.

The various united fronts of the 1967 elections were at least as disparate in ideological complexion as the Congress itself, if not more so. In his analysis of coalition politics following the 1967 elections in North India, Paul R. Brass argues that "inter-party ideological divisions are less decisive in the formation and breakup of governments than intra-party divisions." It thus becomes possible for "independents or party defectors to hold the balance and dictate terms of the established parties. . . ."[2] In Bihar, Uttar Pradesh, and the Punjab, the initial non-Congress governments were broadly eclectic. Ranging across the entire political spectrum, the coalition in each included all non-Congress parties, if not in the government itself, at least in its legislative alliance.[3]

[2] "Coalition Politics in North India," *American Political Science Review*, Vol. 62 (December 1968), p. 1174.

[3] *Ibid.*, p. 1178. Walter Weisburg, in a study of coalition formation in three states, emphasizes the threat of President's Rule and new elections as an impetus to coalition formation. "Coalition Politics in the Indian States: The Case of the Fourth General Elections (1967) in Bihar, Tamilnadu, and West Bengal," unpublished doctoral dissertation, University of Texas, 1972.

Although major ideological cleavages between the parties persist, the parties have shown a willingness to ignore or to compromise matters of principle. Issues not so easily resolved are those involving power—issues related to intraparty factionalism, the relationship of groups within the parties, and the position of such groups in the governments. The formation and collapse of the non-Congress governments depended primarily upon such issues. Defections and multiple floor-crossings introduced a pattern of flux and instability in which floating independents and party defectors held power far greater than their numbers alone ordinarily would command. Between 1967 and 1970, by which time the phenomenon had substantially declined, some eight hundred assembly members had "crossed the flood." Of these defectors, 155 were rewarded with office—84 securing cabinet rank.[4] The coalition governments of North India fell in rapid succession, punctuated by periods of President's Rule and midterm elections.

With half of North India under President's Rule, new elections were coordinated for what was to be a crucial test of the Congress' ability to recoup its strength. The assembly elections held in February 1969 in West Bengal, the Punjab, Uttar Pradesh, and Bihar seemed only to confirm the pattern of the earlier general election. The people's verdict of 1967 was renewed emphatically. The trend toward regional parties and bases of support was bringing an end to the Congress system of one-party dominance in India. The United Front of leftist parties in Bengal was returned to power with an absolute majority. The two Communist parties made decisive gains, and Congress was reduced to 55 of the 280 assembly seats. The Akali Dal, nearly doubling its seats, was returned as the largest party in the Punjab and led the formation of a government in collaboration with other non-Congress parties. In only two states of the four did the Congress emerge as the leading party. In Uttar Pradesh the Congress rallied to secure a near majority and form a ministry. In Bihar, retaining its position as the largest party, though without a majority, the Congress, with the support of minor parties and independents, formed a coalition ministry. After four months in the familiar process of defection, the ministry was defeated. A non-Congress coalition ruled nine days before it too was defeated and President's Rule imposed.

In December 1969, climaxing months of intraparty conflict, the Congress split. Without a Congress majority in the Lok Sabha, the Government of Indira Gandhi was dependent upon external support—notably from the CPI and DMK—and was thus vulnerable to political blackmail, for any one of the segments supporting her could threaten to withdraw and potentially defeat the Government. Seeking a mandate from the peo-

[4] For a discussion of the phenomenon of defection, see Subhash C. Kashyap, "The Politics of Defection: The Changing Contours of the Political Power Structure in State Politics in India," *Asian Survey*, Vol. 10 (March 1970), pp. 195–208, and *The Politics of Defection* (Delhi: National Publishing House, 1969).

TABLE 7–2

THE DISTRIBUTION OF CANDIDATES, SEATS, AND VOTES
IN STATE ASSEMBLY ELECTIONS, 1952–72

Parties	Number of candidates	Number of seats won	% of seats	% of votes
1952				
Congress	3,153	2,246	68.4	42.20
Socialist Party	1,799	125	3.8	9.70
CPI	465	106	3.2	4.38
Kisan Mazdoor Praja Party	1,005	77	2.3	5.11
Jana Sangh	717	35	1.1	2.76
Ram Rajya Parishad	314	31	0.9	1.21
Hindu Mahasabha	194	14	0.4	0.82
Republican Party	171	3	0.1	1.68
Other parties and independents	7,492	635	19.3	32.14
Total	15,310	3,272		
1957				
Congress	3,027	2,012	64.9	44.97
Praja Socialist Party (SP and KMPP)	1,154	208	6.7	9.75
CPI	812	176	5.7	9.36
Jana Sangh	584	46	1.5	3.60
Ram Rajya Parishad	146	22	0.7	0.69
Republican Party	99	21	0.7	1.31
Hindu Mahasabha	87	6	0.2	0.50
Other parties and independents	4,863	611	19.7	29.81
Total	10,772	3,102		
1962				
Congress	3,062	1,984	60.2	43.53
CPI	975	197	6.0	10.42
Praja Socialist Party	1,149	179	5.4	7.69
Swatantra	1,012	170	5.2	6.49
Jana Sangh	1,135	116	3.5	5.40
Socialist Party	632	64	1.9	2.38
DMK (Tamil Nadu only)*	142	50	—	—
Ram Rajya Parishad	99	13	0.4	0.29
Republican Party	99	11	0.3	0.56
Hindu Mahasabha	75	8	0.2	0.24
Other parties and independents	5,313	555	16.8	23.00
Total	13,693	3,347		

TABLE 7–2 (*Continued*)

Parties	Number of candidates	Number of seats won	% of seats	% of votes
1967				
Congress	3,443	1,694	48.59	39.96
Jana Sangh	1,607	268	7.70	8.78
Swatantra	978	257	7.37	6.65
Samyukta Socialist Party	813	180	5.16	5.19
DMK (Tamil Nadu only)*	174	138	3.96	4.34
CPM	511	128	3.67	4.60
CPI	625	121	3.47	4.13
Praja Socialist Party	768	106	3.04	3.40
Republican Party	378	23	0.66	1.53
Other parties	430	195	5.59	4.75
Independents	6,774	376	10.79	16.67
Total	16,501	3,486		
1972†				
Congress	2,558	1,936	70.22	48.02
CPI	329	112	4.06	4.18
Jana Sangh	1,233	104	3.77	8.56
Congress(O)	872	88	3.19	6.75
Socialist Party	678	57	2.07	4.47
CPM	468	34	1.23	4.62
Swatantra	306	15	0.55	1.46
Other parties	999	185	5.26	6.08
Independents	4,742	226	9.65	15.86
Total	12,185	2,757		

* In Tamil Nadu in 1962 the DMK gained 24.3 percent of the assembly seats and 27 percent of the vote. In 1967 it secured 59.4 percent of the seats and 44.66 percent of the vote.
† "De-linked" from the Lok Sabha elections, assembly elections in 1972 were held only in 16 states and 2 Union territories: Andhra, Assam, Bihar, Gujarat, Haryana, Himachal Pradesh, Jammu & Kashmir, Karnataka, Madhya Pradesh, Maharashtra, Manipur, Meghalaya, Punjab, Rajasthan, Tripura, West Bengal, Delhi, and Goa, Daman & Diu.
SOURCES: Adapted from W. H. Morris-Jones, *Government and Politics in India* (London: Hutchinson, 1966), pp. 163–66, and from the Indian Election Commission, *Report on the Fourth General Elections in India*, Vol. 1 (New Delhi: Government Press, 1968), pp. 94–95; and provisional statistics for 1972 provided by the Election Commission of India.

ple in the form of an absolute majority in her own right, the Prime Minister dissolved the Lok Sabha and called new elections for March 1971. Having nationalized the banks and opened attack on princely privilege,

Mrs. Gandhi commanded vast popular support and, moreover, she was at a tactical advantage in holding parliamentary elections separately from the general elections, since the contests for the state assemblies might challenge her search for a stable Congress majority at the Center with distracting local issues. The Prime Minister sought to campaign on national issues, to turn the electorate away from the politics of patronage and manipulation. She sought, in direct appeal to the voters, to bypass the intermediary structures—the village notables and "vote banks"— which had been the base of the old Congress machine.[5] Her efforts, however, were aimed particularly at certain disadvantaged groups—the Scheduled Castes and Tribes, Muslims, and the young. Her message was clear: Garibi Hatao. In opposition, Mrs. Gandhi confronted a Four-Party Alliance of the Jana Sangh, Swatantra, the Samyukta Socialists, and the Syndicate's Congress(O). The Alliance's campaign was based on the removal of Mrs. Gandhi ("Indira Hatao"), and consequently, as W. H. Morris-Jones has observed, the opposition helped the Prime Minister "project a simple personal image throughout the country."[6]

The results were overwhelming. With 44 percent of the vote, Congress won 352 of the 518 seats in the Lok Sabha. The Congress(O), inundated by the "Indira wave," was reduced from 65 to 16 seats and received only 10.5 percent of the vote. The Jana Sangh was cut back from the 35 seats it had won in 1967 to 22 and a 2 point decline in its share of the votes to 7.4 percent. The Swatantra Party secured only 8 seats, compared to 44 in 1967, and a minimal 3 percent of the vote. The heaviest defeats were inflicted upon the SSP. From 23 seats and 5 percent of the vote in 1967, the SSP secured only 3 seats in the new Lok Sabha and 2.4 percent of the vote. The CPI, supporting Mrs. Gandhi with local electoral adjustments, held its own, with 23 seats and 4.7 percent of the vote. The CPM scored well, with an increase from 19 to 25 seats and 5 percent of the vote—but the fact that 20 of the seats came from West Bengal underscored the party's regional dependency.

While the parliamentary elections were for the first time "de-linked" from the state assembly elections, three states, West Bengal, Orissa, and Tamil Nadu, held assembly contests. In these, Congress fared less well. In Bengal the CPM emerged as the largest party, with 111 seats and 32 percent of the vote against Congress' 105 seats and 28 percent. In Orissa the Congress success was limited: 51 seats and 27 percent of the vote compared with 32 seats and 22 percent for the rival Utkal Congress and 36 seats and 17 percent for Swatantra. In Tamil Nadu the Congress had entered into an understanding with the DMK designed to defeat Kamaraj's Congress(O). Congress contested and won only 9 Lok Sabha seats, securing 12 percent of the state's vote. The DMK contested 24

---

[5] See Myron Weiner, "The 1971 Elections and the Indian Party System," *Asian Survey*, Vol. 11 (December 1971), pp. 1153–66.

[6] "India Elects for Change—and Stability," *Asian Survey*, Vol. 11 (August 1971), p. 727.

seats and won 23, with 34 percent of the vote. In the assembly, however, Congress did not contest a single seat, leaving the field wholly to the DMK. In the returns, contesting 201 of the 234 assembly seats, the DMK won 183, with 47 percent of the vote. The Congress (O) contested 194 seats, and though it secured 33 percent of the vote, it was reduced to 15 seats.

By the end of the year Mrs. Gandhi's electoral victories were reinforced by the defeat of Pakistan and the liberation of Bangladesh. The popularity and power of the Prime Minister were unprecedented. In March 1972 sixteen states and two Union Territories went to the polls in assembly elections. Successfully combining populist slogans with the promise of political stability, the Congress, with 48 percent of the vote, won 70 percent of the seats. Of 2,757 seats to be filled, Congress contested 2,558 and won 1,936. In West Bengal, Congress made a dramatic recovery, winning 216 of 280 seats with 49 percent of the vote. The CPM, which had emerged as the state's largest party only a year before, was reduced to 14 seats and 28 percent of the vote.[7] In sharp contrast to the anti-Congress solidarity of 1967, the opposition was divided, enabling Congress to recoup its share of the seats from the 49 percent of 1967 with only a modest increase in its percent of the vote.

Elections

Elections in India have generally been orderly. Given the size of the elections—the world's largest—instances of rioting and violence have been remarkably low, but election violence has been rapidly on the rise. The campaigns are filled with charges and countercharges of assaults, kidnappings, and even murders, though few such allegations are ever brought to court. Stories abound of candidates who have stepped down because they were intimidated or because they were "bought off." Posters and symbols are often defaced, and tensions, aggravated by rumor, often reach the breaking point.[8] The 1967 campaigns were marked by somewhat greater unrest than earlier elections, notably by the serious beating of a leader of the Samyukta Socialist Party and the injury of Prime Minister Indira Gandhi, who was hit by a rock at a public meeting in Bhubaneswar. A number of rallies were disrupted, fasts-unto-death were threatened, and demonstrations and processions occasionally got out of hand. In the 1971 election period, Bengal erupted into widespread violence. Hardly a day passed without a political murder, and on some days as many as ten were reported. The incidents,

[7] For a discussion of Bengal and results by states, see Marcus F. Franda, "India's 1972 State Elections," American University Field Staff Report, South Asia Series, Vol. 16, No. 1 (April 1972).

[8] See S. P. Verma and C. P. Bhambhri, *Elections and Political Consciousness in India* (Meerut: Meenakshi Prakashan, 1967), pp. 87–93.

arising both from Naxalite activity and CPI-CPM warfare, led the press to write of "the great Calcutta killings." The Bangladesh crisis in December 1971 provided the opportunity for military suppression of Bengal's political violence.

The Voting Procedure

The Indian constitution grants all Indian citizens twenty-one years of age or older the right to vote. In 1971 some 275 million people were eligible to vote. From the members of the Central Election Commission down to the local polling officers, about one and a half million people were involved in conducting the election, and there were some 343,000 polling stations, a substantial increase over 1967. The size of the electorate and convenience were major considerations in determining the number and location of the stations. They were spaced so that "ordinarily" no person should have had to travel more than one and a quarter miles to vote. The sheer magnitude of the elections and the inadequacy of transportation and communication facilities have made extended voting periods necessary. The first general elections were held in the winter of 1951–52 over a four-month period. The time was reduced to a span of nineteen days in 1957, and a week to ten days in subsequent elections.

In the first two general elections each voter was given ballot papers for assembly and parliamentary seats. There was a ballot box for each candidate in each contest, and the voter placed the paper in the box marked by the symbol of the candidate he supported. (Some voters reportedly worshipped the ballot box after casting their vote.) The system was confusing and involved a vast number of ballot boxes. A new procedure that provides for marked ballots and a single box in public view was adopted in 1962 and has been used since then. Voters queue at the station, and a polling officer checks each voter's identity slip against his or her name on the electoral roll. The voter is then marked on the finger with indelible ink and receives two ballots, pink for the assembly, white for the Lok Sabha. Marking both ballots secretly with a rubber stamp on the symbol of the chosen candidate, the voter folds the ballots, and drops them into the box. Although the procedure is involved, the number of invalid votes has been relatively small, averaging 3 to 4 percent of the total cast. The whole procedure is scrutinized by polling agents representing each candidate. Their presence and assistance also serve to identify voters and prevent impersonations.

Constituencies and Seats

The States Reorganization Act passed in 1956 provided for the establishment of the Delimitation Commission, consisting of the chief election commissioner and two active or retired judges of the Supreme

Court or a state high court. Their responsibility is to delimit the constituencies for each election. These have varied somewhat with each election, but with the exception of the major changes caused by States Reorganization, there has been sufficient continuity to permit comparative analysis. The Lok Sabha constituencies have been drawn in successive elections to contain from 750,000 to 1,000,000 people. Within each parliamentary constituency are a number of state assembly constituencies, varying in size from state to state, but having an overall average of some 150,000 people. The number of members in the Lok Sabha now totals 524, of whom 506 are directly elected from the states and 15 from the 8 Union Territories. One member is nominated by the President to represent the Union Territory of Arunachal Pradesh, and two are nominated to represent the Anglo-Indian community. There is a total of 3,771 members of the state and Union Territory legislative assemblies.

The Selection of Candidates

Among the conflicts in Indian political life, perhaps none has been more intense or significant than the selection of candidates within the Congress party. The selection process has in fact become increasingly critical, since the election of the Prime Minister has come to depend upon the balance of factional strength in the Lok Sabha. As conflicting interests become more vocal, the Congress is forced to reconcile its pledge to select the "best" candidates with the competing personal and parochial claims of those upon whom its support depends. Ramashray Roy, in analyzing this process in the states of Bihar and Rajasthan, argues that the selection process is "a crucial test of the party's flexibility and adaptability in coping with the pressures and counter-pressures that impinge upon it from both within and without."[9]

FORMAL CRITERIA OF THE CONGRESS

The formal criteria established by the Congress for selecting candidates emphasize (1) the applicant's record of party loyalty; (2) his commitment to the Congress program; (3) his activity in "constructive work" as well as his legislative experience; and (4) reflecting the Congress' concern to broaden its base of support, his representation of groups the Congress may wish to attract.[10] But there has been little agreement in the Congress on the mechanism of selection. Rather, there has been a tug-of-war between the national leadership, which has favored centralization of decision-making, and the lower strata of the party organization, which have pushed for more power. Consequently, different procedures have been adopted for each election. Those party members supporting centralization argue the importance of freeing the

9 "Selection of Congress Candidates, Part I," *Economic and Political Weekly*, Vol. 1 (December 31, 1966), p. 835.
10 *Ibid.*, p. 837.

selection process from local and parochial considerations, while those at the bottom claim that they are in a better position to judge the merits of a winning candidate. In 1952 the district Congress committees played the key role in the selection of candidates, but in 1957 they were relegated to an advisory position and the pradesh Congress committees were responsible for making recommendations to the Central Parliamentary Board, which is responsible for the final approval of all Congress candidates. In 1962 the district organizations were given more importance, but the 1967 procedure placed the pradesh committees in decisive control again.[11] In 1971, in the wake of the Congress split, candidate selection was highly centralized, and many of the candidates were handpicked by the Prime Minister.

FACTIONAL PRESSURES

The Congress ticket is highly coveted, and factional confrontation and intense competition are characteristic of the struggle to win it. In 1962 there were in Bihar, for example, an average of 6.5 applications for every ticket. The various claims put forward often force sharp deviation in prescribed selection procedures. Individual attempts to bend procedural arrangements for personal advantage are likely to be defeated by higher authority, but group efforts, sustained by factional rivalry within the party, are likely to succeed.[12] There is always the fear, however, that the dominant faction at the lower levels may attempt to exploit its hold on the organization by securing all tickets for itself, thus driving out the minority. Under Nehru's consensus-oriented leadership, such conflicts were resolved by central intervention. But with the increasing autonomy of the state parties after Nehru's death, the mechanisms of conflict resolution were threatened, particularly since the central leadership itself was divided. At the demand of state leaders, the selection process for the 1967 Congress tickets was controlled at the level of the pradesh committee, effectively placing the power to draw up the list of Congress candidates in the hands of the Chief Minister and the dominant faction.[13] Isolated from power by the refusal of the dominant faction to accommodate their claims and unable to secure central intervention in their behalf, as they might have done under Nehru, minority factions in various states withdrew from the Congress. Widespread defections led to the formation of rival Jana Congress parties.

At the local level party activists are more concerned with winning than with adherence to the formal criteria of selection and may thus be

[11] *Ibid.*, pp. 838–39, and Stanley A. Kochanek, "Political Recruitment in the Indian National Congress: The Fourth General Elections," *Asian Survey*, Vol. 7 (May 1967), p. 298.

[12] Ramashray Roy, "Selection of Congress Candidates, Part II," *Economic and Political Weekly*, Vol. 2 (January 7, 1967), p. 21.

[13] Stanley A. Kochanek, *The Congress Party in India* (Princeton, N.J.: Princeton University Press, 1968), p. 298.

drawn to the person most likely to command the greatest base of support—even though his party loyalty, constructive work, or commitment
to the Congress program might be minimal. Further, the local organization is more sensitive to the social base of the constituency and thus
more willing to take caste and community into consideration in selecting
their candidate. They also feel that voters prefer a local candidate and
distrust an outsider—no matter how distinguished a Congress record he
may have.[14] Reflecting this view, in contrast to earlier elections candidates now are almost always local.

If the Congress is to retain its position of dominance it must be able
to accommodate the various group pressures, both state and local, in its
selection of candidates. Ramashray Roy identifies four kinds of claims
advanced in the selection process: personal, regional, socioeconomic,
and institutional. Personal demands are those made by individual Congressmen who press for recognition and the reward of a Congress ticket
for their sacrifice, service, experience, and competence. Regional claims
are those that derive from feelings of localism, such as the demand that
the candidate belong to the constituency. Various socioeconomic groups
may also seek to advance their interests by claiming the right to representation among Congress candidates. Institutional demands for representation are made by the various organs of the Congress, such as the
Youth Congress and the Indian National Trade Union Congress. The
failure of the Congress to respond to these conflicting demands might
well mean that even before the election important social sectors are lost
to the opposition. However, factional competition within the Congress
has served to articulate and aggregate these diverse group demands and
to provide them with access to political power and a stake in the political process.[15] Candidate selection thus is a vital recruitment and
mobilization process.

In addition to competition between state and local groups and between factions, there is intense competition between the "old guard"
and young political aspirants. In order to open channels of access there
has been an attempt to insure some degree of turnover by requiring that
one-third of the Congress tickets go to candidates who have not run
before. Although the Congress has frequently been attacked as an aging
party of old men, "the veterans of the freedom struggle are on the wane
and their place is increasingly being taken by newcomers who perhaps
join politics not because it demands sacrifice of them but because it
opens new avenues for the realization of power and/or status."[16] The
drama of the 1969 Congress split reflected something of this genera-
tional conflict.

[14] Roy, "Selection of Congress Candidates, Part II," pp. 22–23.
[15] Ramashray Roy, "Selection of Congress Candidates, Part III," *Economic and
Political Weekly*, Vol. 2 (January 14, 1967), pp. 61–62, 69.
[16] Ramashray Roy, "Selection of Congress Candidates, Part IV," *Economic and
Political Weekly*, Vol. 2 (February 11, 1967), p. 371.

The distribution of Congress tickets also reflects the party's increasing congruence with society. In Bihar, although higher education is still essential for positions of prestige within the party, some 40 percent of the Congress candidates have had very little schooling. The fact that nearly half are landowning agriculturalists reflects the dependence of the party upon the rural sector. But the land is still controlled primarily by the traditionally dominant castes, and they remain dominant within the Congress party. The lower castes, increasingly politically conscious and well organized, are far better represented, however, than are the Scheduled Castes or the Muslims.

The dominant elements of Congress thus are still drawn from the dominant elements of society.

> This means that traditionally entrenched social as well as economic sectors of the society have greater access to positions of power, not only in the party but also in the government, with the result that radical policies of social transformation are bound to be delayed if not sabotaged. The dominance of the vested interests in the Congress, therefore, prevents it from carrying out measures of reforms which may adversely affect the interests of the upper castes.[17]

UNIFICATION OF THE OPPOSITION

While intraparty strife led in 1967 to a decline in the Congress vote in some states, in others it was rather the ability of the opposition to unite that brought down the system of one-party dominance. In earlier elections Congress had been able to capitalize on the splintered opposition. Even in 1967, 184 Congress seats were won by less than 50 percent of the votes—and 80 of these by less than 40 percent.[18] The Congress was vulnerable, and the opposition parties sought to advance their position. The Congress has generally contested all seats, whereas the opposition parties, all-India as well as regional, have followed a policy of selective confrontation. This contest policy of the opposition parties, the result of their limited organization and resources, is a critical element of their election strategy and has influenced the election outcome. It a party's resources are limited, the more seats it contests, the more difficulty it may have in winning anywhere. Consequently, the opposition parties wait until the Congress has announced its final lists of candidates and then take the Congress candidates and constituency strength as their reference points in choosing which seats to contest.

In single member–simple plurality constituencies the candidate with the largest vote wins. Such a system benefited the Congress, with its more extensive organization, but it also motivated opposition to unite.

---

[17] *Ibid.*, p. 375.
[18] Gopal Krishna, "The Problem," in the special issue of *Seminar* on the Congress party, No. 121 (September 1969), p. 14.

In the 1967 elections this "multiplier" effect worked against the Congress. In terms of the total assembly seats in 1967, the Congress fell 5 percent in the votes it received, but 14 percent in the seats it secured. The Congress decline was most dramatic in Tamil Nadu, where it confronted an opposition alliance centered around the DMK and including the Swatantra, the CPM, PSP, SSP, and the Muslim League. The Congress secured a larger percentage of votes than any other party, 41.04 percent, but was reduced from some 67 percent of the assembly seats to 21 percent.

THE SOCIAL BASE OF THE CONSTITUENCY

In the selection of candidates each of the major parties, including the Communist party, is sensitive to the social base of the constituency. When one community is dominant within a constituency—in the traditional terms of landed wealth, ritual status, and political power, or, increasingly, in terms of the modern calculus of numbers—each party is likely to draw its candidate from that community. It has been argued that this practice neutralizes caste as a political factor, but the fact remains that all castes do not have equal access to power.

Dominant castes are themselves arenas of political competition between factions, each of which may try to aggregate the support of other castes. More frequently, a faction will seek vertical support, cutting through caste lines. Thus, the divisions within the dominant caste are mirrored in divisions within each of the other castes that follow traditional patterns of economic dependence and patron-client relationships. In such cases, the candidates, while all from the same community, do not have equal claim to support from within their own caste. When the castes are self-conscious and cohesive in their political behavior, one candidate of the dominant caste may often be clearly identified as the "community man," and other castes will polarize in opposition around the other candidate, even though he is from that same community.

In constituencies in which two or more communities are in relative balance, candidates may be selected from numerically insignificant castes in order to depoliticize the caste factor. Where there are a number of small castes, none of which commands disproportionate influence, the candidate may be selected without regard to caste. In any case, determination of the party candidacy must always take the caste complexion of the constituency into account, and state-wide there may be a conscious attempt to put together a balanced ticket, with each of the major communities represented. The political party that chooses its candidates from the dominant caste of a particular constituency does no more than the American city boss who seeks to aggregate the support of ethnic communities by offering candidacies to their leaders. Few politicians can afford to court a single caste, for in most constituencies no single caste so predominates as to command a majority. Although they may seek to gain the support of a caste by appealing to its particular interest in a given situation, they must do so without alienating the other communities and driving them into united opposition. The appellation "caste man" would severely limit the political horizon of an aspiring office-seeker.

Frequently "dummy candidates," running as independents, are put up to split votes and to draw support away from an opponent. Usually these are more a nuisance than a threat, but in a close election the loss of even a few votes may mean the difference between victory and defeat. An amusing example involved the parliamentary contest in Jaipur in 1962. The major contender was the Maharani Gayatri Devi on the Swatantra ticket. When the nominations were filed, it was discovered that another Gayatri Devi, an illiterate woman from a Scheduled Tribe, was also in the running—probably, it was suspected, at the instigation of others.[19] She polled only a few thousand votes.

The Election Campaign

PARTY FUNDS AND CAMPAIGN FINANCING

Political parties in India derive their funds from a variety of sources: membership dues, contributions, public meetings, and so on. The Congress party is the best financed. Its paid membership (in 1972, nearly 10 million primary members and more than 300,000 active members)[20] provides a substantial portion of its financial backing, but additional contributions must be secured. These come regularly from wealthy supporters and are solicited in fund-raising campaigns. In the days of the undivided Congress the birthday of Kamaraj, for instance, provided the Tamil Nadu Congress with a yearly occasion for bringing money into the party coffers. Contributions were frequently wrested from industry and business, often through considerable pressure. Bus owners, dependent upon the government for licenses, were reportedly "taxed" one thousand rupees per bus, and mill owners were "taxed" by the spindle. It is said that certain wealthy businessmen and industrialists were quietly urged to contribute a portion of their "black money" (income not reported for tax purposes) to the Congress party. Whatever the multitude of sources tapped by the Congress, receipts were staggering. In the celebration week of Kamaraj's sixty-third birthday in July 1965, the main festivals were held in the town of Trichinopoly in Tamil Nadu. Sixty-three arches were constructed at a cost of two thousand rupees each, and a procession under the arches was led by sixty-three cars and included sixty-three bullock carts. In other towns colorful processions were followed by public meetings, poetry competitions, essay contests, distribution of food to the poor, and special *pujas*,

[19] Verma and Bhambhri, *Elections and Political Consciousness*, pp. 69–72.
[20] Membership figures must be approached with some caution, as factional competition has inflated party rosters with bogus members.

or worship services, in the temples. Each of the celebrations culminated in a meeting at which the local Congress leader presented Kamaraj with a "birthday purse" for the Congress campaign fund. Each district was to contribute 63,000 rupees, but in competition to outdo one another, the twelve districts contributed over 1,700,000 rupees ($350,000) during the birthday tour.[21]

The Congress' long control of the Center and the states gave the party a tremendous advantage. Dependent for licenses upon the "permit raj," businesses contributed richly to the Congress. Many have also made sizable contributions to Swatantra, a party with which they might have more ideological affinity. Some, taking no chance with a volatile electorate, have contributed to each of the major parties, right and left. The opposition, however, has generally had far less access to financial support than the Congress.

Each of the parties divides membership dues between the center and lower organizational units. The Congress party's constitution specifies that the central organization is to receive one-eighth of the income from dues; the rest is distributed among the state units. Other parties have similar arrangements, but ones involving considerably smaller amounts. Income from dues fluctuates considerably, since party membership is largest immediately before elections—often the result of mass recruitment or bogus membership arranged by factions to strengthen their bargaining position in the competition for party tickets. The candidates themselves may be expected to make sizable contributions to the party election fund, and tickets are occasionally awarded for a major commitment of financial support. This practice varies considerably from party to party and from seat to seat—for there are clearly a number of candidates from the Congress as well as from other parties without any major source of private income. Levies are also made on the salaries of Parliament and assembly members. Congress MPs contribute forty rupees per month (10 percent of their parliamentary income) to the party. The average Communist MP contributes one hundred rupees each month to his party.[22]

Each of the parties derives some income from publishing. Most successful is the Communist Party of India, which prints several newspapers and operates a publishing house and a chain of bookstores. In addition, the sale of Soviet books and magazines, provided by the U.S.S.R. at minimal cost, brings the Communists considerable profit. The financial capacity of the Communist party has always been a source of speculation and rumor. The CPI is allegedly financed by the Soviet Union, and the CPM was once accused of receiving Chinese support.

21 J. Anthony Lukas, "Political Python of India," New York Times Magazine (February 20, 1966), p. 54.
22 A. H. and G. Somjee, "India," Journal of Politics, special issue on comparative studies in political finance, Vol. 25 (November 1963), p. 692. See also A. H. Somjee, "Party Finance," Seminar, No. 74 (October 1965).

Reports also circulate that the United States has backed specific candidates of various parties through the secret use of Central Intelligence Agency funds. Sources of funds are by no means clear for any party. Swatantra receives substantial contributions from business interests and recently perhaps more money from princes and former zamindars. The Jana Sangh also relies in part on zamindari funds, but the bulk of its contributions probably comes in relatively small sums from professionals, shopkeepers, and government clerks.

The costs of mounting a campaign are high and have increased with each election. In a closely competitive state assembly contest, each candidate may easily spend more than one hundred thousand rupees—considerably beyond the legal limit set by the Indian Election Commission. The laws governing campaign expenses allow up to 35,000 rupees for a parliamentary seat and about 13,500 rupees, depending upon the region, for an assembly seat. The amount of expenses must be filed, but

> no expense, however large the account may be, which is incurred by a party organization in furthering the prospects of a candidate supported by it is required to be entered in the account of the election expenses of the candidate so long as he can make out that such expense was not authorized by him or by his election agent.[23]

In the 1971 Lok Sabha election, it was estimated that the Congress spent a total of about 250 million rupees, or 480 thousand rupees per constituency—more than double that of 1967.[24]

MOBILIZING VOTERS

With each election, Indian political campaigns have become more expensive and intense, a mixture of festival and struggle, penetrating even the most isolated villages. Each candidate, backed by party funds and contributions, builds a team of party volunteers and paid election workers for the campaign. Insofar as possible, local offices are set up throughout the constituency, and transportation, by jeep whenever possible, is arranged. Weeks before the election, posters, painted slogans, and party symbols appear everywhere, competing for available wall space. There is a flood of printed handouts, and children parade through the streets with badges and party flags. Neighborhood party strongholds in villages and in cities prominently display flags, often vying with each other to raise the party flag highest. Jeeps and horse-drawn *tongas*, or carts, bedecked with party flags and the ubiquitous symbol, carry loudspeakers that saturate the air with a jumble of amplified slogans.

Each of the parties has an exclusive symbol by which it is identified. Because of widespread illiteracy and because the symbol, not the name

---

[23] Indian Election Commission, *Report on the Second General Elections: 1957*, Vol. 1 (New Delhi: Government Press, 1959), p. 183.
[24] Morris-Jones, "India Elects for Change—and Stability," pp. 723–24.

of the party, appears on the ballot next to the name of the candidate, emphasis on symbols is a major part of the campaign. The symbol is the critical link in the mind of the voter between the candidate and the party, and for this reason, in the Congress split, the issue of which side got the traditional Congress bullocks was not a trivial one.[25] Figure 7-1 shows the official symbols for the major national parties as allotted by the Election Commission and used in all the states. The symbols are supposed to be neutral but each party strives to attach to them positive or negative connotations.

[25] In January 1971 the Supreme Court ruled that neither claimant was entitled to the old Congress symbol of the two yoked bullocks. After negotiation, the Election Commission allotted the "cow and calf" symbol to Indira Gandhi's new Congress and the symbol of the "charkha (spinningwheel) being plied by a woman" to the Congress (O). For a discussion of the symbol controversy, see *Report of the Fifth General Election in India: 1971–72, Narrative and Reflective Part* (New Delhi: Government of India, Election Commission, 1973), pp. 64–70.

FIGURE 7-1

SYMBOLS OF MAJOR NATIONAL POLITICAL PARTIES

SYMBOL	PARTY
1. Two yoked bullocks	Congress (before 1969)
2. Cow and calf	Congress
3. Charkha being plied by a woman	Congress (O)
4. Sickle and grain	Communist Party of India
5. Hammer, sickle, and star	Communist Party of India (Marxist)
6. Lamp	Jana Sangh
7. Star	Swatantra
8. Banyan tree	Socialist Party

The Government's All-India Radio has not been used by the parties because they cannot agree among themselves on the allotment of time offered to them. Few campaign advertisements appear in the press, probably because of India's low literacy level, although the papers provide detailed election coverage. In reviewing the 1967 elections, Norman D. Palmer commented that "it is doubtful that such complete election coverage has ever been given by the press of any country in the history of democratic elections."[26] While India's principal English and vernacular dailies are free to take an independent, even critical stance, they tend generally to be pro-Government and pro-Congress. Some of the major vernacular newspapers do support opposition parties, however. In addition, each party has its own weeklies in both English and local languages, as have many factions.

Parties often organize mass processions, with decorated floats, elephants, and a throng of party cadres as a means of publicizing their campaign. Torchlight parades evoke memories of early American political campaigns. Parties also make use of traditional folk dramas, particularly for satirical purposes. Some parties, such as the DMK in Tamil Nadu, have successfully used motion pictures to advance their cause. Mass public meetings bring a mixture of politics and entertainment, blending spellbinding orations with renditions of popular film songs. In addition to the luster provided by film stars, national political figures may also make appearances with the local candidates. Depending upon the drawing power of the main speaker and the galaxy of stars present, these meetings may attract several hundred thousand people. Street-corner meetings and spot appearances by a candidate bring the election even closer to the voters, and with each succeeding election emphasis on door-to-door canvassing has increased.[27]

PARTY MANIFESTOES

Each of the parties prepares a manifesto, a formal electoral platform, which may be a statement of minimum ideological agreement or a pledge of aspirations. The manifesto can hardly be expected to have more importance in India, with its mass illiteracy, than does the party platform in the United States. In both nations few voters are aware of the formal party positions on most issues; fewer still ever read these documents. The fact that Indian parties devote such concern to the manifesto, however, may have great significance for legislative behavior if not for popular voting behavior.

The party manifestoes may reflect the changing internal character of the party, the rise and fall of various factions, shifts in ideological stance, and efforts to secure new and broadened bases of support. In the

[26] "India's Fourth General Elections," p. 281.
[27] See Verma and Bhambhri, *Elections and Political Consciousness*, pp. 83–85.

first two elections, the Congress manifesto, like the Congress campaign, emphasized the party as the embodiment of the freedom movement. The Congress stood before the people on the record of its struggle and achievement, and individual Congressmen sought to establish their credentials of sacrifice by citing the time they had spent in British jails. By 1962, however, more than half of the electorate had come to political maturity after the struggle and sacrifice of the nationalist movement. These appeals were lost upon them. To the young the Congress was a party of privilege, wealth, and power, not of martyrdom. Responding to this change in the electorate the Congress, no longer able to trade on history alone, tried to demonstrate that it could satisfy popular demands. The manifesto sought to do this, but it could do so only in terms of real issues.

ISSUES

There have been few national issues in India. In North India, Pakistan has been an issue of emotional concern for many, but it does not stir the South. Cow slaughter has aroused the rancor of the orthodox, but its impact on the general public is fleeting. Corruption has been decried from all sides. Regional nationalism has perhaps provided the most emotive issues. The issue of food scarcity has had considerable impact, but it is more a regional than a national concern, related to the particular problems of drought, rationing, and distribution peculiar to individual states. Inflation and rising prices have aroused national concern.

In 1971 Indira Gandhi sought to raise national issues in her commitment to garibi hatao, but although these larger issues capture the headlines and the concern of party leaders and coffeehouse intellectuals, they are not likely to get out the vote. National, even regional, issues seem remote and arouse little sense of efficacy in most of the electorate. These issues reflect real frustrations, however. Perhaps the *Times of India* is right in suggesting that "there are no all-India issues as such— there are only all-India grievances."[28] To reach the villager or the average urbanite, the campaign must be personalized, made immediate through translation into local issues that affect him and that he feels he can to some extent control. He may know or care little for the problems of food distribution or for the economics of inflation; but he does know that he does not have enough to eat and that he can buy less and less with the rupees he earns.

Although relatively uninformed, the Indian voter is highly politicized. He has increasingly high expectations of government and when frustrated, he will not hesitate to punish those in authority. The reprimand inflicted on the Congress by the voters in 1967, Ramashray Roy writes, was "neither capricious nor ill-conceived." Behind it was "the strongly held feeling that the Congress . . . failed to solve the problems that

[28] February 14, 1967, quoted in Palmer, "India's Fourth General Elections," p. 289.

vitally affect the life of the common man."[29] The voter is becoming increasingly sensitive to a party's capacity to deliver results. Rajni Kothari argues that as "the voters are becoming aware of problems of policy and performance . . . , the appeals that parties make must increasingly be based on concrete items of social and economic change and less and less on either vague manifestoes or reliance on local party organizations and 'vote banks' to deliver the votes, no matter what the party appeal is."[30]

VOTE-BUYING

In the course of the election campaign, party workers attempt to contact each household in behalf of their candidate. In personal contact arguments might be advanced that could never be made publicly—specific appeals to caste loyalty, for example. These electoral efforts are frequently accompanied by payment. "Money politics" is an important lubricant of the Indian political machine. In many constituencies voters have come to expect payment of money by all candidates. It is clear, however, that a candidate cannot buy election by bribing the electorate; a candidate spending a disproportionate amount frequently loses. In the first elections, payments were primarily group-directed. A candidate made a sizable payment to a village or caste leader in return for a promise to deliver a bloc of votes. Such payment sometimes was used for the group's benefit, but more often it simply enriched the leader alone. More recently, as traditional blocs of support fragment, individual contacts and payments are replacing group payments.

Vote-buying is probably less prevalent in cities than in villages, but in urban constituencies cases are reported—particularly among poorer classes—of a few rupees being enclosed in an election leaflet. Many politicians speak of "the price of a vote," complaining that it has risen with each election, but there is no definite pattern of voter response to offers of payment for support. There seem, however, to be four forms of reaction. Some voters will accept money from no candidate. Others will accept payment from all candidates and feel bound to none. Some barter their vote to the highest bidder, negotiating with each candidate to see who will pay the most. Once the bargain is struck, they feel bound to support the candidate. There are others who will accept money only from the candidate to whom they are already committed—a reflection of traditional patron-client relationships. Instances have been reported of money being taken from one candidate and given to another. Because of the Congress' access to greater financial resources, voters are more likely to expect payments from Congress candidates, but few parties are

---

[29] "Elections, Electorate and Democracy in India," *Perspectives*, Supplement to *The Indian Journal of Public Administration*, Vol. 17 (1971), pp. 24, 36.
[30] "The Political Change of 1967," *Economic and Political Weekly*, Vol. 6, annual number (January 1971), p. 250.

exempt. Perhaps only the Communists have successfully avoided this trap.

In the first elections the privilege of voting may have seemed insignificant to many voters. In the course of time, payment for votes has made plain the importance of voting, but as a result payments have less and less effect upon the way voters use their power. F. G. Bailey has described the pervasive cynicism and mistrust among voters in an Orissa hill village. Having the experience of two elections behind them they received the politician's offer of payment for support with the same skepticism with which they received his ordinary protestations of devotion to the public weal.

> Neither the would-be corrupters nor their potential beneficiaries had any faith in one another's probity, and since the ballot was secret there was no check upon individual voters. The voters did not think that they would get the money; the candidates believed that voters accept money from both sides and vote the way they would anyway, without a bribe.[31]

Widespread vote-buying has contributed to attitudes of cynicism, but ironically, money politics impresses the people with the importance of a single vote and serves to draw nonparticipants to the polls. In much the same way, the gifts of the American political machines early in this century politicized new immigrants to the United States and served to integrate them into the society and the political system. As individuals become increasingly involved politically and as voting practice thus becomes institutionalized, payment declines in importance.

APPEALS TO SPECIFIC GROUPS

The adept candidate has done his demographic homework. He has at his fingertips information on the patterns of social cleavage and the numbers and relative strength of each caste and religious group within his constituency. Before he ever arrives in a village, he has attempted by whatever means possible to determine its caste and factional complexion, the degree of his support, and the specific felt needs of the villagers. Since voters may readily pledge to vote for every candidate it may be necessary to get an independent assessment. Candidates therefore may enlist undercover workers in villages and neighborhoods to probe voter feelings. Some even infiltrate the organization of other parties.[32]

On his village tours a candidate may leave his jeep some distance from the village and enter the village on foot, accompanied by an impressive group of party workers. Having previously ascertained what the

---

31 F. G. Bailey, *Politics and Social Change: Orissa in 1959* (Berkeley: University of California Press, 1963), p. 33.
32 A. C. Mayer, "Municipal Elections: A Central Indian Case Study," in C. H. Philips, ed., *Politics and Society in India* (London: George Allen & Unwin, 1963), p. 124.

villagers want most he may well promise them this alone if he is elected, emphasizing his credentials of integrity by *not* offering them everything but, conveniently, just what they want. After a short public speech he may make personal visits to villagers at all levels, particularly those in pivotal or decisive positions. The appearance may then be followed, perhaps some days later, by individual contacts by party workers.

The political candidate must make mass appeals, but, as in the United States, much attention must be directed toward specific groups. If there is a relatively low turnout at the polls or a large number of candidates, victory may hinge on only a small number of votes. Bailey writes that "the structure of traditional society may become the mould within which representative politics operate at constituency level. Old loyalties and allegiances may continue within the new framework of representative politics."[33] Candidates thus may attempt to capture the support of traditional groups that can be guaranteed as a "vote bank" to deliver a bloc of votes on instruction by a leader. The framework of modern politics does not simply foster the continuation of traditional behavior, however. It structures now forms of behavior, and the traditional patron-client ties of the vote bank are weakening as a result. In most cases traditional sentiments are all that remains of the old structures of authority. Unless bloc leaders can reinforce these sentiments by securing for their groups the benefits they demand, traditional blocs are not likely to survive. In all but the most isolated villages, vote banks can no longer be relied upon. Despite pledges of united support, castes and communities are increasingly likely to fragment their support. A candidate for municipal election in central India described the change in his own constituency thus:

> In 1954, people would vote for the man they promised to support. Sometimes they decided this through a council of the sub-caste, sometimes they were brought in through workers, or through the tempo at public meetings. Now people only vote after they have each been reached and persuaded, and they vote because of their own benefit, or because of the person who talks to them; so they can be changed up to the last minute. Maybe in a few years they will vote because of Municipal policies. You see, we are progressing all the time, and our people are learning about elections.[34]

The Indian Electorate

Expanding Participation and the Impact of Competitive Elections

Given the level of literacy in India, political consciousness is remarkably high. Since independence, levels of political awareness and of

---

[33] *Politics and Social Change*, p. 113.
[34] Quoted in Mayer, "Municipal Elections," p. 125.

participation have risen among all segments of the population, and there is evidence on any number of scales that political mobilization is taking place faster in rural areas than in urban areas. That village India has been politically penetrated is revealed in the minimal differences in the levels of partisanship and voter turnout between urban and rural areas. The most dramatic increases have been noted among rural poor and illiterate populations. As an indication of the degree of politicization in India, John O. Field found in survey analysis that 62 percent of his sample identified with some party and two-thirds described themselves as "strong supporters." Fifteen percent were nonpartisan, and 23 percent were parochials, for whom the parties had no meaning whatsoever. These data are confirmed by other surveys. While education and sex are the most salient variables in distinguishing levels of partisanship, Field found that "partisanship is a remarkably diffused attribute." Differences "between the cities and the countryside, the educated and the illiterate, the economically secure and the destitute, even between men and women," are not impressive. "What is really striking," he writes, "are the high levels of partisanship among the least privileged in India, however they are defined."[35]

Expansion of participation in rural areas is closely related to the impact of competitive elections, especially at the panchayat level, in politicizing the village. Elite factions, which once needed only the support of the dominant castes, must now seek a wider base of support to legitimize their traditional position. A critical determinant of the rural turnout is the degree to which local conflicts are identified with struggles at the constituency level. Factions become the vehicle of political mobilization and voting turnout. Almost every village is torn by factionalism, and almost inevitably village conflicts are drawn into the wider political arena. Party struggles thus become an opportunity for each village faction to further its interests and solidify its position within the village.

Factional struggle is by no means new. Land has traditionally been a source of intense conflict; various families in the dominant caste have fought among themselves to enlarge their holdings. Factional conflict has also served to divide castes as vertical relationships of dependence have cut through village society in the formation of client groups. Such factions, although not permanent, have often endured for several generations. The establishment of panchayati raj and the availability of government development money have intensified conflict in the competition for new resources.

Each village faction may try to associate itself with the winning assembly candidate both to command reward for support and to legitimize its local dominance. The Congress, with its own factional division,

35 "Partisanship in India: A Survey Analysis," unpublished doctoral dissertation, Stanford University, 1973, pp. 165, 199, 215. The data are based on a 1966 survey conducted by the Centre for the Study of Developing Societies, New Delhi.

has often been able to command the support of an entire village through the alignment of village factions with various Congress groups, often simply on the basis of polarization. That is to say, one village faction sides with a particular faction within the Congress, so the opposing village faction aligns with the opposing Congress group. A village faction, however, may well extend its support to an opposition party candidate just because the dominant faction of the village supports the Congress. Voting may thus reflect issues and conflicts peculiar to a village alone and virtually unrelated to the issues of the larger constituency.[36]

Levels of Political Awareness

For most of India there is no "public opinion." Although beginning to expand, the identity horizon of most villagers rarely extends beyond the narrow range of personal encounter; their knowledge and concerns remain highly parochial. Local elections are the most likely to arouse enthusiasm, and even assembly elections are contested on highly local issues. Appeals may be calculated in parochial terms, but probably no more so than in any other democratic country.

In early surveys the limited political horizon of most Indians was evidenced in the widespread inability to identify even such well-known national leaders as Nehru. Today there are few Indians in such isolation. Electoral campaigns, bureaucracy, and mass communications have penetrated the villages and expanded the average villager's threshold of political identity. Indians have become increasingly aware of the world beyond the village, increasingly conscious of their vote. Opinions are multiplying and are reflected in growing demands and heightened expectations. If surveys continue to register a large number of "don't knows," the statistics should not be taken to mean that Indians simply have no orientations or sentiments about the matters at issue. Although not articulate, they have real interests of which they are aware.

The attitude of Indian villagers toward politicians is ambivalent. "Peasant communities," Bailey writes, "are proverbially hard and centered upon themselves; within the boundary there is some degree of trust, some rule of morality; beyond the boundary they expect to be cheated or bullied, as they would themselves deal with a stranger. Relationships with outsiders have not yet acquired 'legitimacy.' "[37] The villagers' acceptance of the new framework of government does not rest upon its efficiency alone, but also "on moral judgments about the persons associated with the new institutions."[38] The contrast between the reality of political life in India and Indians' idealized image of the demo-

---

[36] See Myron Weiner, "Village and Party Factionalism in Andhra: Ponnur Constituency," in Myron Weiner and Rajni Kothari, eds., *Indian Voting Behaviour* (Calcutta: Mukhopadhyay, 1963), pp. 177–202.

[37] *Politics and Social Change*, p. 65.

[38] *Ibid.*, p. 68.

cratic process has served to breed a general cynicism. Interest-group activity and responsiveness to group demands are considered immoral. The qualities the legislator *ought* to possess are sacrifice, unselfishness, service, and impartiality. But these are unlikely attributes of a successful candidate—perhaps they are more those of a philosopher-king than a democratic politician. Yet the voters themselves, with little conception of the public interest, demand selflessness of their leaders, while at the same time they project their own code of morality upon all but a very few politicians. Anyone in political life, they believe, must be working for his own betterment; no one would offer himself as a candidate unless he were out to make money for himself.[39]

Although there is a general belief that assembly members ought to be disinterested, Indian voters are primarily concerned with the distribution of benefits. "The voters look to their MLA not for his record and performance as a legislator, but expect him to be their representative, a man who can stand up for them against the local administrators and win favours for them in the distribution of development money or other favours."[40] The voters expect the MLA to be the broker between the masses and the elite.

Many voters have supported the Congress, no doubt as a form of traditional loyalty to the Government: not to do so would be disloyal. Others feel that it is in their personal interest to do so. Many groups consider it to their advantage to vote for "the Government," no matter who it is. Some believe that the Government distinguishes between its supporters and opponents and that they will suffer if they oppose it—or, at least, be deprived of its benefits. These attitudes reflect, in part, a failure to distinguish between the ruling party and administrative services. In the first elections it may have involved as well "an incomplete acceptance of the idea that Governments may be thrown out by means of an election."[41] However, these attitudes also reflect the considerable advantage of the ruling party. Patronage is a powerful political instrument with which to command support. The links between the Government and the Congress party organization have also provided channels of influence and response. Like the Democratic party in the United States, the Congress enjoys association with a variety of services it has established as the party in power. Access to these government services and welfare and development benefits is most often through the intervention of a Congress leader.

Opposition victory might well break this flow of benefits through the party, seriously affecting the ability of the Congress organization to deliver the votes. The political machine operates on the patronage and benefits it can exchange for support. It is fueled, in Bailey's words, "not

---

[39] *Ibid.*, pp. 35–36.
[40] *Ibid.*, p. 84.
[41] *Ibid.*, pp. 23–24. See also Mayer, "Municipal Elections," pp. 128–29.

by moral fervour, but by calculations of profit and advantage."[42] Machine support is contingent; yet it may be the agent not simply of mobilization and integration but, with time, of a party loyalty that transcends the immediate reward. Loyalty to the Congress as Government, long association with the party as the embodiment of the nationalist movement, and the charismatic force of Gandhi and Nehru have served to institutionalize the Congress and to sustain party identity among considerable numbers of voters, who contribute a stable base of political support. In a study of the Indian electorate, Kothari finds that "43 percent 'feel close to' the Congress party, the second closest to the Jana Sangh with 7 percent. . . . Whereas there is a relatively close relationship between identification and voting, it is only for the Congress party that such a relationship has acquired high stability."[43] Even in the widespread defeats of the 1967 elections the actual percentage of Congress votes declined only a few points. Bailey found that in Orissa, Congress support did not rest upon personal interests and parochial issues alone. "Voting for the Congress had become a habit, the same fundamentally irrational—one might call it 'moral'—identification with a party which characterizes party support in the older democracies."[44]

The level of identification with opposition parties is increasing, but they are still primarily dependent upon the politically uncommitted and "floating" voters. The uncommitted, especially among those who are young, urban, and highly educated, are more likely to be drawn to the opposition. For all the stability of Congress support it is an aging party; of all social and economic indicators, age is the most important in explaining variance in party support.[45] With each election, millions of new voters enter the political arena as active participants—a prospect that Congress leaders can only view with unease.

Sheth found that strong partisans, more highly educated and enjoying both economic security and social status, have a relatively high sense of political efficacy. In comparison to weak partisans and the uncommitted, "strong partisans are politically more involved, exhibit greater understanding of competitive politics, participate more in electoral activities, show greater acceptance of parliamentary institutions and display greater satisfaction with the performance of the political system."[46]

[42] *Politics and Social Change*, p. 141.
[43] "The Political Change of 1967," p. 248. John Field found that of his sample, 55 percent identified with Congress—but of the total "partisans" (62 percent), 88 percent indicated Congress support, underscoring the level of party institutionalization. "Partisanship in India: A Survey Analysis," p. 202.
[44] *Politics and Social Change*, p. 85.
[45] Kothari, "The Political Change of 1967," p. 241; and Douglas Madsen, "Solid Congress Support in 1967: A Statistical Inquiry," *Asian Survey*, Vol. 10 (November 1970), p. 1009.
[46] D. L. Sheth, "Partisanship and Political Development," *Economic and Political Weekly*, Vol. 8, annual number (January 1973), p. 268. See also Sheth, "Political Development of the Indian Electorate," *Economic and Political Weekly*, Vol. 5, annual number (January 1970), pp. 137–48. Sheth's conclusions are confirmed by Field. See pp. 391–484.

The new voter, increasingly drawn from lower social and economic groups, lacks both the commitment to a given party and to the system. Perceiving "conventional channels as pre-empted by those who already command political and economic resources," the politically uncommitted participant may turn increasingly to violence and the unconventional modes of political action to which the Government has so often been responsive.[47]

Voting Turnout and Trends

The Montagu-Chelmsford Reforms of 1919 provided for limited franchise based upon property qualifications, the specific criteria varying among the provinces. The total electorate for the various provincial legislative councils was about 5,350,000. Easing the franchise qualifications the Government of India Act of 1935 extended suffrage to include some 30 million people. After independence, the constitution abolished all property qualifications and, in what Rajendra Prasad called "an act of faith," established universal adult suffrage. The electorate has grown from 173 million in 1952 to 275 million in 1971.

While the size of the electorate has expanded with population growth, there has also been a steady increase in the percentage of voting turnout; 45.7 percent[48] in 1951–52, 47.74 percent in 1957, 56.29 percent in 1962, and 61.33 percent in 1967. In the parliamentary elections in 1971, the first unlinked with assembly elections, participation dropped in all states, with an all-India average of 55 percent. Reflecting the greater salience of the assembly for the Indian voter, in 1972 the turnout again rose to 59 percent. (The United States turnout in 1972 was only 55 percent.) Rates of participation vary considerably among the states, from a high of 76.57 percent turnout in Tamil Nadu in 1967 to a low of 44.05 percent in Orissa in the same year. In every state, participation has increased. Probably the most salient variable affecting voter turnout is education, as reflected in aggregate terms at the state level, as well as in individual terms, as revealed in survey data. Urbanization is not a significant variable, at least in studies where other indicators of modernization are controlled. Of variables differentiating voter turnout, sex is one of the most powerful.

Participation by women has increased with each election, although the level of turnout for women is lower in rural constituencies. During the first election many women refused to give their proper names and therefore were not registered. By 1962 two-thirds as many women as men voted, and by 1967 the proportion had risen to three-fourths. The effect of the increasing number of votes cast by women is probably negligible, however, as voting among women generally follows the pattern of one constituency in which "women were not only led to the poll-

[47] Satish K. Arora, "On Acquisition of Political Legitimacy," *Economic and Political Weekly*, Vol. 5, annual number (January 1970), p. 131.
[48] Valid votes only; other figures represent the total number of votes cast.

ing booth by the male members of the family, but in almost all cases voting behaviour was determined by their advice, which was eagerly sought, given, and followed."[49] With increasing education, women may be expected to take a more independent political role, as it is already evident in Kerala. Women played a prominent part in the nationalist movement, and the Congress has encouraged women to enter politics by reserving about 15 percent of its tickets for women. A number of women have served as ministers in the states and at the Center, the most notable of whom is Prime Minister Indira Gandhi.

In 1967 there was an average of nearly five candidates for every parliamentary and assembly seat, but voters tended to ignore all but two or three "serious" candidates. The trend toward fewer independent candidates was reversed in 1967: there were 5,793 independents in the assembly elections that year as compared with 3,888 in 1962. Their number no doubt reflected defections from the Congress. Only 298 won seats, however, and the vast majority forfeited their deposits.[50] In fact, deposits were lost by seven out of eight independent candidates for the Lok Sabha and by five out of every six independent assembly candidates. These defeats register the fact that the electorate has become more party-conscious.

In 1967 some 18,500 candidates stood for Lok Sabha and assembly seats—about 1,000 more than in 1952. In the first general elections approximately one-third of the candidates were independents. There were fourteen national parties and fifty-nine state parties. Of the 17,500 candidates in 1951–52, more than half lost their deposits because they did not secure the needed minimum vote. The largest number of these were independents. The number of forfeitures for independents has increased with each election. While this may reflect "the number of individuals, unable to judge their capacity to translate personal influence into electoral votes,"[51] it also reveals a more rational electorate, unwilling to waste its votes on a variety of minor aspirants. Those states with the highest levels of participation and consciousness, mobilized by party competition, are those in which voters are most party-oriented, with the fewest numbers of returned independents.

The percentage of the Congress vote, despite the 1967 reverses, has remained remarkably stable. It has varied within only seven percentage points, from a high of 47.78 percent in 1957 to a low of 40.73 percent in 1967. Even in the dramatic victory of 1971 Congress secured only

---

[49] J. C. Anand, "Panchayat Elections in the Punjab: A Case Study," *Political Science Review* (University of Rajasthan), Vol. 2 (March 1963), p. 34.

[50] To appear on the ballot, a nomination for a seat from a parliamentary constituency must be accompanied by a deposit of five hundred rupees, for an assembly or council seat by a deposit of two hundred and fifty rupees. (Members of Scheduled Castes and Tribes need deposit only half these amounts.) Unless the candidate receives at least one-sixth of the total vote he forfeits his deposit.

[51] Myron Weiner, ed., *State Politics in India* (Princeton: Princeton University Press, 1968), p. 41.

43.68 percent of the vote. In only a few states has the Congress ever gained an actual majority of the votes. But although Congress has been able to retain a core of support, it has lost significant sectors of the electorate. Congress support seems to show a decline among minorities —Sikhs, Christians, and Muslims—and among various urban middle-class groups, such as students, teachers, and government servants.[52] Most significant are substantial losses from among three groups: those under thirty-five years of age, illiterates, and those with incomes below two hundred rupees per month. The Congress formerly enjoyed a well-balanced base of support, in terms of literacy, age, and occupation, but it has increasingly lost touch with youth and with the lower rungs of the social order.[53] Indira Gandhi reversed this trend in 1971 and 1972, but perhaps only as a brief phase. E. P. W. da Costa's observation, based on the results of 1967, takes on renewed relevance:

> The Indian electorate, believed inert and incapable of dramatic choice, is showing signs of a revolutionary change. The young, the less educated, and particularly the illiterates, the minorities, and, most unpredictable of all, the lowest income groups are all rewriting their basic loyalties. To the candidate this is, perhaps, a struggle for power. To a political scientist it is . . . the beginning of a break with the past.[54]

Political Mobilization and India's Future

The Congress was the architect of political mobilization, but when participation expanded it was no longer able to accommodate it fully. The party organization, although the most extensive in scope, has not successfully provided channels of access to newly participant groups. Because its machine structure made it politically dependent upon the middle-level peasantry and petty landlords, the Congress remained basically unresponsive to those at the bottom, those without land or power. Increasingly isolated from an awakening majority, the Congress organization, captive to narrow interests, was challenged by the Prime Minister in 1969, precipitating crisis and ultimately division. Indira Gandhi turned to the people with the promise to remove poverty, but the radical posture of the Congress was not translated into substantive action. Heightened expectations turned to deepening frustration.

Expanding participation provides the impetus for developing higher levels of institutionalization. The *status quo* in India has been radically

[52] Paul R. Brass, "Political Participation, Institutionalization and Stability in India," *Government and Opposition*, Vol. 4 (Winter 1969), p. 38.
[53] E. P. W. da Costa, "The Indian General Elections 1967" (New Delhi: Indian Institute of Public Opinion, 1967), pp. 2–3.
[54] *Ibid.*, p. 23.

disrupted; yet the emergent system may be capable of attaining a higher level of development. Whether the system has the will to respond to the increasing demands upon it is of course another question. The enhanced capacity of the party system to both generate and absorb change in expanding participation has held the critical balance in India's political development. The parties, in organizing and structuring participation, may provide access to demands, but they cannot wholly satisfy them. The viability of the political system depends upon both the will and the capacity of the Government to respond to these demands. Despite the "fissiparous tendencies" of regionalism and the states' demands for greater autonomy, India's national identity seems increasingly secure. The institutions of government in the years since independence have gained increasing legitimacy. The constitutional framework has been strengthened through its continued operation.

The institutions of government in India, notably the bureaucracy, were grounded in the structure of the British raj. They were designed for administration and for the maintenance of stability; their purpose was to contain demands, not to respond to them. The fundamental problem of transition was to adapt these instruments of repressive order to the needs of social change and democratic response. But rapidly expanding participation and escalating demands quickly outran the capacity of the highly institutionalized structures that India's new leadership had inherited. Control of the Government and the administration, particularly in the states where the masses and the elite met in closest contact, rested largely in the hands of those who sought to resist change, to reinforce the vested interests of the *status quo*, and who lacked the will to respond to the demands stimulated by increasing political consciousness.

As the will to effect a fundamental transformation of society has declined, so, in the face of scarcity, have capacities to meet rising demands. Poverty remains the basic fact of India's existence; scarcity conditions her political life. The party system can order participation only so long as the governmental institutions at the Center and in the states can reasonably meet the aspirations of India's newly conscious, newly participant masses. The comparative order of Indian political life may conceal an unrest that lies just beneath the surface. Economic development, Nehru once said, is "for the growth of the individual, for greater opportunities to every individual, and for the greater freedom of the country." "Political democracy . . . will be justified if it succeeds in producing these results. If it does not, political democracy will yield to some other form of economic or social structure. . . . Ultimately, it is results that will decide the fate of what structure we may adopt in this country. . . ."[55]

---

[55] *Parliamentary Debates—House of the People: Official Report*, Vol. 6, No. 10, Pt. II (December 15, 1952), Col. 2371.

RECOMMENDED READING

Atkal, Yogesh, *Local Communities and National Politics*. Delhi: National, 1971.
> A sophisticated analysis of communications and voting behavior in three communities in western Uttar Pradesh.

* Bailey, F. G., *Politics and Social Change: Orissa in 1959*. Berkeley: University of California Press, 1963.
> Analyzing various levels of political life in a single state, Bailey provides one of the most illuminating studies of political life in India.

Brass, Paul R., *Language, Religion and Politics in North India*. New York: Cambridge University Press, 1974.
> An analysis of political manipulation in the promotion of communal and national interests.

Brecher, Michael, *Political Leadership in India: An Analysis of Elite Attitudes*. New York: Praeger, 1969.
> An examination of elite perceptions of the events surrounding the 1967 election.

Fox, Richard G., *From Zamindar to Ballot Box*. Ithaca, N.Y.: Cornell University Press, 1969.
> A study of social and political change in an Uttar Pradesh market town.

Kashyap, Subhash C., *The Politics of Defection*. Delhi: National Publishing House, 1969.
> A detailed study of defection and floor-crossing in Indian legislatures.

Philips, C. H., ed., *Politics and Society in India*. London: George Allen & Unwin, 1963.
> Papers explore the interaction between society and politics.

* Rosen, George, *Democracy and Economic Change in India*, rev. ed. Berkeley: University of California Press, 1967.
> An analysis of the impact of economic change on India as a whole and on specific groups within Indian society.

Roy, Ramashray, *The Uncertain Verdict: A Study of the 1969 Elections in Four Indian States*. Berkeley: University of California Press, 1974.
> An incisive analysis of political behavior in India, with broad implications for the political system as a whole.

Sirsikar, V. M., *Sovereigns Without Crowns: A Behavioural Analysis of the Indian Election Process*. Bombay: Popular Prakashan, 1973.
> A detailed study of voting behavior in Poona.

Stern, Robert W., *The Process of Opposition in India: Two Studies of How Policy Shapes Politics*. Chicago: University of Chicago Press, 1970.
> An examination of opposition stimulated by specific Government policies.

* Available in a paperback edition.

Verma, S. P., and Bhambhri, C. P., *Elections and Political Consciousness in India.* Meerut: Meenakshi Prakashan, 1967.
>   A comparative analysis of political behavior in two Rajasthan constituencies, urban and rural, with a treatment of election strategy and campaign techniques.

Weiner, Myron, and Field, John O., eds., *Studies in Electoral Politics in the Indian States,* 4 vols. Delhi: Manohar Book Service, 1974.
>   The first volume, by Field and Franda, is on the Communist parties of West Bengal. The remaining three volumes are collections of papers on electoral politics: *Three Disadvantaged Sectors* (princely India, tribal India, and women); *The Impact of Modernization;* and *Party Systems and Cleavages.*

————, and Kothari, Rajni, eds., *Indian Voting Behavior.* Calcutta: Mukhopodhyay, 1963.
>   A collection of constituency studies of the 1962 elections that originally appeared in the *Economic Weekly.*

VIII

THE INTERNATIONAL CONTEXT: CONSTRAINTS AND IMPERATIVES

THE PROCESSES OF MODERNIZATION AND DEVELOPMENT IN ANY NATION ARE fundamentally conditioned by the international context in which they occur. No nation is hermetically sealed in isolation or so strong militarily or economically that it is impervious to influence and challenge from outside. In a world of increasing interdependence the policies and actions of one state may so impinge on others as to determine their domestic policies and developmental prospects. The international economic system has long been under the influence of a handful of nations —the United States, Japan, and those of Western Europe. American fiscal policy, for example, as regards "tight money," has an impact on every nation in the world. But the capacity for influence is not limited to the great powers or to the affluent nations of the West. The energy crisis, brought on by the 1973 Arab oil embargo and the subsequent rise in the cost of oil, was felt throughout the world and significantly affected the character of international politics. Beyond the economic realm, a nation's defense policy is determined largely by the military strength and posture of other, potentially threatening nations. Unfortunately, in the quest for a margin of superiority that will insure security, security itself may be undermined by an arms race.

The study of domestic politics in India cannot be separated from the larger consideration of the international context of development. Development involves the will and capacity to initiate, absorb, and sustain continuous transformation. This necessitates a response to changes within the international system. In that environment India confronts both constraints and imperatives.

Indian Foreign Policy: Nonalignment

In May 1974, in the desert of western Rajasthan, India detonated an underground atomic device and thereby became the sixth member of the exclusive "nuclear club" joining the United States, the Soviet Union, Great Britain, France, and China. Against a specter of nuclear proliferation, many within the international community condemned India's action. Although India has long had nuclear potential the Government has resisted pressure from within the Congress party, as well as the opposition, notably the Jana Sangh, to produce an atomic bomb. India, however, refused to sign the nuclear nonproliferation treaty.[1] The Indian position was that the treaty was discriminatory and that it was as important to control vertical as horizontal proliferation. Significant also was India's security interest *vis-à-vis* China, although Chinese subversion is probably regarded by India as more serious than a nuclear threat. Another factor in India's position was the fact that in a world where "great power" status seems dependent upon having the bomb—as reflected in the deference accorded China by the United States—India was unwilling to relegate itself to an inferior position internationally. Perhaps the main factor in India's decision to go nuclear was its isolation in the 1971 Indo-Pakistani war and its increasing dependency upon the Soviet Union. India's entrance into the nuclear club served to strengthen India's position of nonalignment and to underscore its dominance in the South Asian subcontinent.

Indian foreign and domestic policies are fused in the concern for national security and economic independence. "Eradication of poverty was an important ideal," Prime Minister Indira Gandhi has stated, "but even more important was the preservation of India's freedom—the development of a defense capability against external threats, the building up of infrastructure to strengthen the economy and achieve self-reliance and protect the nation's honor and self-respect."[2]

Having experienced three wars with Pakistan and one with China, witnessing the erosion of "Afro-Asian solidarity," and seeing the world

---

[1] See Michael J. Sullivan, III, "Re-Orientation of Indian Arms Control Policy, 1969–1972," *Asian Survey*, Vol. 13 (July 1973), pp. 691–706.

[2] 1972 speech, quoted in Baldev Raj Nayar, "Political Mainsprings of Economic Planning in the New Nations: The Modernization Imperative versus Social Mobilization," *Comparative Politics*, Vol. 6 (April 1974), p. 362.

influence it commanded during the cold war weakened by *détente*, India is less idealistic, moralistic, and doctrinaire than in the years in which Nehru dominated Indian foreign policy. But the fundamental character of that policy—nonalignment—has not changed.[3]

Indian foreign policy is rooted in two traditions. One is that of British India, with a concern for the territorial integrity and security of South Asia, especially on the Himalayan frontiers. The other is that of the Indian National Congress, evolved from the 1920s almost wholly under the direction of Nehru and focusing on the problems of world peace, anti-colonialism, and anti-racism. In a speech at Columbia University in 1949, Nehru succinctly stated the goals of Indian foreign policy:

> India is a very old country with a great past. But it is a new country also with new urges and desires. . . . Inevitably she had to consider her foreign policy in terms of enlightened self-interest, but at the same time she brought to it a touch of her idealism. Thus she has tried to combine idealism with national interest. The main objectives of that policy are: the pursuit of peace, not through alignment wth any major power or group of powers, but through an independent approach to each controversial or disputed issue; the liberation of subject peoples; the maintenance of freedom both national and individual; the elimination of want, disease, and ignorance, which afflict the greater part of the world's population.[4]

Central to Nehru's concept was nonalignment. Neither a policy of neutrality nor one of isolation, nonalignment by no means precluded an activist stance in the Indian self-interest. In the Indian view nonalignment is a pragmatic policy of independent action. It is simply a refusal to make any commitments, political or military, in advance, to any nation or bloc. Policy positions are made on an *ad hoc* basis according to the merits and circumstances of each case.[5] "India's policy of nonalignment," William Barnds writes, rested on four fundamental considerations:

> (1) The country's major tasks were the internal ones of political, social, and economic development, on which it should concentrate rather than becoming involved in a struggle between the West and the Communist powers that did not directly concern it; (2) taking either side in the conflict would be divisive among a people badly in need of greater national unity; (3) as a weak

---

[3] M. S. Rajan, "India in World Politics in the Post-Nehru Era," in K. P. Misra, ed., *Studies in Indian Foreign Policy* (Delhi: Vikas, 1969), pp. 254–55.
[4] Quoted in William J. Barnds, *India, Pakistan and the Great Powers* (New York: Praeger, 1972), pp. 47–48.
[5] Rajan, "India in World Politics," p. 249.

though large nation, India would lose some measure of freedom if it allied itself with any major power; and (4) as the strongest power in the area, India had no need for external support to bolster its regional position.[6]

Foreign Relations

India came to independence in 1947, having exercised for some thirty years a quasi-autonomous foreign policy. India was a charter member of the League of Nations and the United Nations. Nehru had long made pronouncements on international politics in the name of the Congress, and upon becoming Prime Minister, he retained for himself the portfolio of foreign affairs.

Among the first problems confronting the new Government was its relationship with Great Britain. Nehru overcame strong opposition from those who sought a complete break, and India secured Commonwealth status as a republic by a formula wherein the Crown became the "symbol of free association" among the independent member nations. It was within the Commonwealth, however, that India was to confront its most serious and persistent international conflict—that with Pakistan.

Pakistan

The partition in 1947 presented a host of problems: the division of Indian financial assets; the split within the bureaucracy and the army; and, most critically, the conflict over use of the waters of the Indus basin, which was settled after twelve years of negotiation through mediation by the World Bank. Partition had been accomplished with staggering rapidity and at enormous human cost. But the transfer of almost twelve million people did not fulfill Jinnah's vision of "two nations." Some forty million Muslims remained in India and ten million Hindus in East Pakistan. Throughout the following years there was a continuous annual flow of several thousand Hindu Bengali refugees into West Bengal and Assam, their numbers varying each month with the degree of communal tension. But the focus of the "religious minority problem" as it affected Indo-Pakistani relations was Kashmir.

In 1947 the population of Jammu and Kashmir was about three-quarters Muslim, but the maharajah, a Hindu, resisted the pressure to accede to either Pakistan or India. Pakistan sought to force the issue, first imposing an economic boycott against the state and then supporting Pakistani tribesmen in an invasion of Kashmir. The maharajah's appeal to India for protection was accepted on condition of Kashmir's

6 Barnds, *India, Pakistan and the Great Powers,* p. 63.

accession, with the promise to consult the wishes of the Kashmiri people once law and order had been restored. Nehru reaffirmed this "pledge to the people of Kashmir" and agreed to Kashmiri self-determination through an internationally supervised plebiscite. It was by no means a foregone conclusion that the plebiscite would favor Pakistan, for Kashmir's most popular leader, Sheikh Abdullah of the National Conference, was strongly committed to a secular state and to accession to India. The conditions, mutually acceptable to both India and Pakistan, for such a plebiscite were another matter. Most important for India was a complete withdrawal of Pakistani forces from Kashmir.

In 1949 India and Pakistan accepted the United Nations' cease-fire line, with one-third of the state under the control of the Pakistani Azad Kashmir government. There followed years of continuous negotiation under the auspices of the U.N., but with time, Nehru, himself a Kashmiri Brahmin, increasingly came to regard Kashmir as the guarantee of India's secularism and as a denial of the "two nation" theory upon which Pakistan was founded. The 1954 U.S.–Pakistan agreement brought another factor into the situation, as did Pakistan's strengthened hold on Azad Kashmir. Arguing that the circumstances in Kashmir had changed so completely that the original offer for a plebiscite was no longer valid, India accepted the Kashmir constituent assembly's vote of accession as equivalent to a plebiscite. Article 370 of the Indian constitution had recognized, as a temporary provision, special status for Kashmir within the Indian Union. Kashmir's own constitution, adopted in 1956, specified that the "State of Jammu and Kashmir is and shall be an integral part of the Union of India," but Article 370 remains in force and the precise nature of Kashmir's position within India has yet to be defined.[7]

With communal unrest in Kashmir in 1963–64, Pakistan President Ayub Khan, a decade of American military assistance behind him, embarked on a policy of "leaning on India." In April 1965, following an increase in tension along the cease-fire line in Kashmir, an armed clash occurred in the Rann of Kutch in Gujarat over disputed boundaries in an area alternately marsh and desert but potentially rich in oil deposits. By the end of June a cease-fire was reached, with a mutual withdrawal of forces and an agreement for arbitration. Kutch, however, was but a dress rehearsal. In August, Ayub sent Pakistani-trained guerrillas into Kashmir in hopes of triggering internal rebellion against Indian rule. Pakistani armored units then moved into Jammu, and India launched an attack across the Punjab plain toward Lahore. In

[7] A vast literature is available on the Kashmir dispute. For a succinct discussion, see Charles H. Heimsath and Surjit Mansingh, A Diplomatic History of Modern India (Bombay: Allied Publishers, 1971), pp. 146–83. See also J. B. Das Gupta, Jammu and Kashmir (The Hague: Nijhoff, 1968); Sisir Gupta, Kashmir: A Study in India-Pakistan Relations (Bombay: Asia Publishing House, 1966); and, for a view less sympathetic to India's case, Alastair Lamb, Crisis in Kashmir: 1947–1966 (London: Routledge & Kegan Paul, 1966).

a reversal of Pakistani success in the Rann of Kutch, Pakistani tanks took a heavy beating. The U.S. was chagrined that American arms supplied to Pakistan should be used against another recipient of U.S. military assistance, and both the U.S. and Great Britain cut off further arms shipments to India and Pakistan. China, on the other hand, sided with Pakistan and denounced India's "criminal aggression" with threatening ultimatums. The United Nations Security Council, with the support of the U.S., Great Britain, and the U.S.S.R., called for an immediate cease-fire, which India and Pakistan accepted in September. Soviet Premier Kosygin, seeking to strengthen ties with Pakistan, check Chinese influence, and at the same time maintain traditionally close ties with India, offered the good offices of the Soviet Union to negotiate a settlement. Ayub and Shastri proceeded to Tashkent in January 1966. The agreement, rather than solving the basic problems, represented a return to the status quo before the war. Given Indian success in the war the agreement to withdraw forces was not well received by many in Congress or the opposition. "Yet Shastri's untimely death at Tashkent made it certain that India would not repudiate his last official act."[8] In 1968 a three-member arbitration commission awarded Pakistan about one-tenth of the disputed Rann of Kutch. It was greeted with an angry Indian reaction, but it was accepted.

Indian performance in the 1965 war served to renew the confidence of the army and to restore to it the prestige which had been lost in the 1962 Chinese conflict. Indian anxieties were heightened, however, by the supply of military aid to Pakistan by China. Moreover, despite assurances from the U.S.S.R., India felt uneasy about Pakistani-Soviet *rapprochement* and the limited shipment of Soviet arms to Pakistan.

Within Pakistan, political unrest had measurably increased. In 1969, under pressure, President Ayub Khan stepped down in favor of General Yahya Khan, who pledged to restore democratic institutions. A national assembly would be convened to frame a new constitution for Pakistan, and elections would be held on the basis of universal adult franchise. The formula of voter equality insured a majority of the 313 seats for the more populous East: 169 seats compared to 144 for West Pakistan. The two wings of Pakistan, created out of the Muslim majority areas within the subcontinent, were united by religion but divided by almost every other cultural factor and a thousand miles of Indian territory. West Pakistan, Urdu in language, with a martial tradition and a contempt for the "effete" Bengali, had long exercised what was essentially an imperial relationship over the Bengali East.[9] East Pakistan provided raw materials (notably jute) for world markets, but the larger share of

---

[8] Barnds, *India, Pakistan and the Great Powers*, p. 212.

[9] By the late 1960s the relationship had essentially changed. Rather than an asset, East Pakistan became an increasing economic liability to the West. Although the economies of Pakistan and Bangladesh remain today complementary, Pakistan may well be economically more viable without East Bengal.

foreign earnings were channeled into the industrializing West, for which Bengal provided a ready and captive market. Each year the per capita income gap between East and West widened. To redress Bengali grievances the Awami League of Sheikh Mujibur Rahman advanced a six-point program for the autonomy of East Pakistan and on this basis, in December 1970, contested the elections for the national assembly. The Awami League secured 167 of the 169 seats allotted to the East. In the West, Zulfiqar Ali Bhutto's Pakistan People's Party emerged with 85 seats. Facing an Awami majority and the prospect of Mujib as Prime Minister of Pakistan, Bhutto denounced the six-point program as unacceptable and indicated his intention to boycott the assembly scheduled to meet in early March. Yahya Khan acquiesced and postponed the assembly session. The violent reaction in East Pakistan was met with the imposition of martial law. In mid-March, at Dacca, Yahya entered into talks with Mujib, which, in effect, served as a cover for a massive troop build-up in East Pakistan. On March 25, 1971, Mujib was arrested, and in a wave of terror the heel of the Pakistani army came down upon the people of Bengal.

During the nine months of repression that followed, thousands of Bengalis were killed,[10] and some ten million refugees, most of whom were Hindu, crossed the borders into the northeastern India. The refugee movement created a situation that was economically, socially, and politically unacceptable for India. Moreover, there was the danger that the events in East Bengal might set off communal rioting in India. Fortunately it did not happen. Supplies already "in the pipeline" from the United States continued to flow into Pakistan, and while the U.S. government counselled Indian restraint, the Nixon Administration pursued a policy of "tilt toward Pakistan." Pakistan also found support, not only from the Middle East but from much of Asia and Africa as well—new nations, most of which had their own potential Bangladesh.

In August 1971, India and the Soviet Union signed a twenty-year treaty of friendship and cooperation. Not a mutual security treaty but an agreement for consultation, it served to formalize the relations already existing between the two nations and involved specific commitments of neither.[11] While the U.S.S.R. had condemned Pakistan's actions in Bangladesh, it sought a political settlement of the problem without war. The treaty was intended as a deterrent to Pakistan and China, but it also brought India into greater dependency upon the Soviet Union. India, however, undoubtedly felt bolstered by the treaty, particularly in terms of deterring China's possible entry into the conflict.

West Pakistan began a "Crush India" campaign, and by November

---

[10] Figures vary widely, from tens of thousands to Mujib's claim that three-and-one-half million Bengalis were killed.

[11] See Ashok Kapur, "Indo-Soviet Treaty and the Emerging Asian Balance," *Asian Survey*, Vol. 12 (June 1972), pp. 463–74; and Robert H. Donaldson, "India: The Soviet Stake in Stability," *Asian Survey*, Vol. 12 (June 1972), pp. 475–92.

incidents along the India-Pakistan border, primarily in the East, had become a daily occurrence, as India supplied both aid and sanctuary to Bengali guerrillas. On December 3, Pakistan launched a series of preemptive air strikes from the West against Indian air bases. That night India moved on all fronts against Pakistan. On December 6, underscoring its lack of territorial ambition, India formally recognized the government of Bangladesh. In a blitzkrieg operation the Indian army moved toward Dacca, and on December 16 Indian troops entered the city and accepted Pakistan's surrender. India ordered a unilateral ceasefire on the western front. In disgrace, Yahya was forced to resign. Bhutto became president and, though refusing to recognize the dismemberment of Pakistan, ordered the release of Mujib.

By the early autumn it probably had been clear to India that the liberation of Bangladesh was inevitable. The forces of the Bengali guerrilla Mukti Bahini were growing, but on their own it would be a protracted war with enormous loss of life. For India to sit on the sidelines could prove politically costly. India had a vital interest in the character of the future government of Bangladesh and from the beginning had supported moderate Mujib. Within the Mukti Bahini, however, were Naxalite elements, and anarchy in Bangladesh might invite Chinese involvement. But most immediate was the question of the refugees. If Bangladesh were to be liberated without Indian intervention, it would be highly improbable that ten million, largely Hindu, refugees would be welcomed back to the East. Only by direct military involvement could India insure the return of the refugees to East Bengal.

Immediately upon Pakistan's defeat the refugee return began, and by March 16, 1972, three months after the liberation of Bangladesh, the Indian army was able to complete its final withdrawal. It was yet another month before the United States recognized the new nation of Bangladesh, the last major country to do so, save for China and Pakistan itself.

India was now the undisputed power on the subcontinent. There was a euphoric atmosphere expressed by newspaper headlines proclaiming the liberation as the greatest day since Indian independence. But the war had left many questions unresolved. What was to be the fate of the half million "Biharis," non-Bengali Muslims of Bangladesh who had generally supported Pakistan? There remained too the question of the ninety-three thousand Pakistani troops taken prisoner by India. The Simla Agreement, signed July 2, 1972, by Indira Gandhi and Bhutto, confirmed the new line of control in Kashmir and sought to provide the basis for a "durable peace" between the two countries. A year later agreement was reached between Pakistan and India for the mutual repatriation of prisoners of war and the exchange of Bengali nationals in Pakistan for a substantial number of Pakistanis in Bangladesh. Following Pakistan's recognition of Bangladesh in 1974, a tripartite agreement between India, Pakistan, and Bangladesh was concluded, under which Bangladesh agreed not to try the 195 Pakistani POWs still held for "war crimes." The Bihari question remained.[12]

India continues to regard Pakistan (though reduced in size) as a threat to its security. Pakistan confronts serious internal ethnic tensions that challenge the nation's identity. Against incipient rebellion in Baluchistan, the government has relied upon increasingly repressive measures. The struggle among the Pathans of the Northwest for "Pakhtunistan" has brought Pakistan's hostility toward Afghanistan to the verge of war, arousing deep concern in Iran. Moreover, Pakistan's continued quest for parity with India remains the major plank of its foreign policy. At present, with 10 percent of its GNP going to defense, Pakistan has an army of 365,000 and a greater military capability than in 1971. Its sense of insecurity may serve as an added incentive

> to "invite" India's enemies into the subcontinent on preferential terms. . . . This tends to entangle South Asian regional questions with global international politics and prevent India from considering its *regional* problems independent of its *global* postures. Thus, the United States, China and the USSR have, in turn, complicated India's international security policies due to Pakistan's initiatives.
>
> · · ·
>
> In summary, Pakistan remains a principal security problem for India because of its proximity, its weakness and the foreign policies that flow from its weakness, its irredentist claims to Kashmir, and its ability to involve external powers in Indo-Pakistan competition. No single Indian foreign or security policy posture is adequate to all of these security problems, and India is therefore forced to commit a much larger proportion of its resources—political, diplomatic and military—to Pakistan contingencies than would appear to be the case by simply looking at relative force levels.[13]

The Afro-Asian World and Regional Concern

From the time of Indian independence through the 1950s India assumed a role of leadership in the Afro-Asian world. Special effort

---

12 For a discussion of the war and liberation, see Mohammed Ayood and K. Subrahmanyam, *The Liberation War* (New Delhi: S. Chand, 1972); Wayne Wilcox, *The Emergence of Bangladesh* (Washington, D.C.: American Enterprise Institute for Public Policy Research, 1973); and the two volumes published by the Government of India, Ministry of External Affairs, entitled *Bangladesh Documents* (New Delhi: Vol. I, 1971; Vol. II, 1973).

13 Wayne Wilcox, "Nuclear Weapon .Options and the Strategic Environment in South Asia: Arms Control Implications for India," Southern California Arms Control and Foreign Policy Seminar, 1972, pp. 19–20.

was given to ties with the Islamic states, for India—concerned about its own Muslim population—sought to prevent Muslim unity in support of Pakistan. In the United Nations, India was ever ready to defend the interests of national liberation from the vestiges of imperialism throughout the world. India sought to exert a moral force for peace and to that effect became involved in mediation and "peace-keeping" operations in Korea, Indo-China, the Congo, and Cyprus. India's stance often carried a moralizing tone, and when acting in pursuit of its own interests (as in the invasion of Goa in 1961 after long efforts to dislodge the Portuguese from their enclaves in India), India was regarded in the West as inconsistent, if not hypocritical. But for all India's efforts on behalf of the nations of the Third World, few nations offered even verbal support to India in the 1962 confrontation with China. India's military weakness had been exposed, and in military defeat it suffered a decline in international prestige. Nehru's foreign policy had been based "on global influence without military power."[14] That policy was shattered in 1962. India's position of influence was also affected by the increase in the number of new nonaligned nations and the conflicts between them. Most critically, India's international role was reduced by the end of the cold war and Soviet-American *détente*. Following Nehru's death, India stepped back from its global concerns and turned toward the pressing problems of the economy and national security.

Within South Asia, India's relations with Sri Lanka (formerly Ceylon) have been focused largely upon the persistent problem of the status of the one million Tamils on the island. On the other hand, India's relations with Nepal, Sikkim, and Bhutan have involved matters of vital security concern. As had Great Britain, independent India has sought to maintain a buffer zone in the Himalayas against China.

In 1950, India signed a treaty with Nepal, recognizing its "complete sovereignty." At the same time, however, India exerted enormous influence over the domestic affairs of Nepal and made it clear that India's security parameter included Nepal. In assertion of Nepali independence, the king sought to balance Indian influence by "regularizing" relations with China. The American presence was in turn balanced by an opening to the Soviet Union. By the mid-1960s, as the recipient of aid from India, China, the U.S., and the U.S.S.R., Nepal enjoyed a unique status and considerable political independence.

Sikkim until 1974 was a protectorate of India. In effect, having inherited the status of paramount power from the British, India exercised control over Sikkim's foreign affairs and defense. Although the state formally retained "full autonomy in regard to its internal affairs," India, in fact, exerted extensive influence through Indian administrative officials and advisers to the Maharajah of Sikkim. In addition, India provided an annual subsidy. In 1973–74, when the Nepali majority

[14] *Ibid.*, p. 9.

within the state began to agitate for political rights, India tightened its hold over Sikkim's internal affairs. The Maharajah, stripped of his power, had no choice but to yield. In 1974, in pursuance of the demand by the Sikkim Congress (which held the support of 31 of the 32 members of the Sikkim Assembly), India agreed to provide parliamentary representation to Sikkim. The position of the Indian Government had been that Sikkim was no different from those princely states that acceded to India in 1947, and by the thirty-fifth Amendment to the constitution, India extended an ambiguous "associate" status to Sikkim. Many Indians regarded the move as a step toward Sikkim's eventual incorporation within the Indian Union, and some expressed concern for its international implications, especially in terms of China, which has recognized the "separate identity and political status" of Sikkim.[15]

Bhutan, the most isolated of the Himalayan kingdoms, is an independent state and a member of the United Nations. The British had exercised suzerainty over Bhutan, but in giving to Britain control over its foreign relations, Bhutan had secured freedom from British intervention in internal affairs. In 1949, by a new treaty, Bhutan agreed "to be guided" by Indian advice on foreign relations, but while India provides an annual subsidy, it has chosen not to interfere in the domestic affairs of Bhutan.

Bangladesh, in its weakness and vulnerability, confronts India with potentially serious problems as a major source of political instability within the subcontinent. With seventy-five million people, Bangladesh is one of the world's most densely populated nations—and one of the poorest. A victim of both nature and mankind, Bangladesh has been ravaged by cyclone, war, floods, and corruption. Its economic situation is desperate, and the political situation, discouraging. Midwife to the liberation, India feels a sense of responsibility for Bangladesh, but its capacity to provide aid in cash or resources is limited, and the burden already imposed on India's economy by the refugees, the war, and reconstruction assistance has been enormous. Nevertheless, resentment against India is widespread within Bangladesh. Many East Bengalis hold India responsible for the smuggling that threatens the economy with collapse. Others find fault with India over the issue of the Farakka barrage, a low dam to flush out the heavily silted port of Calcutta by diverting a portion of Ganges water from its course into East Bengal.

The Farakka dispute is the most difficult specific problem between the two countries, but the deteriorating economic and political situation in Bangladesh is of deep concern to India, for it involves a number of potential dangers. Muslims of Bangladesh, in search of a scapegoat, might turn on the Hindus, so many of whom as refugees were returned under the protection of the Indian army. Another concern arises from the links already established between Maoists in Bangladesh and their

15 See, for example, the *Hindustan Times'* editorial, August 30, 1974.

Naxalite counterparts in West Bengal. A "left" Government in Dacca, or simply anarchy, might well provide sanctuary for Bengali guerrilla insurgents in the West, or for tribal insurgents in India's ethnically unstable Northeast. Moreover, the thirty-mile wide district of Cooch Bihar separates Bangladesh from Sikkim, cutting off Assam and the Northeast from the rest of India. Possible *rapprochement* between Pakistan and Bangladesh, or, most significantly, the intrusion of China —already aiding Naga rebels—compounds these Indian concerns.

China

India's first encounters with the new government of the People's Republic of China were clouded by the reassertion of Chinese suzerainty over Tibet. India had inherited the British concern for a Himalayan buffer zone and sought to maintain Tibetan autonomy. Despite Peking's denunciation of India as an imperialist lackey, Nehru worked for improved relations. In 1954, recognizing Tibet as a "region of China," India negotiated an agreement with China, setting forth the five principles—*Panchsheel*—which were to be the basis of their friendship and, as reaffirmed at the Afro-Asian Conference at Bandung in 1955, a cornerstone of Indian foreign policy: (1) mutual respect for each other's territorial integrity and sovereignty; (2) nonaggression; (3) noninterference in each other's internal affairs; (4) equality and mutual benefit; and (5) peaceful coexistence.

From 1954 until 1959 India continuously declared its friendship for China. But in 1959, revolt in Tibet and the Dalai Lama's flight into India served to expose serious tensions between India and China. India had long been aware that Chinese maps showed large areas claimed by India (some 40,000 square miles) as parts of China, regions which had at one time been under Chinese imperial hegemony. The areas claimed by China included nearly all of the North East Frontier Province (now Arunachal Pradesh), small pockets along the India-China border between Nepal and Kashmir, and the Aksai Chin plain of eastern Ladakh in Kashmir. In the East the dispute focused on the legitimacy of the McMahon Line, defining the border between NEFA and Tibet, which was drawn in 1914 by the Simla convention. Even in its position of weakness at that time China had refused to sign the convention. In Ladakh, China's claim to the vast and desolate Aksai Chin, again historical, disputed the imperial frontier imposed by Great Britain upon China. Far more important for China, however, was the strategic position of the Aksai Chin, for along the old caravan route was China's most secure access to Tibet. The Aksai Chin occupied a position of strategic importance to China in terms of both internal security within Tibet and the perceived threat posed by the Soviet Union, particularly as directed against Sinkiang. Chinese concern deepened with Tibetan unrest and the intensification of the Sino-Soviet controversy. In 1957 China completed an all-weather road across the Aksai Chin, linking

Sinkiang with Tibet. A year later Indian patrols discovered the road, but it was not until the Tibetan revolt and border clashes along the Tibet-NEFA border in 1959 forced the issue that Nehru revealed to Parliament the full extent of the dispute with China.[16]

In 1960 Nehru and Chou En-lai entered into "talks" on the border problem. The Chinese proposed to abandon their claims in NEFA in exchange for the Aksai Chin, already under Chinese control. By this time the dispute had become a matter of emotional intensity in India. India was unwilling, and politically unable, to accept the proposal. Despite its comparative military weakness, India embarked on a "forward policy" on the frontier "intended to check Chinese advances everywhere and, if possible, force Chinese withdrawals in Ladakh."[17] In an effort to force India to negotiate and give up claims to the Aksai Chin, China in the fall of 1962 began a push along the NEFA frontier. On October 20 the invasion of NEFA began. The move in the Northeast was clearly designed to secure a *quid pro quo* in Ladakh, and on October 24 Chou En-lai proposed a cease-fire and a mutual withdrawal of forces from the current line of contact, to be followed by negotiations. In a position of weakness, negotiation for India could only mean capitulation. In preparation for continued war with China, the Government of India proclaimed a state of emergency.

Within a month, Indian defenses collapsed: China had penetrated 150 miles below the McMahon Line. India's lack of military preparedness and the debacle in NEFA became a national scandal, and defense minister V. K. Krishna Menon, Nehru's closest friend, was forced to resign.[18] The United States and Great Brtain rallied to India's aid with emergency airlifts of arms and supplies. The U.S.S.R., as well, reaffirmed its commitment of military assistance to India. On November 20, as Chinese troops stood on the foothills above the Assam valley, China announced a unilateral cease-fire and withdrawal of forces to the 1959 "line of actual control." And there the matter has remained, with China's *de facto* occupation of the Aksai Chin.

While India now seeks to normalize relations with China, most

---

[16] For discussions of the border question, see Margaret W. Fisher, Leo Rose, and Robert A. Huttenback, *Himalayan Battleground: Sino-Indian Rivalry in Ladakh* (New York: Praeger, 1963); Alastair Lamb, *The China-India Border: The Origins of the Disputed Boundaries* (London: Chatham House, 1964); and Parshotam Mehra, *The McMahon Line and After* (Delhi: Macmillan, 1974). For the ideological context of the dispute, see Mohan Ram, *Politics of Sino-Indian Confrontation* (Delhi: Vikas, 1973). A particularly fascinating account of the border dispute and of the war itself, though highly critical of India's position, is Neville Maxwell's *India's China War* (New York: Anchor Books, 1972). For an Indian rebuttal by the former director of the Intelligence Bureau, see B. N. Mullik, *The Chinese Betrayal* (Bombay: Allied Publishers, 1971).

[17] Heimsath and Mansingh, A *Diplomatic History of Modern India*, p. 467.

[18] Various accounts by Indian generals have appeared, including B. N. Kaul, *The Untold Story* (Bombay: Allied Publishers, 1967); J. P. Dalvi, *Himalayan Blunder* (Calcutta: Thacker, 1969); and J. N. Chaudhuri, *Arms, Aims, and Aspects* (Bombay: Manaktalas, 1969).

Indians regard China as a continuing threat, with the power, motives, and opportunities to challenge Indian security.

> The power is both in nuclear weapons and in the ability to support guerrilla insurgency in the Himalayas and the Northeast. The motives range from national competition to ideological fervor. The opportunities lie in the extreme left in Indian politics, the exposed position of Indian forces on the frontiers, and the "open door" of Pakistan and nuclear blackmail.[19]

The U.S. and the U.S.S.R.

Relations between India and the United States have been broadly characterized by strain, punctuated by periods of friendship and cooperation. The point of contention, most frequently, has related to Pakistan. During the period of the cold war, the U.S. had sought to forge a chain of alliances from Europe to the Far East for the containment of Communist expansion. India, committed to a policy of nonalignment, was unresponsive. Pakistan, seeing the opportunity to escape Indian hegemony within the subcontinent, was very interested. In 1954 the U.S. and Pakistan signed a mutual defense treaty, and in the next year, Pakistan was linked to the Southeast Asia defense system through SEATO and to that of the Middle East through CENTO. The U.S. regarded Pakistan as the eastern flank of the "northern tier," an indispensable link in the containment of Soviet aggression against the Middle East.

Although Eisenhower assured Nehru that the arms supplied to Pakistan would never be used in aggression against India, India regarded U.S. military aid to Pakistan as a threat to the peace and stability of South Asia, opening the subcontinent to foreign penetration, and as a challenge to its own security, for Pakistan commanded easy access to Kashmir and occupied part of the plain upon which New Delhi itself was situated. Even in the improved relations of the late 1950s and the Kennedy years of the 1960s, which witnessed a substantial economic assistance program and the inauguration of military aid to India, India deeply resented the parity accorded India and Pakistan by the United States. India was, after all, a nation with four times Pakistan's population, and in the military sphere the U.S. attempt to balance Pakistan's capacity with that of India could only be a source of instability and potential armed conflict. That conflict came in 1965, when Patton tanks were used by Pakistan against India in the Rann of Kutch and later in Kashmir. Even though the U.S. cut off arms to both Pakistan and India during the 1965 war, the shipment of spare parts and nonlethal military equipment to Pakistan was subsequently resumed. In October 1970 an agreement was reached between the U.S. and Pakistan under which a

[19] Wilcox, "Nuclear Weapon Options and the Strategic Environment in South Asia," p. 21.

limited quantity of weapons (largely armed-personnel carriers and some aircraft) was to be shipped to Pakistan. The U.S. described this as a "one time, limited exception to the embargo," an explanation not readily acceptable to India.

Bangladesh brought Indo-American relations to an all-time low. That the U.S. allowed those shipments already in the pipeline to continue into Pakistan, knowing that they would be used for the suppression of East Bengal, was regarded as outrageous to India—and to many people in the United States as well. The U.S. appealed to India for restraint and with Pakistan counselled for a political settlement. Although the American press denounced Pakistani atrocities in Bengal and members of Congress and many State Department officials urged the White House to exert all leverage on Pakistan to release Bengal, the administration remained publicly silent. Privately, Nixon ordered the "tilt toward Pakistan," even at such time that Pakistan's defeat was inevitable. In a final act of futility, the U.S. aircraft carrier *Enterprise* was ordered into the Bay of Bengal, with the ostensible purpose of evacuating American and foreign nationals at the port of Chittagong.

U.S. action during the Bangladesh crisis has been explained variously as the product of concern that American access to China through Pakistan not be jeopardized; that the U.S. stand by an old friend and ally in gratitude for the American air base at Peshawar; and that it was the result of "personality"—Nixon's personal regard for Yahya Khan and his distaste for Indira Gandhi. Whatever reasoning was involved, American interests were ill served. India was forced into increasing reliance upon the Soviet Union, and American prestige and influence in South Asia reached rock bottom. (In Pakistan, a lower point was probably reached in 1965, with the arms embargo.)

As the ferment of Bangladesh receded, India and the United States sought to explore the terms of a new relationship. It had already been in the making when so rudely interrupted. The U.S. was assuming a "low profile" in India, a position of less visibility, reflected, for example, in the cutbacks in bilateral aid and in the reduction of American personnel in India. This lower profile rested fundamentally on the understanding that the United States had no vital strategic interests in South Asia. The U.S. recognized "legitimate" Soviet and Chinese geopolitical interests in the region, and American concerns were directed toward countering the dominance of any one super power in the area. While Indo-American relations improved, points of tension remained, as in the efforts of the United States Navy to establish a base at Diego Garcia in the Indian Ocean. In opposition the CIA and others argued before congressional committees that an American build-up in the Indian Ocean would only invite a Soviet response, opening the region to the dangers of a Soviet-American confrontation. This position reflected the concern of India and other littoral states, embodied in a United Nations resolution, that the Indian Ocean be preserved as a "zone of peace," free from big-power rivalries that might affect the political stability of the region.[20]

Soviet interests in South Asia are in large part geopolitical. During the cold war, in the struggle to win the "hearts and minds" of the emergent peoples of the Third World, both the U.S. and the U.S.S.R. regarded India as the key to the Afro-Asian world, the nation that might well determine the direction all others would take. Today, with *détente*, the Third World has been given a lower priority, but for the Soviet Union, India remains of vital strategic interest *vis-à-vis* China. Both Soviet and Chinese involvements in South Asia are fundamentally a product of their mutual hostilities and security concerns.

Although Nehru had long expressed his admiration for the Soviet Union, especially in its industrial development, India was initially viewed by the Russians with suspicion, as a tool of "Anglo-American imperialism." By 1952 Soviet policy began to change, and with support for India in Kashmir (and subsequently on the Goa issue), the foundation of Indo-Soviet friendship was laid. The exchange of various delegations was soon followed, in 1953, by the Indo-Soviet trade agreement and, two years later, by the exchange of visits by Nehru and Khrushchev and Bulganin and by the Soviet commitment to construct the Bhilai steel works, the first of a number of highly visible projects in India. (By contrast, U.S. aid was aimed principally at increasing food production in rural areas.) Indo-Soviet relations served, in the domestic context, to undercut the CPI and to "domesticate" the Communist movement in India. But Nehru's eagerness to secure Soviet friendship came, at points, under sharp criticism from within India as well as from abroad—most notably, in India's defense of Soviet repression in Hungary in 1956.

In 1960, as the Sino-Soviet controversy began to deepen, the U.S.S.R. began to supply arms to India. As India's own conflict with China approached war the Soviets agreed to supply MIG fighters to India and to set up a plant within India for their production. (The first Indian MIGs were completed in 1968.) Although Soviet aid to Pakistan, designed to counter increasing Chinese influence, was a source of anxiety to India, the Russian position of neutrality in the 1965 war eased the way for the Tashkent Declaration, a triumph of Soviet diplomacy. In the course of the Bangladesh crisis, the Soviets, while condemning Pakistan, continued to supply economic assistance. Even the 1971 Indo-Soviet treaty of friendship and cooperation did not wholly undermine Pakistani-Soviet relations. Indeed, with the dismemberment of Pakistan, the enormous costs imposed upon India, the tragedy borne by East Bengal, and the loss of prestige inflicted by the U.S. upon itself, the Soviets emerged as the only real "winners" in the 1971 conflict.

---

[20] U.S. interest in the Indian Ocean is essentially an extension of strategic concern for the Middle East and specifically for the oil sheikhdoms of the Persian Gulf. See K. Rajendra Singh, *Politics of the Indian Ocean* (Delhi: Thompson Press, 1974).

Dependency and Self-Reliance

India occupies a position of international dependency, a vulnerability to external leverage within both areas of the defense and the economy.

While India's dependency in the weapons field is dispersed widely among a number of nations, the Soviet Union is its major outside source of armaments. But whatever dependencies may now exist, either in the supply of arms or in "protection" extended by a super power, India is committed to strategic as well as political independence. In India's perspective, nonalignment, as a policy of self-interest, has not declined with Soviet-American *détente*. India seeks self-reliance, knowing that ultimately it cannot rely on any outside protection, nor would such reliance be consistent with its self-image of national integrity. India's entry into the nuclear club in 1974 must be seen in this light.

Arguing against the conception that there is an inverse relationship between defense and development, strategic analyst Susir Gupta has pushed for greater defense expenditure. Small wars, he writes, can only wear India down economically.

> India's defence policy must not seek to win wars: it must seek to make wars impossible to contemplate so far as her neighbours are concerned. It must be stated, however, that deterrence does not automatically mean the use of one's most developed weapons and a decision to escalate the war's level the moment the enemy launches such a war: it means acquiring an option in this regard.[21]

India's nuclear power and space programs do not refer to weapons implications or to defense choices, "but despite India's assurance that nuclear energy would be used only for peaceful purposes, many analysts see the programs as directed toward a thermonuclear warhead missile by about 1980."[22] Because a nuclear weapon without a credible delivery system would only increase India's vulnerability, its nuclear "option" is limited fundamentally to the ICBM. But India is a poor country facing desperate economic problems, and the development of a nuclear defense system involves enormous and essentially indeterminate costs. Wayne Wilcox has written that

> defense spending, diplomatic agreements and arms limitations are addressed to the same goal—national security. Army, navy, air force and atomic energy department expenditures are also addressed to the same goal—optimum defense postures at the lowest possible cost. What makes a reconciliation between these

---

21 "India's Defence: A Plea for an Integrated Approach," in K. P. Misra, ed., *Studies in Indian Foreign Policy*, p. 270.
22 Wilcox, "Nuclear Weapons Options and the Strategic Environment in South Asia," p. 30.

seemingly contradictory aspects of national security impossible is strategic uncertainty. The power relationships between states are not self-managing, and the structures by which they are moderated appear less and less able to control violence.[23]

As in defense, India has committed itself to economic self-reliance. Prime Minister Indira Gandhi has announced her Government's determination to move to a position of "zero net aid" by the end of the Fifth Plan in 1979, that is, to accept continuing aid only for debt repayment. This in itself now amounts to about one-half of India's annual foreign aid receipts. Although most countries that have provided aid to India have rescheduled debts, repayment remains one of India's most serious problems. For 1974–75 the World Bank has recommended that India receive a total of 1.4 billion dollars in foreign aid. Of this amount, 700 million dollars will go to debt repayment. The remaining portion is earmarked for economic development.

In all, since the beginning of the First Plan, India has received roughly 10 billion dollars in foreign aid, half of which has come from the United States. In addition, under Public Law 480 the U.S. has provided nearly 5 billion dollars worth of food and agricultural commodities to India. This has involved more than 50 million tons of wheat, and at the program's height in the mid-1960s, one-fourth of the American wheat crop went to India.

Although figures vary from source to source, over the past few years India has received about 1.1 billion dollars per year in foreign aid. The largest single contributor has been the World Bank, with an average of about 500 million dollars, its greatest commitment in loans and credits to any single nation. The Consortium, organized by the World Bank in 1958 to coordinate aid to India by various Western nations and Japan, accounted for about 500 million dollars. The Soviet bloc put in another 100 million. Within the Consortium, the U.S. had initially been the major contributor, but by the late 1960s, with the assumption of a "low profile" in India, the U.S. portion diminished yearly. In 1973–74 the American contribution was about 30 million dollars for debt relief, and under the Food for Peace program of PL 480, wheat was provided with a value of about 80 million dollars. In terms of Consortium aid to India the U.S. now ranks even below Canada. As bilateral aid to India from the United States declined, that of the Soviets increased. In 1973–74 it totalled about 200 million dollars. While U.S. aid through the Consortium has been reduced the American contribution to the World Bank's assistance to India has remained relatively stable, approximately 160 million dollars annually. The United States continues to be India's largest creditor and aid source, but of all Western nations, only Italy spends a smaller portion of its GNP on foreign aid.

[23] *Ibid.*, p. 33.

The net aid component of India's projected Fifth Plan represents 4.6 percent of the public sector investment. Though a smaller portion than in previous plans (it was 13.6 percent in the Fourth Plan), it remains a critical component. Beyond debt repayment, India confronts an increasing deficit in the balance of payments, arising principally from world inflation exacerbated by the energy crisis and from India's continuing need to import ever more costly food.

It is within the international economic system that India's most critical dependency is exposed, and here it is least likely to free itself for it is here least able to control its position. India's vulnerability to the flux of the world market, to the erection of trade barriers against Indian manufactured goods, to monetary revaluations, and, above all, to inflation imposes overwhelming constraints on India's development capacity.

India's dependency is the product not simply of economic backwardness but of the historical pattern of the international economy as sustained by a stratified system of power relationships.[24] As with the social evolutionists of the nineteenth century, contemporary social scientists often assume that development occurs in a succession of stages and that "today's underdeveloped countries are still in a stage, sometimes depicted as an original stage, of history through which the now developed countries passed long ago." A. G. Frank contends that "underdevelopment is not original or traditional and that neither the past nor the present of the underdeveloped countries resembles in any important respect the past of the now developed countries."[25] The now developed countries, though surely once undeveloped, were never *under*developed in the sense of the relationships of cultural, economic, and political dependency that bind the nations of the Third World today to foreign powers.[26]

Development involves more than growth alone; it involves the structural transformation of the society, the economy, and the political system. But the international constraints which India confronts in its development efforts are enormous. The responsibilities are not those of India alone. Economic and technical assistance in themselves cannot change the character of the international economy or the pattern of

[24] For a discussion of the theory of dependency, as arising from the Latin American context, see James D. Cockcroft, André Gunder Frank, and Dale L. Johnson, *Dependence and Underdevelopment: Latin America's Political Economy* (New York: Anchor Books, 1972).

[25] "The Development of Underdevelopment," in *Latin America: Underdevelopment or Revolution* (New York: Monthly Review Press, 1969), p. 4. For a discussion and critique of stage theory, see James A. Bill and Robert L. Hardgrave, Jr., *Comparative Politics: The Quest for Theory* (Columbus, Ohio: Charles E. Merrill, 1973), pp. 50–62.

[26] For an examination of India's history of underdevelopment, see Barrington Moore, Jr., *Social Origins of Dictatorship and Democracy* (Boston: Beacon Press, 1966), pp. 314–410.

world trade by which India is disadvantaged. And however vital population control may be to India's future, the great bulk of the world's resources, energy, and food is consumed by the far less populous nations of the developed world. The United States alone, with 6 percent of the world's population, consumes 40 percent of the world's resources.

India is part of a global ghetto. In a world of interdependence, India cannot, as some have suggested, be allowed to sink—for we would all go down together. Years ago Rabindranath Tagore wrote:

> Power has to be made secure not only against power, but against weakness; for there lies the peril of its losing balance. The weak are as great a danger for the strong as quicksand for an elephant. . . . The people who grow accustomed to wield absolute power over others are apt to forget that by so doing they generate an unseen force which some day rends that power to pieces.[27]

"The question before the advanced nations," Indira Gandhi has said, "is not whether they can afford to help the developing nations, but whether they can afford not to do so."[28]

[27] Quoted in an address by Indira Gandhi in *Aspects of Our Foreign Policy: From Speeches and Writings of Indira Gandhi* (New Delhi: All-India Congress Committee, 1973), p. 72.
[28] Address before the Second United Nations Conference on Trade and Development, New Delhi, February 1, 1968, in *Aspects of Our Foreign Policy: From Speeches and Writings of Indira Gandhi*, p. 72.

RECOMMENDED READING

Ayoob, Mohammed, *India, Pakistan and Bangladesh: Search for a New Relationship.* New Delhi: Indian Council of World Affairs, 1974.
    An analysis of the international politics of South Asia after 1971.

———, and Subrahmanyam, K., *The Liberation War.* New Delhi: S. Chand, 1972.
    Of the literature on Bangladesh, one of the best.

Bandyopadhyaya, J., *The Making of India's Foreign Policy.* Bombay: Allied Publishers, 1970.
    A study of the policy process, focusing on the Ministry of External Affairs and the personal role of the Foreign Minister.

Barnds, William J., *India, Pakistan and the Great Powers.* New York: Praeger, 1972.
    An examination of the international politics of the subcontinent, with particular concern for America's role in South Asia.

Brecher, Michael, *India and World Politics: Krishna Menon's View of the World.* New York: Praeger, 1968.
    A portrait, based on extended interviews, of the man and his impact on India's foreign policy.

Brines, Russell, *The Indo-Pakistani Conflict*. London: Pall Mall, 1968.
A detailed study of the mutual insecurities that have fed continuing conflict.

Burke, S. M., *Pakistan's Foreign Policy: An Historical Analysis*. New York: Oxford University Press, 1973.
The major study of Pakistan's foreign relations.

Heimsath, Charles H., and Mansingh, Surjit, *A Diplomatic History of Modern India*. Bombay: Allied Publishers, 1971.
A comprehensive account of Indian foreign relations, with emphasis on the Nehru era.

* Maxwell, Neville, *India's China War*. New York: Anchor Books, 1972.
A fascinating account of the 1962 war, with a well-argued case for the Chinese position.

Misra, K. P., ed., *Studies in Indian Foreign Policy*. Delhi: Vikas, 1969.
An excellent collection of previously published articles.

Nehru, Jawaharlal, *India's Foreign Policy: Selected Speeches, September 1946–April 1961*. New Delhi: Government of India, Publications Division, 1961.
Major statements of India's policy by the man who shaped it.

* Palmer, Norman D., *South Asia and United States Foreign Policy*. New York: Houghton Mifflin, 1966.
Though now dated, still an important and highly useful study of United States–Indian relations.

* Sen Gupta, Bhabani, *The Fulcrum of Asia: Relations Among China, India, Pakistan and the USSR*. New York: Pegasus, 1970.
A perceptive study of the international politics of South Asia.

Stein, Arthur, *India and the Soviet Union: The Nehru Era*. Chicago: University of Chicago Press, 1969.
Examines the factors leading to the development of close ties between India and the U.S.S.R.

Verma, S. P., and Misra, K. P., eds., *Foreign Policies in South Asia*. New Delhi: Orient Longman, 1969.
A useful collection of papers on various aspects of foreign policy among the states of the region.

* Wilcox, Wayne, *The Emergence of Bangladesh*. Washington, D. C.: American Enterprise Institute for Public Policy Research, 1973.
A brief study of the liberation, its background and implications, by a most perceptive observer of the South Asian scene.

* Available in a paperback edition.

RESEARCH GUIDE*

General Bibliographies

Guide to Indian Periodical Literature.
> A major reference source in the social sciences for India. Published monthly since 1964. (Gurgaon, Haryana)

Index India.
> This periodical index, published quarterly by the University of Rajasthan, is an extremely valuable source for research in contemporary politics.

Indian Books in Print.
> A selected bibliography of English language books printed in India.

Indian National Bibliography.
> Quarterly and annual. Two sections—"Books and Articles" and "Government Publications"—each with an index. Exhaustive listings of all items published In India in all languages. Useful for students who are engaged in fairly specialized research or who read an Indian language.

Indian News Index.
> Quarterly guide to English newspapers in India.

* Adapted from a research guide originally prepared by Lloyd I. and Susanne H. Rudolph, the University of Chicago. Their permission is gratefully acknowledged.

International Guide to Periodical Literature.
> An important guide to scholarly articles. Useful for book reviews.

Journal of Asian Studies.
> Since 1956, this scholarly quarterly has published a fifth bibliographical number. A most useful guide to the literature.

Mahar, J. Michael, *India: A Critical Bibliography*. Tucson: University of Arizona Press, 1964.
> Outstanding annotation. Strongest on history, philosophy, and religion. Unfortunately Mahar lists books only.

Patterson, Maureen L. P., and Inden, Ronald B., eds., *Introduction to the Civilization of India; South Asia, an Introductory Bibliography*. Chicago: University of Chicago Press, 1963.
> The most comprehensive bibliography. A good place to start. Includes a section on general and specialized bibliographies.

Public Affairs Information Service, *Bulletin.*
> An invaluable guide to the literature of public policy around the world. Lists books, articles of a scholarly and a more popular nature, and publications of the United States and other governments, international agencies, and private research groups. Indexing and cross-indexing are particularly valuable.

Special Bibliographies

Alexandrowicz, C. H., ed., *A Bibliography of Indian Law*. Madras: Oxford University Press, 1958, 69 pages.

Case, Margaret H., *South Asian History, 1750–1950*. Princeton, N.J.: Princeton University Press, 1967.

Cohn, Bernard S., *The Development and Impact of British Administration in India: A Bibliographic Essay*. New Delhi: Indian Institute of Public Administration, 1961, 88 pages.

Goil, N. K., *Asian Social Science Bibliography*. Delhi: Vikas, 1970.

Leonard, T. J., "Federalism in India," in William S. Livingston, ed., *Federalism in the Commonwealth: A Bibliographical Commentary*. London: Cassell, 1963.
> An excellent bibliographic essay, ranging far beyond federalism itself to include Indian politics and government generally.

Matthews, William, *British Autobiographies: An Annotated Bibliography of British Autobiographies Published or Written Before 1951*. Berkeley: University of California Press, 1955, 376 pages.
> Indexed by subject; thus works that deal with India can readily be located.

Morris, Morris David, and Stein, Berton. "The Economic History of India: A Bibliographical Essay." *Journal of Economic History*, Vol. 21 (June 1961), pp. 179–207.
> An excellent guide. Includes a discussion of needed research concerning theory and approaches.

Muin ud-din Ahmad Khan. "A Bibliographic Introduction to Modern Islamic Development in India and Pakistan 1700–1955." Appendix to *Journal of the Asiatic Society of Pakistan*, Vol. VI, 1959, 17 pages. (Dacca)

Select Bibliography on Electoral Behavior in India. Jaipur: University of Rajasthan, 1966.

Select Bibliography on Indian Government and Politics. Jaipur: University of Rajasthan, 1965.

Sharma, Jagdish S., *Indian National Congress: A Descriptive Bibliography of India's Struggle for Freedom.* Delhi: S. Chand, 1959, 816 pages.

————, *Jawaharlal Nehru: A Descriptive Bibliography.* Delhi: S. Chand, 1955, 421 pages.

————, *Mahatma Gandhi: A Descriptive Bibliography.* Delhi: S. Chand, 1955, 565 pages.

————, *Vinoba and Bhoodan, A Selective Descriptive Bibliography.* New Delhi: Indian National Congress, 1956, 92 pages.

Shulman, Frank J., *Doctoral Dissertations on South Asia, 1966–1970: An Annotated Bibliography Covering North America, Europe, and Australia.* Ann Arbor: Center for South and Southeast Asian Studies, University of Michigan, 1971.

Spencer, Dorothy M., *Indian Fiction in English: An Annotated Bibliography.* Philadelphia: University of Pennsylvania Press, 1960, 98 pages.

Zelliot, Eleanor, "Bibliography on Untouchability," in J. Michael Mahar, ed. *The Untouchables in Contemporary India.* Tucson: University of Arizona Press, 1972, pp. 431–86.

Reference and Sources

All-India Reporter.
    The official reports of high court and Supreme Court cases.

Asian Almanac.
    Weekly abstract of Asian affairs. (Singapore)

Asian Recorder.
    A very useful archive of public events based on a collation and reproduction of the English press in Asia. Published in India, its coverage of India is extensive and detailed. The index is well done.

Census of India.
    1891, 1901, 1911, 1921, 1931, 1941, 1951, 1961, 1971.

Conparlist.
    Monthly survey of major constitutional and parliamentary developments. Published by the Institute of Constitutional and Parliamentary Studies. (New Delhi)

Foreign Affairs Record.
    Monthly of the Indian Ministry of External Affairs.

Foreign Affairs Reports.
Monthly of the Indian Institute of World Affairs. (New Delhi)

ICSSR Journal of Abstracts and Review.
An important source on current research in Indian anthropology and sociology.

ICSSR Newsletter.
Published by the Indian Council of Social Science Research. (New Delhi)

India, A Reference Annual. New Delhi: Ministry of Information and Broadcasting.
Convenient summaries of all aspects of government. For research purposes see the bibliographies of each chapter collected at the end of each annual volume. They contain an excellent inventory of major government reports.

Indian Annual Register: An Annual Digest of Public Affairs of India. 1919–1947.
The major source for political events in the inter-war years. A contemporary archive.

Indian Behavioural Science Abstracts.

Indian Dissertation Abstracts.
Quarterly published by ICSSR.

Indian Economic Diary.
A digest of economic events. (New Delhi)

Indian Information.
A fortnightly record of the activities and official announcements of the Government of India. (New Delhi)

Indian Press Index.
Index of Indian newspapers.

Indian Recorder and Digest.
Formerly *Indian Affairs Record.* Published by the Diwan Chand Institute of National Affairs. Gives synoptic chronologies of events on a monthly basis, including national, state, and party affairs. Includes excellent monthly bibliographies. A most useful research tool.

Kessing's Contemporary Archives.
An extremely useful, objective, and detailed record of national and international events, including extensive selections from speeches and public documents. Its Indian coverage, both domestic and international, is quite good. Excellently indexed. Published in Bristol, England.

Lok Sabha Secretariat. *Abstracts and Index of Reports and Articles.*
Quarterly. (New Delhi)

Monthly Commentary on Indian Economic Conditions.
Published by the Indian Institute of Public Opinion. (New Delhi)

National Diary.
A biweekly record of Indian events, with an index.

Public Opinion Survey.
Indian Institute of Public Opinion organ, published monthly.

Quarterly Economic Report.
Published by the Indian Institute of Public Opinion. (New Delhi)

Research Abstracts Quarterly.
Reports on findings of projects sponsored by the Indian Council of Social Science Research.

South Asia.
Monthly news review of the Institute for Defence Studies and Analyses. (New Delhi)

Times of India Directory and Yearbook, Including Who's Who.
Very useful. Published annually since 1914.

Scholarly Journals

The journals listed below regularly publish articles on India.

Asian Economic Review.
Quarterly journal of the Indian Institute of Economics. (Hyderabad)

Asian Survey.
Published by the University of California, it is one of the best sources of current developments.

Behavioural Sciences and Community Development.
Journal of the National Institute of Community Development. (Hyderabad)

Cohesion.
Quarterly of the Nehru Institute of National Integration.

Community Development and Panchayati Raj Digest.
Quarterly of the National Institute of Community Development. (Hyderabad)

Contributions to Indian Sociology.
A major international journal of Indian social science, published by the Institute of Economic Growth, University of Delhi.

Demography India.
Journal of the Indian Association for the Study of Population. (Delhi)

Eastern Anthropologist.
A scholarly journal of high standards that often contains articles of first-rate interest and importance. (Lucknow)

Economic and Political Weekly.
India's foremost periodical of the social sciences. Indispensable for contemporary politics and economics. (Bombay)

India Quarterly.
Published by the Indian Council of World Affairs, it is one of the best Indian journals in the field of international politics.

Indian Anthropologist.

Indian Economic and Social History Review.
Published by the Delhi School of Economics, the journal is one of the best in India and regularly carries contributions from Western scholars.

Indian Economic Journal.
Published by the University of Bombay.

Indian Economic Review.
    The biannual journal of the Delhi School of Economics.

Indian Historical Quarterly.
    (Calcutta)

Indian Journal of Political Science.
    Journal of the Indian Political Science Association.

Indian Journal of Politics.
    Published by Aligarh Muslim University.

Indian Journal of Public Administration.
    Published by the Indian Institute of Public Administration in New Delhi,
    the journal maintains good standards and carries articles on a broad variety
    of topics on public policy.

Indian Journal of Social Research.
    Published three times a year. (Meerut)

Indian Journal of Social Work.
    A quarterly devoted to the promotion of professional social work, scientific
    interpretation of social problems and advancement of social research. (Bom-
    bay)

Indian Journal of Sociology.

Indian Political Science Review.
    Quarterly, published by Delhi University.

*Indian Press: Quarterly Journal of the Indian and Eastern Newspaper
Society.*

Indian Sociological Bulletin.

Indian Studies: Past and Present.

Institute for Defence Studies and Analyses Journal.
    Quarterly. (New Delhi)

International Studies.
    Quarterly publication of the Indian School of International Studies, Jawa-
    harlal Nehru University. Good standard journal. Extensive bibliographies in
    the manner of *Foreign Affairs.* (New Delhi)

Journal of African and Asian Studies.
    Quarterly, University of Delhi.

Journal of Asian and African Studies.
    An international quarterly of sociology and anthropology.

Journal of Asian Studies.
    Formerly the *Far Eastern Quarterly.* Sound and scholarly. Its book review
    section is excellent and its annual bibliographic number very useful.

Journal of Commonwealth Political Studies.
    Published by the Institute of Commonwealth Studies. (London)

Journal of Constitutional and Parliamentary Studies.
    Quarterly of the Institute of Constitutional and Parliamentary Studies.
    (New Delhi)

Journal of the Indian Anthropological Society.

Journal of Indian History.
    Published three times a year by the University of Kerala. (Trivandrum)

Journal of the Maharaja Sayajirao University of Baroda.
    A social-science journal.

Journal of the Society for Study of State Governments.
    (Varanasi)

Man in India; A Quarterly Record of Anthropological Science with Special Reference to India.

Modern Asian Studies.
    Quarterly, published by Cambridge University.

Modern Review.
    Monthly. (Calcutta)

Pacific Affairs.
    An established and lively scholarly journal.

Parliamentary Studies.
    Published by the Indian Bureau of Parliamentary Studies.

Political Science Review.
    Biannual journal of the Department of Political Science, Jaipur.

Public Opinion Surveys of the Indian Institute of Public Opinion.
    The most important source of survey data on India. Monthly.

Quarterly Journal of Indian Studies in Social Sciences.

Quarterly Journal of the Local Self-Government Institute. (Bombay)

Social Scientist.
    Monthly journal of the Indian School of Social Sciences; Marxist. (Trivandrum)

South Asia.
    Australian journal of the South Asian Studies Association.

South Asian Studies.
    Published by the Department of Political Science, University of Rajasthan. (Jaipur)

Strategic Digest.
    Published by the Institute for Defence Studies and Analyses. (New Delhi)

Journals of News and Opinion

Backward Classes Review.
    Monthly of the All India Backward Classes Federation.

Blitz.
    Sensational and exposé oriented, with a strong leftist (pro-Moscow) perspective. (Bombay)

Capital.
By its own admission, India's leading financial newspaper devoted to the development of industry and commerce. Weekly.

Commerce.
Weekly magazine of news, business, and industry. (Bombay)

Current.
Exposé oriented; conservative. Weekly. (Bombay)

Eastern Economist.
Another Birla enterprise, it is not unaware of an English journal of the same name. Its political and economic commentary, reporting, and criticism are quite good and its statistical data most useful.

Economic and Political Weekly.
Probably India's premier journal of analysis and opinion. Indispensable for contemporary politics and economics.

Everyman's.
Weekly newspaper, with Jayaprakash Narayan as chairman of the editorial board. (New Delhi)

Far Eastern Economic Review.
An important weekly of political and economic events for the whole of Asia.

Fortnightly Review.
Published by FICCI (New Delhi)

Forum.
Monthly. (Bombay)

Frontier.
A well-edited weekly magazine reflecting a quasi-Maoist position somewhere to the left of the CPM. (Calcutta)

Gandhi Marg; A Quarterly Journal of Gandhian Thought.
Published by the Gandhi Peace Foundation. (New Delhi)

Hind Mazdoor.
Monthly of the Hind Mazdoor Sabha.

Illustrated Weekly of India.
India's *Life* magazine, published by the Times of India. Kushwant Singh, editor. (Bombay)

India Weekly: Journal of Politics, Commerce and Industry.
Moderate; independent. (New Delhi)

Indian and Foreign Review.
An independent government publication. Semimonthly. (New Delhi)

Indian Left Review.
Monthly. (New Delhi)

Indian Worker.
Journal of the Indian National Trade Union Congress (INTUC), affiliated with the Congress party. Weekly. (New Delhi)

Link.
> Published in Delhi since 1959, *Link* models itself on *Time*, but with a CPI orientation. It publishes "inside dope" and digs out stories not otherwise available but should always be checked out against more staid sources. Particularly valuable for its treatment of politics in the states. (New Delhi)

Mainstream.
> Leftist. Relatively good quality. (New Delhi)

Now.
> Weekly journal of opinion.

Peasant and Labour.
> Monthly of the All-India Kisan Sabha.

Quest.
> An Indian version of *Encounter* and is backed by the same organization, the Congress for Cultural Freedom.

Radical Humanist.
> Weekly, founded by M. N. Roy. (New Delhi)

Sarvodaya.
> Monthly of Vinoba Bhave's movement. (Thanjavur)

Seminar.
> A monthly edited by Romesh Thapar, a regular contributor to *Economic and Political Weekly*, where his views can be sampled. *Seminar* examines one topic per issue. It tries to get a good range of opinion on it and includes most useful bibliographies on each occasion.

Shankar's Weekly.
> India's established political *Punch.*

Thought.
> An informed journal of independent but conservative opinion. Covers literature as well as politics.

Voluntary Action.
> Sustaining the viewpoint of Jayaprakash Narayan.

Yogana.
> Publication of the Indian Planning Commission.

Newspapers

Amrita Bazar Patrika. (Calcutta)
> Reflects the views of the Congress Bengali middle class.

Hindu. (Madras)
> A conservative paper, with thoughtful editorials and extensive coverage.

Hindustan Times. (New Delhi)
> Birla owned and generally pro-Congress, it often exercises a tough-minded independence and is critical of the Government. Good coverage and features.

Indian Express. (Bombay)
Conservative and with sympathy for Jayaprakash Narayan, it is generally critical of the Government.

National Herald. (New Delhi)
Founded by Nehru, generally reflects the views of Indira Gandhi.

Overseas Hindustan Times. (New Delhi, weekly)
This airmail edition provides good independent coverage.

Patriot. (New Delhi)
Daily companion to *Link*, expresses the views of V. K. Krishna Menon and is generally pro-CPI.

Statesman. (Calcutta)
Somewhat elitist, but with good, reliable coverage. Before independence, it was the voice of the British community.

Statesman. (Calcutta, weekly)
Airmail edition, extensive coverage, good features.

Times of India. (Bombay)
Perhaps the best coverage of any paper, with an independent, but generally pro-Government viewpoint. Excellent features.

Party Periodicals

(AICC) Economic Review.
Published by the All-India Congress Committee of the National Congress, it provides a lively and useful forum for the discussion of policy issues even though a party publication.

Call.
Published on behalf of the Central Committee of the Revolutionary Socialist Party. (Delhi)

Congress Bulletin.
Issued by the Indian National Congress.

Janata.
Weekly journal of the Socialist Party (PSP).

Liberation.
The official publication of the Naxalite CPI (ML) Monthly. Proscribed. (Calcutta)

Mankind.
Socialist Party quarterly founded by Lohia.

New Age (weekly).
Journal of the Communist Party of India. Primarily news.

New Age (monthly).
Political monthly of the Communist Party of India. Longer, more analytic, and more theoretical articles than in the weekly *New Age*. Ceased publication.

Organiser.
> Weekly journal of the Jana Sangh. Tries to include a broad range of conservative opinion.

People's Democracy.
> The official publication of the CPM. Weekly. (Calcutta)

Political and Economic Review.
> Weekly organ of the Indian National Congress. (New Delhi)

Socialist Congressmen: A Journal of Congress Socialist Opinion.
> Semimonthly. (New Delhi)

Socialist India.
> Congress party weekly.

Swarajya.
> The unofficial weekly journal of the Swatantra party. (Madras)

Swatantra Newsletter.
> Official monthly of the party.

FILM GUIDE

India's foremost film director is Satyajit Ray. His films (in Bengali, with English subtitles) are not specifically political, although more recent films like *Distant Thunder,* dealing with the Bengal famine of 1943, and *The Adversary,* set against the backdrop of unemployment and Naxalite terrorism in Calcutta, confront the political situation. Ray's films provide a sensitive study of Indian life, urban and rural. His films include the brilliant "Apu trilogy" (*Pather Panchali, Aparajito,* and *Apu Sansar*), *Mahanagar,* and *The Adversary,* and are available through:

> Audio-Brandon Films
> 34 Macquesten Parkway South
> Mt. Vernon, N. Y. 10550

Two documentaries on Gandhi and the nationalist movement are Burton Benjamin's *Gandhi* (CBS), 27 minutes, b&w, and David Wolper's *Gandhi,* 26 minutes, b&w. Both are available through:

> Alden Films
> 5113 16th Ave.
> Brooklyn, N.Y. 11204

Film Rental Library
Syracuse University
1455 East Colvin St.
Syracuse, N.Y. 13210

Also available through Syracuse University is the best documentary on village India: A *North Indian Village*, 32 minutes, color, produced by P. J. and J. T. Hitchcock.

BBC-TV produced a series on the British Empire, with three fine 55-minute color segments devoted to India: *Remember Cawnpore*, on the mutiny; *Raj*, on the British in India; and *The Long Farewell*, on the nationalist movement and independence. For information, contact:

Life-Time Films
43 West 16th St.
New York, N.Y. 10011

A brilliant film of India's capital is James Ivory's *Delhi Way*, 45 minutes, color, available through:

Film Images
Radim Film Inc.
17 West 60th St.
New York, N.Y. 10023

One of the finest film documentaries ever made on India is Louis Malle's controversial *Phantom India*. Originally made for BBC-TV, the film is in color and is in seven parts, totalling 6 hours. An additional Malle film, *City of the Dreadful Night*, deals solely with Calcutta. The films are distributed by:

New Yorker Films
43 West 61st St.
New York, N.Y. 10023

Another BBC-TV production is the superb film interview, *Indira Gandhi of India*, 52 minutes, color, available from Life-Time Films.

The Government of India Films Division produces documentaries of the highest quality. Among those most relevant to Indian politics are *India Goes to the Polls, General Elections 1971, Mahatma Gandhi, Time Capsule on Jawaharlal Nehru*, and *Our Indira*. For information, contact:

Information Service of India
2107 Massachusetts Avenue, N.W.
Washington, D.C. 20008

Information Service of India
3 East 64th St.
New York, N.Y. 10021

Information Service of India
215 Market St.
San Francisco, Calif. 94005

INDEX

Abdullah, Mohammed, 48, 215
Agriculture: *see* Economy
Ahmed, Fakhruddin Ali, 51
Ahmedabad, 136
Akali Dal, 90, 91, 120, 169, 172–73, 181
Aksai Chin, 222–23
All-India Congress Committee, 147, 157
All-India Kisan Sabha, 123
All-India Manufacturers' Organization (AIMO), 128
All-India Muslim League, 119–20
All-India Railwaymen's Federation, 126
All-India Student Federation, 132
All-India Trade Union Congress (AITUC), 125
Ambedkar, B. R., 34, 44, 51, 64, 101, 122
Amritsar thesis, 162
Andhra Pradesh, 88, 93, 118, 150, 161, 164, 165, 180
Anglo-Indians, 187
Anna DMK, 172
Annadurai, C. N., 170, 171
Appleby, Paul, 68, 69, 70, 86
Arunachal Pradesh, 93, 187, 222
Arora, Satish, 60
Arya Samaj, 23
Assam, 11, 91–93, 214, 222-23
Associated Chambers of Commerce and Industry of India (Assocham), 128
Atlee, Clement, 37
Austin, Granville, 47, 50, 54
Awami League, 217
Azad, Maulana Abul Kalam, 39, 45
Azad Kashmir, 215

Bailey, F. G., 98, 199, 200, 202, 203–04
Banerjea, Surendranath, 24, 25, 27
Bangladesh, 26, 63, 80, 155–56, 185, 217–19, 221–22
Barnds, William, 213
Basu, Jyoti, 163
Beals, Alan, 8
Belgaum, 94
Bengal, 11, 23, 26, 86–87, 93, 94, 118, 124, 134, 150–51, 156, 158, 164, 165, 179, 181, 184–85, 214, 216–17, 218, 221, 222, 225
Bentinck, William Cavendish, 20
Besant, Annie, 29
Bharat, 168
Bharatiya Jana Sangh: *see* Jana Sangh
Bharatiya Kranti Dal (BKD), 154, 173
Bharatiya Lok Dal (BLD), 160, 173
Bhave, Vinoba, 110, 134–35, 158
Bhoodan movement, 135, 158
Bhutan, 221
Bhutto, Zulfiqar Ali, 217, 218
Bihar, 93, 131, 136, 160, 169, 173, 177, 178, 180–81, 188–90, 218–19
Birla, G. D., 129
Bombay, 90, 100, 105, 150

Border disputes, India-China, 222–24
Bose, Subhas Chandra, 32, 35, 158
Brahmins, 8, 20, 121, 170
Brahmo Samaj (Divine Society), 22
Brass, Paul R., 144, 180
Brecher, Michael, 62, 151
British East India Company, 17, 21
British India
  historical background, 16–17
  nationalism, awakening of, 21–30
  rise to power, 17–21
  Sepoy mutiny, 20–21
  westernization, 19–20
Bureaucracy, 68–71, 80–81
Business community, 127–30

Cabinet, 52, 56, 62–65, 81
Candidates, selection of, 187–92
  criteria of Congress, 187–88
  factionalism, 188–90
  opposition and, 190–91
  social bases and, 191–92
Caste system, 7–8, 104, 111, 114–16, 191–92, 199–200
Central Administrative Pool, 68
Central Election Commission, 186
Central Parliamentary Board, 188
Central Secretariat, 64
Central Services, 65–66
Centralization of government, 46, 84–87
Chanda, Asok, 84
Chandigarh, 91
Charter Act of 1833, 24
Chaudhuri, T. K., 51
Chavan, Y. B., 125
Chief Minister, 97
China, 76, 132, 162–63, 166, 193, 212, 216, 217–18, 220, 221, 226
  border disputes with India, 48, 222–24
  see also Foreign relations
Chou En-lai, 223
Christians, 23, 120
Civil disobedience, 30–37, 136, 160
Class, 60, 67, 78–80, 116, 121, 137–38
Collector, 100
Commonwealth, 46–47, 214
Communalism, 116–20
  Hindu, 116–18
  Muslim, 118–20
Communism, 49, 54, 123–24, 125, 129, 132, 143, 154, 161–66, 221, 226
Communist Party of India (CPI), 94, 137, 161–66, 181, 184, 186, 193, 199
Communist Party of India (Marxist) (CPM), 94, 163–65, 180, 184–86, 191, 193
Communist Party of India (Marxist-Leninist) (CPI-ML), 166; *see also* Naxalites
Community Development Program, 102